Critical
Multiculturalism

Critical Studies in Education and Culture Series

CRITICAL MULTICULTURALISM

Uncommon Voices in a Common Struggle

Edited by
BARRY KANPOL

and
PETER McLAREN

Critical Studies in Education and Culture Series
EDITED BY HENRY A. GIROUX AND PAULO FREIRE

BERGIN & GARVEY
Westport, Connecticut • London

Library of Congress Cataloging-in-Publication Data

Critical multiculturalism : uncommon voices in a common struggle /
  edited by Barry Kanpol and Peter McLaren.
    p.   cm. — (Critical studies in education and culture series,
  ISSN 1064–8615)
    Includes bibliographical references and index.
    ISBN 0–89789–307–7 (alk. paper). — ISBN 0–89789–308–5 (pbk. :
  alk. paper)
    1. Critical pedagogy. 2. Multicultural education.   I. Kanpol,
  Barry.   II. McLaren, Peter.   III. Series.
  LC196.C756   1995
  370.11'5—dc20   94–29021

British Library Cataloguing in Publication Data is available.

Library of Congress Catalog Card Number: 94–29021

ISBN: 0–89789–307–7 (alk. paper)
      0–89789–308–5 (pbk.)
ISSN: 1064–8615

First published in 1995

Bergin & Garvey, 88 Post Road West, Westport, CT 06881
An imprint of Greenwood Publishing Group, Inc.

Printed in the United States of America

The paper used in this book complies with the
Permanent Paper Standard issued by the National
Information Standards Organization (Z39.48–1984).

10 9 8 7 6 5 4 3 2 1

To my mother, Pearl Kanpol,
who taught me the value of reading.
To my father, George Kanpol,
who taught me the values of hard work,
self-discipline, and motivation.

Barry Kanpol

To Jenny McLaren,
the inspiration for all of my work.

Peter McLaren

Contents

Series Foreword

Within the last decade, the debate over the meaning and purpose of education has occupied the center of political and social life in the United States. Dominated largely by an aggressive and ongoing attempt by various sectors of the Right, including "fundamentalists," nationalists, and political conservatives, the debate over educational policy has been organized around a set of values and practices that take as their paradigmatic model the laws and ideology of the market place and the imperatives of a newly emerging cultural traditionalism. In the first instance, schooling is being redefined through a corporate ideology which stresses the primacy of choice over community, competition over cooperation, and excellence over equity. At stake here is the imperative to organize public schooling around the related practices of competition, reprivatization, standardization, and individualism.

In the second instance, the New Right has waged a cultural war against schools as part of a wider attempt to contest the emergence of new public cultures and social movements that have begun to demand that schools take seriously the imperatives of living in a multiracial and multicultural democracy. The contours of this cultural offensive are evident in the call by the Right for standardized testing, the rejection of multiculturalism, and the development of curricula around what is euphemistically called a "common culture." In this perspective, the notion of a common culture serves as a referent to denounce any attempt by subordinate groups to challenge the narrow ideological and political parameters by which such a culture both defines and expresses itself. It is not too surprising that the theoretical and political distance between defining schools around a common culture and denouncing cultural difference as the enemy of democratic life is relatively short indeed.

This debate is important not simply because it makes visible the role that schools play as sites of political and cultural contestation, but because it is within this debate that the notion of the United States as an open and democratic society is being questioned and redefined. Moreover, this debate provides a challenge to progressive educators both in and outside of the United States to address a number of conditions central to a postmodern world. First, public schools cannot be seen as either objective or neutral. As institutions actively involved in constructing political subjects and presupposing a vision of the future, they must be dealt with in terms that are simultaneously historical, critical, and transformative. Second, the relationship between knowledge and power in schools places undue emphasis on disciplinary structures and on individual achievement as the primary unit of value. Critical educators need a language that emphasizes how social identities are constructed within unequal relations of power in the schools and how schooling can be organized through interdisciplinary approaches to learning and cultural differences that address the dialectical and multifaceted experiences of everyday life. Third, the existing cultural transformation of American society into a multiracial and multicultural society structured in multiple relations of domination demands that we address how schooling can become sites for cultural democracy rather than channeling colonies reproducing new forms of nativism and racism. Finally, critical educators need a new language that takes seriously the relationship between democracy and the establishment of those teaching and learning conditions that enable forms of self and social determination in students and teachers. This suggest not only new forms of self-definition for human agency, it also points to redistributing power within the school and between the school and the larger society.

Critical Studies in Education and Culture is intended as both a critique and as a positive response to these concerns and the debates from which they emerge. Each volume is intended to address the meaning of schooling as a form of cultural politics, and cultural work as a pedagogical practice that serves to deepen and extend the possibilities of democratic public life. Broadly conceived, some central considerations present themselves as defining concerns of the Series. Within the last decade, a number of new theoretical discourses and vocabularies have emerged which challenge the narrow disciplinary boundaries and theoretical parameters that construct the traditional relationship among knowledge, power, and schooling. The emerging discourses of feminism, post-colonialism, literary studies, cultural studies, and post-modernism have broadened our understanding of how schools work as sites of containment and possibility. No longer content to view schools as objective institutions engaged in the transmission of an unproblematic cultural heritage, the new discourses illuminate how schools function as cultural sites actively engaged in the production of not only knowledge but social identities. *Critical Studies in Education and Culture* will attempt to encourage this type of analysis by emphasizing how schools might be addressed as border institutions or sites of crossing actively involved in exploring, reworking, and translating the ways in which culture is produced, negotiated, and rewritten.

Emphasizing the centrality of politics, culture, and power, *Critical Studies in Education and Culture* will deal with pedagogical issues that contribute in novel ways to our understanding of how critical knowledge, democratic values, and social practices can provide a basis for teachers, students, and other cultural workers to redefine their role as engaged and public intellectuals.

As part of a broader attempt to rewrite and refigure the relationship between education and culture, *Critical Studies in Education and Culture* is interested in work that is interdisciplinary, critical, and addresses the emergent discourses on gender, race, sexual preference, class, ethnicity, and technology. In this respect, the Series is dedicated to opening up new discursive and public spaces for critical interventions into schools and other pedagogical sites. To accomplish this, each volume will attempt to rethink the relationship between language and experience, pedagogy and human agency, and ethics and social responsibility as part of a larger project for engaging and deepening the prospects of democratic schooling in a multiracial and multicultural society. Concerns central to this Series include addressing the political economy and deconstruction of visual, aural, and printed texts, issues of difference and multiculturalism, relationships between language and power, pedagogy as a form of cultural politics, and historical memory and the construction of identity and subjectivity.

Critical Studies in Education and Culture is dedicated to publishing studies that move beyond the boundaries of traditional and existing critical discourses. It is concerned with making public schooling a central expression of democratic culture. In doing so it emphasizes works that combine cultural politics, pedagogical criticism, and social analyses with self-reflective tactics that challenge and transform those configurations of power that characterize the existing system of education and other public cultures.

Henry A. Giroux

Introduction:
Resistance Multiculturalism and the Politics of Difference

Barry Kanpol and Peter McLaren

Only within the last few years, at a time in which it has become increasingly clear that schools are determined to exile everything from their curricula that is not marketable, has the critical education literature reflected dramatic and important conceptual turns and theoretical advances in what could be loosely described as a criticalist enchantment with and embrace of emergent strands of postmodern social theory. While desirous of change or condemned to it, critical educationalists have advanced our understanding of the relationship among schooling, cultural formations, and the production of subjectivity. Despite their formidable attempt to bring critical social theory into the educational debate as a means of deepening educators' appreciation for the complexity of the relationship among classroom practices, institutional structures, and the change in capitalist formations, they have found the quest for a common vision and united political agenda to be a slippery journey and increasingly fraught with unforeseen obstacles. For these critics, it has become an age of impossible options as the multitemporal heterogeneity and self-referentiality of postmodern cultures, in devouring the origins of their own power, have enabled existing elites to manage uncontested the vital intersections of desire, meaning, and history.

Working within what could generally be described as a postmodern purview, educators have found themselves trapped between the Scylla of the imminent collapse of humanism under the weight of its own totalizing productions and the Charybdis of the decline of those powers that, entrapped by the modern code, possess the power to create the real. In other words, educators face a world both seduced and sanctioned by the enlivening power of dead signs that have given Karl Marx's dream of worker autonomy and mastery the form of a fatal attraction. The new vicissitudes that make up the imponderability of everyday life include forms of alienation and power undreamt by Marx and his followers. If, in the new world of the simulacrum, freedom is always illusory and autonomy and self-management are seen to be the delusions of bourgeois theorists, what then are leftist educators to make of the vision of social emancipation that has guided their forebears?

The world of radical educational politics has moved into new theoretical realms. It is no longer a question of challenging Maoist or Leninist positions or the irredeemably dogmatic Castroist and Guevarist theory of *foco* and revolutionary struggle as being unfit or unrealistic for deployment in U.S. sociopolitical contexts, but rather an acknowledgment that individuals are now "produced" within Western forms of hegemony that make them less capable of dismantling their ideological scaffolding and developing strategies and practices of resistance. Certainly it is the case that in Western societies hegemonic social and cultural formations are the result of new articulations brought about as much by the revolution in the media industries as by the transformation of capitalism on a global scale. In emphasizing this point, we do not claim that these new hegemonic formations do not have axial and functional disturbances (since all forms of hegemony, despite their seeming invincibility, are constituted with leaks and fissures), but suggest that their civilizing mission and ideological deployment are linked to artic-ulatory practices that are difficult to identify, let alone interrogate and trans-form. Hence the need for theoretically sophisticated and committed leftist scholars and cultural workers in general, and for mature and dedicated leftist educational critics in particular.

While the educational Left can no longer be described as simply an am-algam of subterranean arguments and self-justifying manifestos, having recently reached a respectable level of transdisciplinary theoretical sophisti-cation, it remains the case that the brute facts of mass poverty and exploi-tation still haunt its emergence as a voice of mature expression and shape the contours of the struggle that needs to be waged. Faced with this all-too-familiar reality, critical educationalists (those who have been identified as "resistance postmodernists") suggest not the abandonment of this strug-gle but rather its configuration and revitalization in new terms (Giroux, 1992; Aronowitz and Giroux, 1991; McLaren, 1993). Further, they signal the need to develop a new ideology of needs and a theoretical framework that can better explain and eventually prove more capable of transforming a world in which the signifier has become its own referent (Baudrillard, 1975) and the defining binarisms, significative dualisms, and seriality of di-chotomies of modernist cultural knowledge have placed under siege the identities and opportunities of women and people of color.

Recent issues of journals such as *Educational Theory, Educational Foun-*

dations, Harvard Educational Review, Journal of Education and *Urban Review*, among others, have been devoted to postmodern criticisms of both mainstream and leftist educational theory and practice. With the exception of the important work of Henry Giroux and a few others, only a scarce number of these theoretical criticisms have touched on the urgency of establishing a political agenda for educational and social emancipation. Yet at the same time we do not want to underestimate the significance of these journals in the ongoing establishment of alternative and sometimes transgressive viewpoints (Kanpol, 1992; Kincheloe, 1993; McLaren, 1986, 1993; Giroux and McLaren, 1993; Lanshear and McLaren, 1993; McLaren and Lankshear, 1993; Burbules and Rice, 1991; Beyer and Liston, 1993; Giroux, 1988, 1992; McLaren and Hammer, 1989; Lather, 1989; among many others) and heated and sometimes volatile debate (Ellsworth, 1989; Giroux, 1992; Lather, 1991; McLaren, 1994; among others).

While acknowledging the utmost importance of scholarly debate and the exchange of ideas, critical postmodernists need to make a more concerted effort to build genuine dialogue among competing theoretical factions and explore the idea of what a common emancipatory struggle might look like. Regrettably, there has been little consistency in the production of these new ideas, except that they have all tremulously attached a negative sign to the totalizing forces of liberal humanism and established a healthy irreverence for correspondence theories that establish a mimetic relation of truth between reality and language.

Our own situatedness within postmodern theory is closely aligned to what has been described as resistance or critical postmodernist discourses (Aronowitz and Giroux, 1991; Giroux, 1992; McLaren, 1993; Kanpol, 1992), in distinction from those "ludic" discourses, which reduce agency to a multiplicity of playful signs that, in their cavalier and adventitious clusterings, purport to invent experience and produce the arbitrariness and negotiability of reality. It is as if by freeing signs from the buried archives of history and mixing them with those that have been pillaged in the cultural present that ludic postmodernists profess to have discovered political agency. The convulsing melange that is produced assumes a transgressive role only in its disquieting excess, and not because it has established the grounds for a project based on the referents of social justice and cultural struggle (Zavavzedeh and Morton, 1991). In turn, we reject those postmodern suavities that simply exalt theory as a type of travelogue, as a form of fatal attentiveness to *difference* and infinite heterogeneity, and that posit experience as the basis of developing a political project.

Here the responsibility of the state to subalternalized groups is reduced to a bourgeois individualist form of noblesse oblige. In addition, bourgeois postmodernist practices too often recapitulate the project of high modernist vanguardism. In distinction from the provocative irreverence and fashionable apostasy of the postmodernist avant-garde, we believe experience to be important but only insofar as such experiences can be understood as being constituted within regimes of commodified signs and overdetermined social relations. In other words, experiences need to be engaged in terms of a theory that takes oppression, resistance, and liberation seriously. Our position follows Laclau and Mouffe (1985) in arguing that necessity is produced out of its relation to contingency. Identities are only necessary in that such "necessity" is constituted by what is peripheral or marginal to it. This concept of identity as multiple and open-ended suggests that it is not some unitary, metaphysical essence, but the result of overdetermined equivalences of difference or structural logics organized around specific antagonisms.

Following this understanding of identity, we recognize that there are good reasons why a radical politics of solidarity has been difficult to conceptualize over recent years, let alone strategize and accomplish. History, it seems, has intervened (and not ended, as some recent conservatives would proclaim!) in a way that has made the idea of a coordinated social transformation less plausible. For instance, recent historical events such as the collapse of the Soviet Union and anticapitalist and antiimperialist movements around the world have further weakened consideration for Marxist-based reform, most certainly among the educational left in the United States. We are referring here, of course, to the development of flexible specialization or accumulation that has followed in the wake of the decline of the manufacturing industries in the developed economies. The corresponding expansion of the informal economy and service sectors (i.e., subcontracting and an emphasis on consumption rather than production) that has accompanied deregulation, the multinationalization of capital, an increased monopolization of markets and broadcasting centers, and the fragmentation of our heterogeneous societies pose new and serious problems for social and educational reformers.

Alain Touraine (1988) remarks that today there appears on the Left to be more emphasis on social contradiction, exclusion, and marginalization than on conflict, domination, oppression, and social movements. The idea of state intervention is losing the little credibility that it once had and the discourse of the marketplace and "choice" has tightened its grasp on the direction of educational reform. Schools, curricula, and even students themselves have been turned into social texts and commodity signs competing for a share of the market. Democracy has been turned into one large advertising campaign with no product to sell except a share of its own commodified sales pitch, as it works to compose structures of equivalence between signs and meanings (i.e., Rambo and patriotism; profits and civic duty), to assemble distinctly "American" values and fetishistically encode them in particular ways that have real market values not for democracy but rather for the idea of democracy.

Radical teachers ask themselves if they can become free of state control while at the same time develop a praxis of emancipation that moves beyond both the call and the thrall of marketplace ideology. Certainly the global transformation of capitalism has posed a serious challenge to traditional ways of conceiving social movements and socialist change, but this does not necessarily have to sound the death knell for the idea of social movements. Scholars, including Touraine, have noted that whereas the older social movements were associated with the concept of revolution, there exist today new social movements more concerned with the idea of democracy. This speaks to the possibility of new forms of social action and reform strategies in which teachers and other cultural workers can rediscover themselves as agents rather than passive subjects and identities.

Within the context of this debate (or lack thereof), critical pedagogy along with feminist pedagogy continue to play a crucial role. For instance, critical pedagogy has been inscribed as the means by which teachers both in and out of the academy can be used as vehicles for developing "border identities" (McLaren, 1993) and a sense of historical agency as "transformative intellectuals" (Giroux, 1992) as well as strategies of hope and possibility, and for developing a politics of refusal and resistance with respect to society's race, class, and gender antagonisms (Kanpol, 1992). In short, critical pedagogy has emerged on the scene over the last fifteen years in order to participate in the struggle for human/social agency within highly bureaucratic institutions and wage a pedagogical campaign for creating a radical democratic citizenry.

Of course, the educational Left is not solely or even largely composed of educators within the tradition of critical pedagogy, although it is probably not an overstatement to say that critical pedagogy is perhaps one of the most contentious educational perspectives (if we take into consideration, among other things, its penchant for attracting critics). As some exponents of this perspective attempt to engage the debate over postmodernism, it has become clear that critical pedagogy needs to address the problem of bringing together various political and theoretical constituencies and their social or cultural differences. While we believe that critical pedagogy needs to play a greater part in reformulating the role of historical agency in the postmodern era, we stress that it must concomitantly take pains to avoid becoming yet another master narrative or essentialist form of truth construction.

While the emergence of Latin American social movements—such as the black movement in Brasil; the indigenous movements in Ecuador, Colombia, and Mexico; the Mothers of the Plaza de Mayo in Buenos Aires; and the recent noble exploits of El Ejérolo Zapatista de Liberacion Nacional led by poet revolutionary el subcomandante Marcas—are often romanticized in the United States through *ad populum* discourses, possibilities do exist in North American public spheres for social movements to take a more active role in the struggle for civil society. We believe schools are necessary but not sufficient sites where such struggles need to be waged.

As criticalists, we accept the position that we invariably claim to know what our own logic of analysis says is impossible and unknowable; knowledge, in other words, cannot be spoken from some objective, all-embracing standpoint of absolute authority. That is, it can never be made preontologically available or complete; *au fond*, knowledge is not some dramatic *passe-partout* that can serve as an Archimedean point of certainty or evaluation, but is always in flux, moving and partial; it is always situated and enunciated from some position or politics of location; it is necessarily representational of multiple subjectivities and positionalities. Such a perspective often leads to a feeling of frustration about the intellectual disparities within the criticalist field in education in this current historical juncture, since many of the theoretical trajectories are moving away from what is now often disparagingly referred to as "modernist" narratives of human emancipation that not only engage race, class, and gender differences, but are motivated if not always designed to reduce oppression, alienation, and subordination, including our very own, and no less!

When, after reading G.W.F. Hegel, V. I. Lenin (1960, p. 412) pronounced that "truth is concrete" he meant, *inter alia*, that truth does not reside in some metaphysical vault or transcendental reserve but rather is bound up in human joy, pain, strife, and struggle. Criticalists take such an insight to heart, as they attempt to develop self-reflexive standpoints that acknowledge their own ideological interests. Here we emphasize Seyla Benhabib's (1990) assertion that the privatized knowledge of epistemic subjects is not enough to formulate minimal criteria of validity for discursive and material practices; rather, what is needed are public signifying activities of a collection of subjects. Recently, Benhabib (1992, p. 228) has elaborated on what she calls "interactive universalism," which is based on a proceduralist form of rationality and refers to "situated knowledge for a global community." An interactive universalism allows for recognition of a generalized other through acknowledgement of the moral identity of a concrete other; every generalized other, in other words, is also a concrete other (pp. 164–165). Like Benhabib, we feel that the practice of interactive universalism means that sometimes we must articulate our vision "from outside the walls of the city" (p. 228).

It is the idea of a common vision or common ground of understanding that weaves together many different truths or "truth effects" that has driven us to collectively dialogue across differences. Who we are as a critical pedagogical movement in these difficult economic, social, and cultural times needs some greater clarity (what *is* already clear is that we are institutionally and politically fragmented) and the periphrases that often accompany the new language of theory in recent times have certainly not hastened the furthering of this end. Understanding the process of identity formation and the construction of subjectivities (and this includes the subjectivities of those who theorize about teacher and student identity) within the larger narrative of social and cultural reproduction needs a more sustained and nuanced theoretical effort put forth by educational researchers in order for a cultural politics of the classroom to be developed and appreciated as part of a wider politics of liberation.

We also realize that one cannot include all political factions of critical pedagogy in one volume, despite our efforts to include other researchers and cultural workers who reflect some of these different viewpoints. What is vital to this project is to accomplish a political statement that combines both theory and practice, and constructs at the same time different voices. While we realize that in doing so we cannot be totally "essentialist free," we must own up to and reflect on any essentialist forms of truth or "nominal essences" that we might stumble into. Second, we wish to build theory, but also disseminate it into practice, while simultaneously considering the construction of difference and strategies of emancipatory practice. Theoretically informed practice is important and, together with hope, forms the cornerstones of emancipatory praxis. We must remember that pedagogical praxis is always a form of advocacy. We must recognize, additionally, that there are many forms of advocacy occurring in the nation's classrooms. The vital question for us is: What is the nature of such forms of advocacy and in whose interest do they serve? We are aware that amid the fractious antipathy that currently infects leftist educational constituencies, we give up what little space we have to the reactionary forces of the right. These forces constitute a new *Gleichschaltung* (bringing-into-line) of the discourses of sameness and a monumentalization and homogenization of culture. They are dangerous forces and need to be understood and contested by teachers who recognize the dangerous mix of totalizing discourses and the ideology of fascism.

Across all "critical" dialogue about schools and the academy, the age-old question about democracy is still a much-debated issue. For critical pedagogists steeped within the postmodern dialogue, democracy is never final, is always in flux and under constant theoretical and practical negotiation. Perhaps Laclau and Mouffe's (1985) description of the "democratic imaginary" best depicts our own notion of democracy: democracy exists not in all places at one time but in many places, instances, and events where people struggle to undercut and alleviate the oppression, alienation, and subordination they and others experience. In schools this occurs in many ways as teachers and students work individually and collectively to redress institutional inequities (Weiler, 1987; Kanpol, 1992). Common elements of struggle for a more just and caring society also prevail in the name of democracy on a global scale. Therefore, how postmodernism, democracy, and difference intersect, especially in relation to materiality of struggle, is of serious concern to us.

Chantal Mouffe (1992b) makes the important point that the "we" that represents a radical democratic community must necessarily be one that requires the correlative notion of the common good. However, a notion such as the common good must always be "conceived as a vanishing point, something to which we must constantly refer but that can never be reached"

(p. 30). The concept of the common good is therefore a nonsubstantive one. What holds the form of political community together should not be a concept of the common good but, rather, as Mouffe argues, the idea of a *common bond*. The notion of common bond here refers to a sense of collective concern. Such a concern leads to a collective form of identification among a variety of democratic demands (i.e., from women, African Americans, gays, ecologists) that are linked to the principles of liberty and quality that are, in turn, designed to construct a chain of equivalence articulated through the principle of democratic equivalence. Mouffe stresses that such a relation of equivalence does not eliminate difference. Rather such a view of citizenship becomes "an articulating principle that affects the different subject positions of the social agent while allowing for a plurality of specific allegiances and for the respect of individual liberty" (p. 32).

We want to make clear that our concern with developing a critical pedagogy consistent with the articulating principles of a radical democracy is not to remain content with merely presenting opportunities for students and teachers to engage in forms of ideology-critique (although this is certainly a worthwhile challenge in any critical pedagogy), but rather to explore how individuals make *affective investments* in events, practices, and representations. We take our cue here from Lawrence Grossberg's (1992) work on the structure of the affective plane (what anchors people in particular experiences, meanings, pleasures, and what constitutes the nature of their caring and passion in relation to them). How do students and teachers construct affective spaces and intensities—"mattering maps"—and what constitutes the various ways that investments can possibly play in the construction of a democratic citizenry? Ideological relations are not simply internalized through some passive form of absorption as if students or teachers were simply passive dupes of dominant discursive regimes and social and bureaucratic arrangements. Rather, as Grossberg points out, it is the construction of the affective investment that enables ideological relations to be internalized.

Daily life, in other words, constitutes complex relations among ideological, economic, historical, material, discursive, and affective articulations. These articulations operate within various narrative forms that constitute particular affective sensibilities in which people assume the authority to shape their identities and locate themselves within certain circuits of power (although always within the limitations of the contexts in which these occur). Grossberg (1992, p. 86) notes that "the affective investment in certain sites demands a very specific ideological response, for affect can never define, by itself, why things should matter." In other words, ideology always serves to legitimate *why certain differences matter over others*. We feel that it is important to engage critical pedagogy with the challenge of developing forms of "affective empowerment." Grossberg states:

Affective empowerment is increasingly important in a world in which pessimism has become common sense, in which people increasingly feel incapable of making a difference, and in which differences increasingly seem not to matter, not to make any difference. Affective relations are, at least potentially, the condition of possibility for the optimism, invigoration and passion which are necessary for any struggle to change the world. (p. 86)

Grossberg is aware that the transformation of capitalism from Fordist variants to interconnected forms of global economy, which concern themselves not with the production of goods but the production of value itself (which reflects the decline of industrial capital and the growing autonomy of finance capital), effectively denies the relationship between the productivity of value and an ethics of responsibility and social justice. In an era in which individuals have become forms of "human capital" produced "through fragmenting machines of capitalization," the question of what forms of affective investment individuals will produce both in classrooms and in the sphere of popular culture cannot be ignored by critical educators.

Following Grossberg's lead, we have become aware of the limitations of various articulations of identity politics in the struggle for educational and social reform. The competing claims and struggles of various groups cannot, we believe, be organized around a single referent such as democracy. Any of the various strategies designed to construct a "we" that can speak across a multiplicity of identities and subjectivities is problematic, Grossberg warns, because such strategies "must always reinstate relations of power within the struggle itself, thus splitting it back into fragments" (p. 377). Identity politics establishes social conflicts rather than political antagonisms and this, according to Grossberg, fails "to provide sufficient ground to organize both opposition and alternatives to the contemporary conservative hegemony" (p. 377).

While we are certainly interested in the politics of identity and experience in terms of its importance in understanding the production of subjectivities within differential relations of power and structured opportunities for economic and social advancement, we do not feel that it should be the primary site of struggle. Rather, we need to create affective alliances beyond the legitimacy of identity/experience alone. We need to construct a politics of agency and practice rather than identity insofar as it is possible to transform schools into "the production of spaces of articulation and places of investment." Such spaces and places need to become sites for the production of "common affective structures and antagonisms."

The "we" of common struggle is not a universal referent that is designed to subsume all differences under a common clarion call to freedom; rather, following Grossberg, it serves as a "floating sign of a common authority and commitment to speak and to act" (pp. 379–380). Ethnicity, in this view, becomes not the representation of ideological subjects, but rather their mobilization through structures of affect located within the plane of political commitment that have the power to organize social movements.

Our politics must never follow unreflectively from our particular identities. Our identities can never guarantee that our political commitments will be mobilized in the service of social justice. Affective investment put into the service of liberation is more than simply the practice of changing the political consciousness of students and teachers (although this is certainly important) but rather transforming the axiomatics of capitalism (whether in their pre-Fordist, neo-Fordist, global Fordist, or post-Fordist incarnations) that condition the acts of knowing that accompany the practices of everyday life. As Grossberg argues:

If people are to change history, it is their passions that must be awakened, for the crisis of the Left is not ideological. It is a matter of people's affective involvement, of the intensity people are willing to invest in their political beliefs and struggles, and of the vectors which increasingly discipline and regulate their everyday lives. (p. 394)

Our own analytical framework for understanding schools, classrooms, communities, and cultures necessarily takes the form of a postmodern conjuncturalism (Grossberg, 1992). We follow here R. Frankenberg and L. Mani (1993, p. 306), who stress a political project that "centers the analysis of object formation and cultural practice within matrices of domination and subordination." Moreover, a postmodern conjuncturalism "asserts that there is an effective but not determining relationship between subjects and their histories, a relationship that is complex, shifting and yet not "free" (p. 306). In other words, the relationship between subjects and their histories and experiences *is an articulated one*, one that is contextually embedded in social practices and relations of power and is geopolitically specific. We agree to a certain extent with poststructuralists who argue that there is no essential self that preexists signification. At the same time we do not want to reduce human subjects simply to the positions that are provided for them in language.

How does such a politics and perspective deal with the pressing question of racism? This is an important challenge to critical educationalists, especially given the proliferation of racialized discourses of white supremacy among our youth. How are teachers and students going to be able to unfix the history of racialized expression through the construction of economies of affect and forms of political commitment and mobilization within new spaces and places of democratic struggle? David Theo Goldberg (1993, p. 207) reminds us that within this era of flexible accumulation, sociocultural and spacial boundaries have become more porous and there seems to be more room for "conditions of possibility for moving through, for transgressing, the established racialized limits of spatial confines and political imagination." Yet at the same time Goldberg notes that racism has become a form of private circulation as "commitments to diversity in the public domain have been displaced by privatizing univocality, exclusion, and exclusivity" (p. 207). Goldberg rejects both the formalist universalism of modernist morality and the particularism of the postmodernist as grounds for developing resistance to racist exclusions and expressions.

We agree with Goldberg that we need multiple strategies to resist racism and these will depend on the contextual specificity of the forms in which racist expressions and practices occur. Goldberg's position is a cautious move toward the pragmatism of the "Critical Race Theorists" and constitutes a transformative project that seeks to avoid abstract, transcendental ideals associated with the sameness of the transhistorical subject, atemporal universals, and fixed social foundations linked to liberal humanism, while at the same time avoiding the forms of communitarian particularism associated with postmodernism. Grounding his praxis in a "principled pragmatism," Goldberg argues that principled pragmatists refuse "any grand teleological narratives specifying in deterministic fashion . . . the social state in which all social tensions and difficulties will purportedly be resolved" (p. 215). Moreover, they are concerned "with and about the contingent and transforming relations between knowledge and power, with resisting the discursive conditions and determinations of domination and exclusion, and with setting the contingent grounds for instituting and promoting liberatory self-determination for all people" (p. 216).

Situating his project within a "pragmatics of praxis," Goldberg rejects the universal ideals of nonracialism of the liberal (and also postmodern bourgeois liberal), which fails to recognize racial distinctions. Further, he supports the neopragmatists' practical principle of antiracism. His concern is "to end racist exclusions and the conditions that give rise to and sustain such exclusions, however and whatever they manifest" (p. 217). The ideals for such antiracist practice are not foundational but necessarily and always revisable—they are "warranted assertions and contingent generalizations" rather than "necessary truths or universal essences." We must, maintains Goldberg, be attentive to "the possible transformations available to the specific conjuncture at hand" (p. 218).

Following this thesis, we believe that it is productive for critical educators and cultural workers to work toward the realization of what Goldberg calls "incorporation." He uses this term in contrast to the notions of assimilation or integration. Incorporation refers to "the dual transformations that take place both in the dominant values and in those of the insurgent group, as the latter insists on more complete incorporations into the body politic and the former grudgingly gives way" (p. 220). Cultural space in this view is continually renegotiated. Cultural sites such as schools become arenas for cultural negotiation, translation, and contestation through forms of "transformative incorporation" in which imposed identities and racist cultural practices and policies are resisted.

We find Goldberg's antiracist strategies consistent with Mouffe's (1992a, p. 380) notion of radical democratic citizenship defined as "the construction of a common political identity that would create the conditions for the establishment of a new hegemony articulated through new egalitarian social relations, practices and institutions." In our view, what is urgently needed in our pedagogical projects is a greater space for the articulation of different struggles against oppression, including those waged by feminists of color. This volume was created to provide, in part, a modest space for the articulation of struggles against oppression and for developing within public sites such as schools a vision of democracy underwritten by a politics of difference and "pragmatics of praxis."

In Chapter 1 Svi Shapiro reminds us that common struggles for school reform are not always identical. In order to build what he describes as a political imaginary, moral and spiritual discourses in schools must be translated into the everyday life-world. The only avenue for democratic possibilities in schools exists in the form of a social bloc, one that connects "the suffering of one group of humans to another," one that creates, again broadly, a shared human identity, one that must speak to "real needs, anxieties, tensions and feelings of insecurity." In short, Shapiro reminds readers of these needs within the current state of moral and social decline.

Michael Peters poses a fundamental question in relation to what he describes as a "commodified democracy." How, he asks in Chapter 2, is it possible to build community and citizenship without "succumbing to an ideology of individualism?" It might also be said that in the face of diversity, how does one build social relations that are not predicated on narcissism and market values? If "real" communities are to flourish in these "new times," Peters argues, a politics of "differences" rather than a universal and utopian idea of the social self must be developed in diverse educational arenas so as to confront the decaying social conditions of the times. Peters argues that differences must be treated as variations and not exclusivities, and can also be connected to a common and shared emancipatory goal.

Beverly M. Gordon's Chapter 3 illuminates what a politics of difference, representation, and sharedness may indeed look like. In this sense, Gordon views the African American feminist struggle as decisively different from the struggle of white feminists or the plight of African American males. She argues that a politics of difference, democracy, and representation must include a multitude of voices, not only the privileged white middle-class feminist or African American male voices. Otherwise these discourses run into the possibility of becoming controlling essentialist narratives, dominant and "masculine" in their power. Gordon argues that if we take history seriously, we will see how other voices, particularly those of African American women, have struggled against the grain to contribute to a politics of both community and other, to a posthumanist democratic imaginary. Gordon's call is for a totality of vision, without ever losing sight of the particular struggle of the marginalized, while concurrently coming to grips with the multiple constructions of the social (not only white middle-class America, but also historically oppressed groups such as African American females), as well as a communal vision of "We are therefore I am—I am therefore we are."

Related to the above arguments is an increasingly national concern with the often-bandied term "multiculturalism." Much debate around multiculturalism in the United States has centered around a discussion of implementation strategies within schools and universities and has focused primarily on affirmative action policies. Like the concepts of "empowerment," "excellence," or "effective teaching," multiculturalism also has its various political and ideological constituencies. Conservative and liberal positions on multiculturalism assume justice is ultimately reachable through an equal distribution of wealth. We believe that critical pedagogy needs to move beyond conservative and liberal positions on multiculturalism that operate within modes of intelligibility that reproduce the logocentric thinking that reinitiates the logic of domination and oppression. We also believe that the way in which multiculturalism is related to democracy and the postmodern politics of difference is vital to an emancipatory agenda that must include both different and similar points of view.

A basic assumption of this book is that justice is not evenly distributed and cannot be so without a radical and profound change in social structures and in terms of a development of historical agency and a praxis of possibility. The multiculturalism espoused by the authors in this volume can be described as a critical or resistance multiculturalism. While differing in some areas, these authors stress the importance of understanding how language and identities are represented both historically and experientially.

An extremely interesting position is taken up by Carl A. Grant and Judyth M. Sachs in Chapter 4. They discuss ways in which various multicultural discourses should be made available to students in order that they be able to deconstruct their own and other cultures. Grant and Sachs also attempt to create a theoretical common ground dialogue for an emancipatory struggle that is based on *academic* solidarity. Instead of creating intellectual barriers to knowledge, they imply, borders of understanding need to be built that are more amenable to democratic dialogue and politics.

Henry A. Giroux argues in Chapter 5 that in order for a critical multiculturalism to survive, "white supremacy" must be deconstructed. Giroux maintains that too much attention has been focused on minority deficits. More serious scrutiny must be placed on the discursive construction of white supremacy in order to develop what Giroux terms "border institutions"— places like schools that can translate and negotiate, demonstrate and recognize the multiple sets of positionalities that students occupy. The Los Angeles uprising, perhaps as symbolic of the moral decline of a public and democratic discourse, is used as an example from which teachers and other cultural workers can learn.

Kris Gutierrez and Peter McLaren engage in a dialogue about minority struggles in classrooms, communities, and the larger development of global capitalism. Their dialogue in Chapter 6 suggests ways to rethink the concept of multiculturalism outside of conservative or liberal accounts with the intent to pragmatize experience (for any ethnicity) that is not essentialist, but open to multiple interpretation.

In her discussion of adult education in Chapter 7, Daniele D. Flannery argues that before we can create a multicultural "adult" society, serious consideration must be given to rethinking the theoretical components of learning theory. Flannery builds on the postmodern notion of difference so as to illuminate how recent learning theory is "objectified" at the expense of the more subjective, narrative-driven, and representational realities of different adult learners. She suggests that a more holistic approach to adult learning can and should include critical postmodern tenets if emancipatory ideals are to be realized. Flannery also makes clear that only when the present "text" of learning theory is deconstructed can adult education better approach a critical and resistance multiculturalism.

The later chapters of this volume attempt to apply some advances in critical postmodernism to classroom narratives and case study material. How critical multiculturalism and radical democracy can be used as an empowering and practical agenda is central to our project, particularly as related to this section of the book.

Bonny N. Peirce recounts the story of Maria in Chapter 8. Maria's story is about the failure of multiculturalism in one school district (the closing of this predominantly "Italian"-student-populated school) and about Maria's struggle for identity as an Italian-Canadian. What we learn from Peirce's enlightening piece, among other things, is that if there is a lack of community support for other cultures besides the WASP mainstream, funding will affect the official policies of the Canadian Multiculturalism Act. As Peirce states, "Maria is aware that this discourse on multiculturalism negates the lived experience of ethnic minorities in Canada." The story of Maria invites readers to reflect upon and reconsider founding sets of binarisms, such as Wop/WASP, ethnic/dominant, and subordinate/dominant.

Barry Kanpol's case study material in Chapter 9 raises interesting phenomonological as well as critical dialogue about multiculturalism. He argues not only for understanding "similarities within our differences," but also for a way to construct how we might go about incorporating, learning from, disseminating, and enjoying difference, while maintaining an eye to what binds difference—acts of oppression, subordination, and alienation. Kanpol argues that critical educators must scrutinize the social construction of empathy—how empathy is or can be intersubjectively interrogated and used for emancipatory purposes. The case study material suggests that in order to construct border pedagogies of resistance and solidarity, educators on all levels must be prepared to internally investigate similarities within their differences.

Fred Yeo continues Kanpol's argument by connecting empathy, difference, and marginalization to urban schools. In Chapter 10, Yeo describes his personal triumphs and tribulations in an inner-city school in Compton in South Los Angeles. Yeo argues that despite the often-decrepit conditions of inner-city schools (described by Kozol, 1992, among many others), "dialogue across differences is possible, but occurs in a spectrum of lived experiences across a broad range of shifting positions that constitute ephemeral connectivities." For Yeo, as a former teacher in the inner city, borders between his African American students and his Anglo students could be built only by deviating from official (and often meaningless) curriculum to a dialogue that brought empathy into play. Yeo suggests that there is a connection between critical elements of postmodern (resistant and critical) multiculturalism and inner-city school realities. Not to make these connections, Yeo suggests, omits the possibilities of building cultural borders.

In Chapter 11 Suzanne SooHoo describes how predominantly Hispanic students became coresearchers with her. In doing so, these students were able to learn about the construction of their subjectivities within the confines of institutional constraints. SooHoo argues that these students are not familiar with just one common learning paradigm—it is precisely their cultural heritage that must be understood within different experiences in order to allow critical research to be conducted and coresearched. SooHoo poses some illuminating images and symbols of student learning. She concludes that student learning, especially (but not limited to) of different cultures, cannot be confined simply to one theoretical paradigm or one particular experience. That is, the intersection of constructivism, feminism, and critical theory is in itself one way we can understand how students learn and how they experience.

In the final chapter, Jeffrey Cinnamond constructs an ethnographic portrait of a school whose faculty is trying to produce and foster teacher "empowerment." Using Foucault's notion of discourse and power, Cinnamond argues that one can view power only in the contextual specificity of its production. That is, empowerment can be understood only in the context of the political project in which its meaning is constructed and given legitimacy. While Cinnamond describes how teacher-perceived empowerment "clouded their consciousness" of power relationships, he also argues that teachers have the opportunity to live within a life-world that includes multiple sets of empowerments that are never fixed and always in flux. To realize that power is never centralized becomes, for Cinnamond, one of the important features of empowerment. Only then can teachers better understand the process of critical reflection on practice with the intent to "change" and/or modify institutional concerns, such as race, class, and gender inequities as well as bureaucratic constraints.

The major intent of this volume was together "different" authors who in their artificial separate fields of interests (both in theory and in practice) would come together to dialogue in solidarity across differences. Our hope is that readers will find much in common with our collective emancipatory intent, and that further dialogue of this sort can be established across borders of difference.

REFERENCES

Aronowitz, S. and Giroux, H. (1991). *Postmodernism and Education: Politics, Culture and Social Criticism.* Minneapolis: University of Minnesota Press.

Baudrillard, J. (1975). *The Mirror of Production.* St. Louis: Telos.

Benhabib, Seyla. (1990). "Epistemologies of Postmodernism: A Rejoinder to Jean-François Lyotard." In L. Nicholson (ed.), *Feminism/Postmodernism* (pp. 107–130). New York: Routledge.

———. (1992). *Situating the Self: Gender, Community and Postmodernism in Contemporary Ethics.* London: Routledge.

Beyer, L. and Liston, Daniel (1993). "Discourse or Moral Action: A Critique of Postmodernism." *Educational Theory,* 42(4): 371–394.

Burbules, N. and Rice, Suzanne (1991). "Dialogue across Differences: Continuing the Conversation." *Harvard Educational Review,* 61(4): 393–416.

Ellsworth, E. (1989). "Why Doesn't This Feel Empowering? Working through the Repressive Myths of Critical Pedagogy." *Harvard Educational Review,* 59(3): 297–324.

Frankenberg, R. and Mani, L. (1993). "Crosscurrents, Crosstalk: Race, 'Postcoloniality' and the Politics of Location." *Cultural Studies,* 7(2), 292–310.

Giroux, H. (1988). "Border Pedagogy in the Age of Postmodernism." *Journal of Education,* 170(3).

———. (1992). *Border Crossings: Cultural Workers and the Politics of Education.* New York: Routledge, Chapman & Hall.

Giroux, H. and McLaren, P. (eds.) (1989). *Critical Pedagogy, the State, and Cultural Struggle,* Albany: State University of New York Press.

———. eds. (1993). *Between Borders.* London: Routledge.

Goldberg, D. T. (1993). *Racist Culture: Philosophy and the Politics of Meaning.* Oxford: Blackwell.

Gore, E. (1990). "What Can We Do for You? What Can "WE" Do for "You"? *Educational Foundations,* 4(3): 5–26.

Grossberg, L. (1992). *We Gotta Get Out of This Place: Popular Conservatism and Postmodern Culture.* London: Routledge.

Kanpol, B. (1992). *Towards a Theory and Practice of Teacher Cultural Politics: Continuing the Postmodern Debate.* Norwood, NJ: Ablex.

Kincheloe, J. (1993). *Toward a Critical Politics of Teacher Thinking: Mapping the Postmodern.* Westport, CT: Bergin & Garvey.

Kozol, J. (1992). *Savage Inequalities.* New York: Crown Publishers.

Laclau, E. and Mouffe, C. (1985). *Hegemony and Socialist Strategy: Towards a Radical Democratic Politics.* London: Verso.

Lankshear, C. and McLaren, P. (eds.) (1993). *Critical Literacy: Politics, Praxis, and the Postmodern*. Albany: State University of New York Press.

Lather, P. (1989). "Postmodernism and the Politics of Enlightenment." *Educational Foundations*, 3(3): 7–28.

———. (1991). *Getting Smart: Feminist Research and Pedagogy with/in the Postmodern*. London: Routledge.

Lenin, V. (1960). *Selected Works*, vol. 2: *Notes to Hegel*. London: Lawrence and Wishart.

McLaren, P. "White Terror." *Strategies*. In press.

McLaren, P. (1986). "Postmodernism and the Death of Politics: A Brazilian Reprieve." *Educational Theory*, 36(4): 389–401.

McLaren, P. (1993). *Schooling as a Ritual Performance*, 2nd ed. London: Routledge.

McLaren, P. (1994). *Life in Schools*, 2nd ed. White Plains, NY: Longman.

McLaren, P. and Hammer, Rhonda (1989). "Critical Pedagogy and the Postmodern Challenge: Towards a Critical Postmodernist Pedagogy of Liberation." *Educational Foundations*, 3(3): 29–62.

McLaren, P. and Lankshear, C. (1993). *Politics of Liberation: Paths from Freire*. London: Routledge.

McLaren, P. and Leonard, P. (1993). *Paulo Freire: A Critical Encounter*. London: Routledge.

Mouffe, C. (1992a). "Citizenship and Political Identity." *October*, 61: 28–32.

Mouffe, C. (1992b). "Feminism, Citizenship and Radical Democratic Politics." In Judith Butler and Joan W. Scott (eds.), *Feminists Theorize the Political*. London: Routledge.

Touraine, A. (1988). *Return of the Actor: Social Theory in Postindustrial Society*. Minneapolis: University of Minnesota Press.

Weiler, K. (1987). *Women Teaching for Change*. New York: Bergin & Garvey.

Zavarzadeh, M. and Morton, R. (1991). *Theory, (Post)Modernity, Opposition*. Washington, DC: Maisonneuve Press.

1

Educational Change and the Crisis of the Left: Toward a Postmodern Educational Discourse

Svi Shapiro

INTRODUCTION: BEYOND THE TOTALIZING VISION

There is something that must be confessed at the outset of this chapter. Call it masculine hubris or intellectual arrogance perhaps. The intention was to find and offer a language or vision for education that would express all aspects of our hopes and commitments for educational renewal and change. This discourse would tie together our concerns with a *single* thread. We felt capable of finding the one powerful, resonant image or representation of educational purpose and goals that could claim the allegiance, and capture the imagination, of the broad mass of citizens in this country at this moment in time. Indeed, we feel impelled to discern the unitary overarching demand for education that might unleash the political will and drive for educational reform—one that would connect educational changes to the impulse for changing our society in directions that are more socially just, democratic, and compassionate. It seemed that our combined visionary power and perspicacity would inevitably allow us to unlock the discursive secret for mobilizing wide public support and sympathy for transforming the goals of education in the United States in progressive directions. As will become clear, our response to this challenge is more complex and rests less on a simple formula or clear cut notions than perhaps we may have liked to have achieved.

Perhaps our desire or confidence of the possibility of finding such a language was the legacy of what has been called "totalizing" political thinking that, especially in the twentieth century, has promised to provide us with some key to social change.[1] It is a kind of thinking that has self-confidently assumed that there is always an historically correct strategy that a group of committed political individuals can discern. On the political Left this has meant, very often, the belief that there is a single, preeminent motive that when galvanized can bring a society toward its own transformation. Left intellectuals, in particular, have long operated under the assumption that with the acquisition of a critical level of cultural, economic, and political understanding, it becomes possible to uncover the secret of social transformation; that armed with their often-prodigious knowledge of a society's nature and development, the mechanism of social change can be ignited and the quest for human emancipation will roar to life and renew its historical quest.[2]

This belief has been one component of the often-frantic intellectuality of Left intellectuals convinced that perhaps a final or complete grasp of the whole social situation is within reach—and, based upon that, contains the wherewithal to make social change, or educational change, happen. The failures, losses, and unpredictability of events in this century—not the least of which have been the revolutionary changes in Europe at the end of the 1980s—have surely introduced great caution into this faith. They have, or should have, tempered our belief in our capacity to know and steer the hearts and minds of the masses (a term that itself reeks of the separation between that privileged group that provides intellectual and moral guidance and the rest who may receive it).

Yet, and despite our own admission here, the difficulty of keeping faith with the promise of this project and provide some straightforward, clear, and evocative language by which to stir educational revolt or insurgency is a disappointment, even a bitter pill. Of course this recognition is not ours alone. We are quite aware that it is no more than a number of our thoughtful colleagues and comrades in struggles have also found. The pages of some of the most creative Left publications such as *Tikkun* magazine in the United States or *Marxism Today* in Britain are testimony to this.

The world is too complex, the range of views too wide, and the diversity of concerns too differentiated to imagine that there can, any more, be some simple unanimity of goals or interests that unites all of us who have some concern for deep political social, economic, cultural, and educational change. Or can all of those who are now apathetic, cynical, detached, or even hostile to social change be mobilized around some all-embracing want, or can hope be won over by some transcendent image, representation, or vision of the future?

Of course, as we have already noted in admitting such difficulties, it is also possible to conclude, as have some critical scholars, that there is nothing left to unify us; no common human goal or vision is now possible. There is indeed nothing for those of us on the Left to attend to and support but the endless proliferation of different voices, each of which is trying to find some justified place in the sun after its imprisonment in silence, denial, or exclusion.

We in no way wish to diminish the recognition of the multiplicity of ways that human beings have been oppressed, their dignity undermined, and the full realization of their humanity thwarted. After the imperial discourse of social class—the so-called real font of oppression and exploitation—we have, at last, entered a world where the multiple ways in which human beings suffer and are dehumanized is achieving its proper recognition. Yet, and we will return to this later, something is lost in this radical discourse of "difference." Where are the bridges that connect the suffering of one group of human beings to another? Where is the sense of commonality among different people—not just within the *particular* oppressed group itself?[3] If we all speak only from within our specific situations and identities (the sexually oppressed, native peoples, the old, the mentally disabled, women) who speaks for humanity?

While the socialist tradition of emphasizing working-class struggles may have arrogantly ignored or dismissed so many other forms of human pain and struggle, it did, at least, maintain some kind of universal human vision. We will need to decide whether the claim that all such universal visions are part of man's megalomaniacal desire for power and uniformity, or part of the deep failure of political nerve that now afflicts so many on the Left. The catastrophic failures of revolutionary social experiments in the twentieth century certainly can be seen as giving credence to either argument or position.

FRAGMENTATION OR DIVERSITY: RECONSTITUTING A POLITICAL IMAGINARY

Of course, the question of a universal human vision is connected to the difficulty of articulating an alternative radical discourse about education among what is undoubtedly a fragmented, divergent public. In this sense, we have come to accept the implication of what might be called our postmodern reality.[4] Our identities in the world are overdetermined in a way that makes a "call to arms" to fight a clearly focused, unique opponent— an outmoded discourse inapplicable to the particular social, cultural, political, and economic conditions we now encounter in the United States. More and more we have come to understand ourselves as "positioned" in the world in complex and contradictory ways with allegiances, concerns, and needs that are anything but given, static, or singular.

It has become increasingly misleading to see individual identities as fixed by one or another sociological category and people as having predetermined ways of looking at or making sense of their world. Neither those whom we might envisage as our "natural" allies in the struggle for our own survival as human beings, nor those who we come to see as our necessary nemeses or opponents, is foretold by history. One only has to consider, for example,

Elie Wiesel's assertion that today "all of us have become Jews." Today all of humanity can be seen as victims living under a Damocles sword of a word in the process of destroying its delicate web of life-giving resources. The carcinogenic effect of the pollution of water and food, the erosion of the ozone layer, among other environmental ills, places even the wealthiest and most powerful among us at risk. In this sense, at least, much of humanity faces the death-dealing prospects of its own making. If it is self-interest that motivates collective action, then the extent of people who may be attracted to a socially transformative political—or educational—agenda might be very much wider than we often assume.

The sometimes surprising and unexpected nature of political commitment in the contemporary world is surely demonstrated in what is now frequently referred to as "green" politics. We have seen how such politics, as well as the closely related antinuclear and peace movements, have received their major support from the professional middle classes.[5] It is these relatively well-educated groups who have what the German political thinker and activist Rudolf Bahro has termed the "surplus consciousness" that allows them to consider, and be attentive to, far more than the immediate needs and imperatives of their existence.[6] Such groups can be concerned about the destruction of the Brazilian or African rain forests because their consciousness (and conscience) radically expands the time and space coordinates that locate what is experienced as threatening or endangering to them.

Much more than the oppression of a nation, a class, a race, or some other relatively circumscribed social entity, it is humanity itself that is under the gun, facing not just exploitation but global, annihilation. The focus of struggle becomes the future of the Earth itself; what is at stake is the continuity of our species life. When considered in this way there is a common human struggle—one that positions all of us as possessing a common and shared human identity.

Bahro's analysis has taken on particular significance in light of the successful uprisings against Stalinism and bureaucratic socialism in Eastern and Central Europe. The role of professional and white-collar middle-class groups, as well as artists and intellectuals and their concern with issues of ecological deterioration, peace, and cultural freedom, was obviously an important, even crucial, element in the transformation of the states in these countries. Quite obviously, too, these concerns were conjoined to working-class concerns for a poor and deteriorating standard of living and oppressive work conditions.

In Western capitalist societies, the enormous growth of the state is both the product of, and the catalyst for, a vast expansion and proliferation of social struggles. Traditional Marxist notions of class struggle at the point of production have been supplemented (if not replaced) with the multiplicity of popular movements that demand from government an expansion of their social, economic, political, and cultural rights.[7] Demands to address AIDS sufferers, questions of abortion rights for women, protecting consumers, providing for the needs of senior citizens, maintaining financial support for students, or offering health care to those who cannot afford to buy it in the marketplace are among the many such areas of struggle. Each struggle organizes and mobilizes a distinct and different social entity; each need constitutes a new and different identity of want or deprivation. While the range of political struggles expands and embraces a larger and larger span of our complex lives, the potential for social fragmentation, divisiveness, and competition grows space. Politics is paradoxically more pervasive and more insinuated into our everyday lives while becoming more particularistic, limited in its immediate concerns, and mean-spirited as each constituency defines its objectives in highly parochial ways.

Out of the ways in which we come to perceive our place among other human beings, we develop what Douglas Kellner has called our "political imaginary."[8] This, he says, is the cognitive and moral mapping that gives individuals a vision of the existing state of their world, and what it should or could become, as well as providing the sense of identification as to who does, or does not, share our needs and concerns in the world. The imaginary offers specific ways of seeing and interpreting the events and issues people must deal with in their everyday lives. On the basis of what we have said, it is clear that the imaginary can be shaped and constituted in many diverse ways—though it is not infinitely elastic. It must in some ways speak to the real needs, anxieties, tensions, feelings of insecurity, and so on, that people are facing (though quite obviously these can be understood and made sense of in many different ways). Thus, for example, to see the world as threatened, and humanity itself as victims, makes it possible to see ourselves in fundamentally different ways and in a new kind of relationship to others (and perhaps to nature itself). With the emergence of alternative ways of imaging our situation, different kinds of human concerns are articulated, unrecognized or unfulfilled desires come to the fore, new voices are heard, and new forms of outrage and indignation are expressed.

The question of what kinds of discourse govern how citizens think of and define education belongs to this larger question of what kind of political imaginary—what kind of cognitive and moral map—governs our understanding of the existing state of our world and what it should or could become. The question of the public discourse about education is then nothing less than the question about what kind of world we live in, what we wish it to become, and who may favor or obstruct such possibilities. Of course, as we have argued previously, the relationship of the public discourse about education to the larger questions of culture and society have typically been treated with varying degrees of obfuscation, denial, and mystification. The dominant tendencies have ranged from the assertion by some of the need for education's moral and political neutrality (obviously something we think is impossible) to the overwhelming centrality of an economic rationale for education (the "human capital" view of schools' purpose), to the Right's demand that education should act as a brake on the moral and cultural disintegration of the nation.[9]

While we disagree with the prescriptive nature of the latter's claims—its coercive, parochial, and chauvinistic view of education—we believe nonetheless that it is appropriately arguing for a moral/cultural vision of education's purpose. It places education on what is for us the correct and most desirable discursive terrain; education must primarily be defined in terms of its relationship to the community's moral vision. For us this is necessary because it places education squarely in the context of the critical, social, and human conditions of our time—a context that reflects our desire for an education that is rooted in a prophetic commitment to social awareness as to the dangers and suffering of our world, and in the praxis of deep personal and social change. More than our own normative preference, however, it is the belief that the struggle for a genuinely new public discourse of education depends on our capacity to offer a cognitively convincing and, more especially, a morally compelling vision of possibilities as a culture and a society. The struggle for transformative social challenge—whether about education or anything else—depends now on a politics that is ready and able to articulate the future in terms of a compelling moral vision rooted in the material, emotional, and spiritual needs of our lives.

POLITICS AND THE RIGHT: MORALITY AND COMMUNITY

The effectiveness of a moral vision is one of the lessons of the political success of the Right in the 1980s and 1990s. This argument has been eloquently and forcefully made by *Tikkun* editor Michael Lerner, who notes that the thirst for moral meaning is one of the deepest in American life. Moral vision, he says, far from being a "soft tissue," is potentially the guts of American politics.[10] It powerfully fuels the "traditional values" crusade of the Right, which continues to haunt and obstruct attempts at a more progressive politics. It is precisely by its constant failure to grasp this fact—by staying away from the moral needs of the people—that the Left in America is unable to mobilize a strong sense of commitment. The power of the Right discourses has been that its moral language addresses the psychological deprivation that has grown out of the failure of communal life in the United States. While, says Lerner, liberals and *the Left* have championed the poor and those facing overt racial and sexual oppression, they have ignored the pain that many—especially middle-class people—have experienced in the not strictly legal or economic arenas, in their families, in the absence of community and an ethnical frame of life. In particular, argues Lerner, implicit in conservatives' "pro-family" and "traditional values" politics is a compassion that counteracts the self-blaming that dominates personal life today.

Whether in terms of personal happiness, economic well-being, or social success and recognition, everything is supposedly in the hands of the individual. The pop-psychology formulation of "take responsibility for your own life" and "you cam make it if you really try," he says, reinforces in new ways the deepest belief in American ideology—the belief in meritocracy. If you want happiness, you will get it; if you don't have it, you have only yourself to blame. Being contrary to this conservative politics, argues Lerner, depends not on the specifics of its program but on the way that it acknowledges the crisis in personal lives while pointing the finger at a set of social causes (feminism, gays, "liberal permissiveness") that are not the fault of individual Americans. Lerner continues:

While strongly rejecting the conservatives' scape-goating, we can also see that by encouraging people to find a social cause for family crisis they decrease self-blame and increase self-compassion. This analysis helps to understand the popularity of Reagan in the first six years of his presidency. Reagan's picture of an America in which people could find true community and pride in their lives offered a seductive alternative to self-blaming. We need not adopt or accept a similar patriotic chauvinism, but we do need to be able to understand the seductiveness of such an appeal.[11]

It is easy to see similar factors at work in the Right's educational agenda: the homogeneity and uniformity of a core curriculum and a common standard of cultural literacy, the question of prayer in school or the demand for an end to bussing, a return to neighborhood schools, and the demand for explicit inculcation of "traditional" moral values in schools. The conservatives' moral language is a call for a communal life that would buffer the insecurities and uncertainties of daily life.

Paradoxically, of course, it is a desire that is undermined by the very economic system that the Right itself trumpets unquestioningly. While, as Lerner notes, decent human relationships depend on trust, caring, and the ability to give to others, today the "successful" American spends much of his or her day manipulating and controlling others. The kinds of people who will be rewarded with promotions, clients, and customers must learn to continually manipulate and sell themselves. This must inevitably develop personalities in which their own feelings and emotions become distant and alienated; antithetical to authentic and deep relationships with other human beings, whether in families or in friendships. And the conservative philosophy of selfishness and individualism expressed in a worship of the capitalist marketplace and its disdain for the poor contradicts relationships that are open, loving, and caring—the cement of a compassionate and supportive communal life.[12]

Notwithstanding the distortions of conservative discourse and the phony remedies of the Right political agenda, there are important lessons here for those of us who stand on the Left. Not the least of these is the power and importance of rooting our concerns in a vision that speaks to our moral and spiritual needs as a community; one that is inclusive of not just the usual focus of our compassion, but also those we so often exclude or are even contemptuous of. Without this vision, liberal politics becomes what it so often is: a laundry list of worthy but desperate issues (health care, equal pay, day care, environmental protection, tax reform, etc.). It is a set of unquestionably important concerns but without the moral and spiritual vision that moves people, and in which people find themselves affirmed.

The Left's current preoccupation with "difference" reduces politics to the clamor of a willing tribalism. Far from a communal moral and spiritual vision, it offers an image of a world Balkanized into the endless proliferation of those who can claim some history of oppression and exclusion. Such oppression becomes a jealously guarded experience about which no one outside of it dare speak (without the accusation of acting imperiously and arrogantly). Again, our goal here is not to disregard the "difference," a denial of the experience, language, and distinctiveness, of people's lives. The world, as we know too well, has been hideously deformed by the way whole groups of human beings have been silenced and made invisible through the power of other people's discourse. Yet the validation of these disregarded voices is a necessary though not sufficient condition for radical social change. It too easily becomes a politics that divides people, excludes, and emphasizes our separation. It becomes a holier-than-thou sectarianism, very far from the image of a world in which we can all see ourselves valued and loved. And while we emphasize irreducible differences and distinctiveness, the Right and the religious fundamentalists will bludgeon us into a "recognition" of our common heritage, tradition, and values.

Perhaps the image of the "quilt" with its validation of the distinct patches whose singularity is enhanced by their continuity with others, and the richness of the whole, is the metaphor for a liberating communal life we like the best and think appropriate for our time. Despite what we have seen in the multiplicity of identities in modern society and the complexity of demand, claims, needs, and wants, we should not imagine that this lessens the power or significance of a morally and spiritually rooted communal vision as the leitmotif for a renewal of a politics of progressive social change.

SUBJECTIVITY IN CRISIS: FINDING THE LEFT CONSTITUENCY

Of course the struggle for a different definition of the purpose and goals of education in many ways turns on the matter of social agency; *who* will support and respond to an alternative language or vision of educational concerns?[13] Yet we have entered the postmodern world, as it is sometimes called, which makes it harder than before to clearly find and identify some kind of "natural" Left constituency.[14] For example, who are we to see or identify as the victims of oppression and who the perpetrators? Who will respond with enthusiasm for an alternative educational discourse and agenda that concerns itself, say, with issues of social justice, social responsibility, and democratic empowerment?

The shifting, more fluid nature of identity in today's culture, and the multiple forms of suffering, indignity, and deprivation felt by human beings in the world, make the ground on which we struggle to banish or at least mitigate oppression and pain a slippery one, which refuses any secure or stable point from which we may situate ourselves and understand who we are in relation to those around us. The human catastrophes of drug addiction or emotional illness, for example, create among those who are touched by their pain new forms of solidarity among people separated in other ways by social class, race, or other forms of identification. It creates new contexts in which human beings find themselves united in shared desperation and need. Within this context, different kinds of politics can emerge that pose questions about society, its compassion, and its supportiveness. Questions about addiction and emotional illness highlight deep veins of suffering and need that run through the society; forms of indignity and exclusion that crisscross the culture, signaling the breadth and scope of current pain and oppression. Like the crisis of the environment it represents a context of human experience that lends itself to new forms of shared concerns and expectations, and thus to new languages and images that may reorient the larger vision for our society, as well as our expectations and hopes for education.

Of course, while we wish to emphasize here the fluid and relatively open way in which political struggles—including those around education—might be constituted, it would be foolish to suggest (as some have) that the lines that distinguish oppressor and oppressed have lost all meaning or relevance; that we are all, for example, equally culpable for the ills and injustices in the world. The exploitation of labor by capital continues to be readily discernible. Corporate greed and disregard for the needs of the working and middle classes are all too visible. Military and political elites in this country support and supply material to authoritarian governments in the Third World that continue to suppress those who call for more equitable and democratic social and economic systems. At home, women suffer the structural violence of poverty and economic injustice, and the personal violence at the hands of men, for whom there are real social, cultural, and economic advantages in the existing gender arrangements.

While in some ways we may all be responsible for the current degradation of nature, this must not be confused with the guilt of those powerful political and economic interests who plunder the Earth's limited resources. Yet in spite of all this, none of us operate in sealed and all-dimensional social spaces. We slide quickly from roles where we exploit and dehumanize others to those where we ourselves are the object of other's instrumental attitudes and exploitative treatment. In the complexity of the contemporary world we occupy, others become for us targets of our prejudice, venality, or manipulation. In the loose and shifting sands of our world, there can be few of us who do not find ourselves scarred by the indifference, callousness, and indignity that are epidemic to both the private and public worlds we inhabit. Of course, for some, this process of psychic and spiritual wounding is more visible, more unrelenting, and sometimes more total. For people of color, women, gays and lesbians, the handicapped, the aged, the mentally ill, the poor, and all those who come to be, in our society, designated as "other," the pains of exclusion and abuse are obviously palpable.

Even domination, however, exacts its price in suffering. Robert Bly and others have, for example, begun to make the case for a male liberation for the drivenness and emotional stuntedness of masculine middle-class life, whose consequences are male rage, which more and more seems to explode on our streets and in our homes.[15] The rapid spread of reevaluation counseling among professional, middle-class men and women speaks also to the stored-up emotional and psychic distress, along with those who are, by society's standards, relatively successful. Again, we do not wish to suggest that all of the suffering in this society is on a par. The deprivations of homelessness, or poverty, or racism, or sexual abuse are certainly more brutal and more terrible than other forms of human suffering. The issue here is not whether we may find equivalence in the forms of pain and oppression. For some, oppression and victimization are unrelenting, in which survival itself is a matter of unrelieved struggle. Elsewhere, while survival itself may not be at issue, psychological mutilation is so great that any meaningful sense of personhood and of human agency is in doubt or has to be won in the face of society that constantly endangers it.

What we do wish to recognize is that there is no "privileged" bearer of oppression or suffering in our society. There is no simple duality that distinguishes people as *either* those who dominate, exploit, or inflict pain on others, or those who are its recipients. Political topographies that want to categorize the world in this way end up with rigid, predetermined images of "us" and "them," or "us" versus "them." They lead us to the reassuring simplicities of "enemy thinking." These maps have demographically carved up the population so that it is assumed from the outset who is politically "progressive" and who is not. The political images and understandings that people adopt are, from this point of view, foretold, mainly waiting in the wings for the curtain to rise before making their appearance according to an already rehearsed dramatization. Yet such interpretations, in their rigidity and dogmatism, start by ignoring the complexity of human experience and identity and therefore the increasingly problematic nature of our political affiliations and reference.

It is not unlikely, as Sharon Welch courageously acknowledges, to be at once both oppressor and oppressed. She writes as both a woman in a patriarchal culture and a professor at an elite university that is a cornerstone of the system of class privilege in the United States. Such contradictions are not uncommon in many of our lives. We may move routinely between positions that seem privileged and offer us authority and status to situations in which we are degraded, disempowered, and victimized. Such is the routine character, for example, of many women's lives.[16]

To understand all this is to appreciate the importance of Michel Foucalt's critique of the Marxist concept of power and categorization.[17] There is no *single* axis around which all relationships of power and domination, struggle and resistance, are plotted. There are instead a multiplicity of fields in which human beings struggle for freedom, justice, dignity, and a fuller realization of their lives. These fields overlap and cut across one another, producing a complex social map of human aspirations and struggles. Such struggles have their own dynamic, character, and set of possibilities. Families, schools, religious communities, neighborhoods, workplaces, cultural institutions, state institutions, and so on sustain and focus deep, even explosive, tensions.

While such tensions are fueled by the unrealized aspirations and disappointed hopes generated from within the culture, they cannot easily be assimilated to one another, reduced to one overarching problem that if resolved would herald a utopian transformation of the world—solving, at one stroke, all our problems and concerns. Relinquishing such an apocalyptic tale of revolutionary change may be disappointing to those who hunger for the simple, the universal, and the either/or explanation of events. Yet, nor does it diminish our sense of radical possibility and the hope of human transformation and social change. Quite the opposite. Relieved as we are from the old Left fixation on finding the historically "privileged" agent of social change or revolution, or the one real focus for radical struggle, we can now open our eyes and see a world replete with human aspirations for fulfillment, plenitude, dignity, justice, compassion, love, and spiritual significance, and the struggles to realize such possibilities in modern society. Of course, our different situations infect our hopes and struggles in different ways. The possibilities for change are shaped and delimited by the multiple discourses that share the diverse realities we confront each day.

Even within the life of one person, relative satisfaction at work, say, might give way to fury and agitation at the inability to be safe from harassment on the streets; economic well-being might be accompanied by the fear of family disintegration or the despair of a spiritual emptiness; or patriotic sentiments might coexist with a religious faith that impels one to work for the sanctuary of those who are the victims of U.S. collusion with fascist governments in Central or South America.

The politics that emerge from the fluidity and complexities of identity in contemporary America do not, it must be emphasized, negate those historically important social struggles. We in no sense wish to underestimate, for example, the long and difficult struggles by labor in this country to ameliorate exploitative economic relations or to advance the welfare and occupational conditions of working people. Likewise, nor do we wish to detract from the crucial value of movements like those for racial justice, for peace, or for sexual equality. Our goal is, however, to offer an educational language—and later an agenda—that can be as inclusive as possible, to recognize the fullest possible range of human struggles and concerns at this juncture in time.

A NEW DISCOURSE FOR THE LEFT: BEYOND MODERNITY

We believe that life in the United States at this time has become so anguished, alienating, ethically compromised, and spiritually impoverished that we are compelled both morally and politically to insist that education speak first and foremost to this human and social crisis. The crisis is pervasive and multidimensional in its effects—sometimes material, sometimes psychological and emotional, and sometimes spiritual (and often all of the above). It reaches into the corners and crevices of our society, producing the pauperization of some and misery of many.[18] Its consequences are in the form of shame, deprivation, indignity, and psychic distress. The desperate need for a transformative politics and an educational vision and language that is commensurate with this leads us to attempt to construct a discourse and an agenda that can speak to the widest range of people who might be responsive to the need for deep social change; who might recognize that our present cultural, moral, and economic paths as a nation (and as a planet) are destructive and dehumanizing.

This is not a time to speak to the converted (as sadly so much of critical educational scholarship tends to do), or to stay within the predictable and expected social constituencies, or to seek what is ideologically "correct" but politically ineffective.[19] We wish to emphasize that our struggles here are not ours alone. They belong to all those who are sincerely attempting to renew a Left vision and language where, for many, they are felt to be irrelevant, moribund, or antithetical to the "good" life. Among what we think are the best of these is a recognition that a Left renewal means to seriously question the tried and traditional language of Left politics and the subjects of such politics.[20] We are convinced, for example, that an "economic" discourse alone—that is, the question of how wealth is to be divided up between classes—is necessary but insufficient to mobilize the kind of support that is needed. Nor is it enough to attach Left politics solely to the language of political, civil, or social rights, or to the expansion of a democratic culture. As important as this is, such an emphasis does not speak clearly enough to the emotional distress and spiritual despair that comes from a world that

does not offer the support, solidarity, and compassion of a loving community.[21]

As important as is the language of economic justice it implies, in and of
itself, it says little about how we should reinterpret human beings' relationship to nature and the Earth; nor how we should break out of the ecodes-
tructive conditions of industrial societies that currently bind both working
class and the captains of industry to a global path that is suicidal.[22] Nor can
we find convincing any more the equation of the Left vision with the image
of a world that is thoroughly rational and therefore fully engineered.

For many of us, especially the young, what seems especially attractive is
rather a world in which the spontaneous, the unpredictable, and the ecstatic
flourish, in which individualism and freedom find deep and vibrant expression. What has been called the post-Fordist phase of capitalism with its com-
puterized capacity for unprecedented novelty, diversity, and creative fluidity
has made the old heroic production (oriented images of socialism) seem
repressive and archaic. In such conditions, the demand for diversity and
pleasure in everyday life cannot be derided as purely romantic escape or
capitalist excess.[23]

Nor is there much to find attractive in the Marxian promise of a society
wherein everything is fully transparent and accessible to reasoned intellect.
Such a vision seems positively perverse in its denial of the mysterious, the
unfathomable, and the wondrous. While, for example, we might insist on
women's reproductive rights, we need also to acknowledge the difficulties
and dilemmas that do indeed surround the question of how and when we
might assert that the precious phenomenon of human life comes into being.
As our life-world is corroded and subjected by the technocratic order with
its depersonalization and abstract rationalities, so men and women under-
standably turn to the religious, the spiritual, and the mystical as means of
asserting the ineffable qualities of human life and experience.[24]

The Left's long marriage to modernism with its narratives that are so
determinedly secular, rationalistic, and instrumental has wrought a vision
that finds itself at odds with many of the most powerful and moving discourses of human freedom and resistance in the world today.[25] But to accept
and include such discourses in its own language of transformation and
change means to shed any remaining illusions about our capacity to describe
the world as it really is, rather than in *metaphors* that offer resonant and
evocative images concerning human existence and possibilities.

Perhaps the difficulty of doing this is reflected in the Left's (and particular
Left intellectuals) reluctance to fully embrace the language that has emerged
from liberation theology and feminist and creation spirituality—surely some
of the most moving and powerful revolutionary discourses in existence today.[26] To include the spiritual and the religious in our language of social or
educational change is to acknowledge that political struggle is not so much
about "truth" but about how we and others can image or reimage the

world. It is about the way we can envision human possibility, to identify a meaningful existence. Just at the moment when the Left has come to recognize so clearly the mass psychic impoverishment that both capitalism and bureaucratic socialism have wrought, it has been captured by a sensibility that is increasingly cynical and increasingly reluctant to articulate the value of universal human rights, of liberation, community, and social justice.[27] Such notions are dismissed by critics as but part of the metaphysics of modernity and so-called enlightenment. What is offered is instead nothing but the endless transgression of cultural limits and the proliferation of differences among people. Yet for many people this "postmodern bazaar" is repulsive and terrifying. It is part of the problem not the solution. It offers little that validates tradition; it provides little that connects us across time and space; and it says little about what might transcend the particular, the local, and the contingent and be able to speak to the whole human condition.[28]

CONCLUSIONS: TRANSFORMING THE PUBLIC DISCOURSE ON EDUCATION

For those for us critical intellectuals in education, then, the struggle must be for a public discourse that privileges no one group of people; one that tries to speak to and include the experience, needs, and hopes of a broad spectrum of people in our society who together can constitute what Stuart Hall has referred to as a "social bloc"—a political movement comprising a diverse set of social groups who might favor deep social and educational change.[29] The language we need is one that is broad and inclusive and attempts to be rooted in aspects of our national culture; one that seems to make possible the articulation of the multiple concerns of human beings who, in obviously different ways, might be moved by a vision of education whose overriding task is what has been called *tikkum olam*, the healing and repair of our society and the world.

In this sense, we seek here to offer a discourse for education centered in a broad moral language that can embrace and express the variety and complexity of wounds, indignities, and exclusions that are the experiences of our fellow citizens. To construct this "social bloc" means to find ways by which dissimilar people with distinct, sometimes divergent, interests can come together and find common ground. It means to seek a language, and an agenda, for education that reflects the particular struggles and aspirations of social groups and can reconcile their differences without denying or subordinating any of them.

To talk of a transformative educational discourse means to offer a language and an agenda for educational reform that insists that the most important purpose of what we do in our schools is to educate the young for a socially just, socially responsible, democratic, and compassionate community. In proposing that the work of education be conceived of in these terms means, on the one hand, to envisage an education that works for the transformation of our culture in ways that emphasize the overarching moral imperative of a compassionate, solidaristic, and participatory society. Yet, at the same time, this vision must not turn into some monolithic, moral, strait-jacket while dictating educational concerns in narrowly defined ways. The struggle for a fuller, deeper, and more humane community may in some set of circumstances mean the insistence that education be about ensuring lit-eracy; elsewhere it may mean the possibility of jobs; or in some other places political participation and empowerment.

Given what we have stressed is the complex nature of identity and the diversity of ways that people are concerned with humane transformation of our culture and the world, we want to ensure that our educational language be an agenda that is not confused with the dead hand of some program-matically "correct" instructional methodology curriculum or form of ped-agogy. The overriding concern for an alternative, appealing, and catalytic public discourse for education is to be understood as quite distinct from questions of exactly what and how we teach in the classroom (even when this is conceived in the radical forms of critical or feminist pedagogy). Our concern here is not to advocate a particular methodology or form of ped-agogy. Of course, this is not irrelevant to reshaping education; but it should not be confused with our present task, which is to formulate and offer a broad and inclusive discursive framework through which a diversity of peo-ple can see the concerns and hopes they have for themselves and their chil-dren, given expression and related to the purposes of education in this country.

The struggle here is not about pedagogy as much as it is about education's place in what we earlier referred to as the political imaginary. It is about how to conceive of the purpose and goals of education. It is about winning the minds and hearts of people to a different set of goals for education—an education that is explicitly linked to the transformation of the social and cultural reality in which we live. And this is not to be reduced to matters of classroom methodologies, modes of teaching, and such. Notwithstanding the obvious importance of these matters to the actual process of education, we do not want to be caught in the trap of technique, an obsessive focus on matters of practice, or questions of how to do things in the classrooms. And in order to do this it is worth running the risk of urging a different kind of conversation—one that might be dismissed as removed from real school concerns, but that insists on referencing the larger human, cultural, moral, and spiritual vision within which we wish to educate our children. It does not aim to displace matters or questions of practice but only to act as the reference point (or points) for how we are to conceive of the value and purpose of what education ought to be in this society at this time.

Educational work is made more meaningful and vital by its situatedness in this vision. The political effectiveness of this vision (i.e., the extent of its appeal and support) depends on how well it is capable of drawing in and articulating the diverse and divergent needs and concerns of ordinary people. It depends on how well an education oriented to this vision can be seen as speaking to their lives and, more importantly, to the lives of their children. This, it is worth recalling, was almost certainly the failure of those socialist-dominated London borough councils that decided to place so many of their educational eggs in the basket of antisexist, antiracist or antihomophobic curricular changes. It was not that such changes were wrong. Of course, such concerns are important dimensions of a progressive agenda for education. But they appeared to be entirely sectional in their concerns, responding to the demands of a limited set of political constituencies. They appeared to speak to radical educational or political interests and at the expense of, or disregard for, many working-class or middle-class parents, who say their policy or curriculum changes are antithetical to their interest or concerns.[30] As such, the educational agenda of the Left in these places rapidly became subject to an "us" versus "them" kind of politics in which the concerns of the majority of people were portrayed (and experienced) as being slighted by the insurgent and divisive demands of radical political interests.

Whatever the deliberate distortions and manipulations of information and images by a right-wing press and politicians in such circumstances there was, at the same time, the every real phenomenon of an educational language and agenda that seemed to exclude many from its concerns; to not speak to, or articulate, the real issues and needs of many within the society. The same danger is apparent in the emphasis today in radical education circles within critical or feminist pedagogues, or defining educational change in terms of revitalizing what it means to be a citizen and in the pursuit of what has been called a critical democracy. Again the issue is not that these are not valuable and valid aspects of what we on the Left have to offer education in the present situation. It is that they are too limited in what is emphasized, too circumscribed in who they address, too one-sided in their definition of what constitutes educational renewal. The result is, as is quite clear from the limited enthusiasm or acceptance of the whole critical pedagogy project, an agenda for education that is simply not sufficiently resonant with the concerns of many people.[31] Indeed, it is one that is glaring in its disregard for a whole range of human concerns such as the role of tradition, the spiritual, community and obligation, responsibility and discipline (concerns that loom large in some of the major antimodernist revolts in recent times around the world).

In this regard it is worth noting what we believe has become the inadequate emphasis in recent post-Marxist, socialist political thinking (such as that found in the influential book by Ernesto Laclau and Chantal Mouffe) on making the expansion of democratic life the leitmotif of radical social change in contemporary society.[32] Our response again is that such concerns are necessary but insufficient as the way to image our future social reality.

Radically extending popular empowerment in economic, cultural, and political life is a crucially important goal of a society that is more and more subject to a quality of existence emptied of any meaningful democratic experiences; in which most of us are increasingly moved from any real opportunity to shape or control our collective future.

The project of directing our reform or changes in education to a deepening of the meaning of democratic rights and responsibilities in the public sphere is certainly a crucial concern for those of us on the Left. Yet we are convinced that the concept of an education that can speak to a healing and a repair of our world must say more than this if it is to be heeded. It must be capable of touching people's spiritual and emotional lives through what have been called the feminine moral images: of wholeness, compassion, care, and responsibility. This the notion of social rights and democratic empowerment cannot do. They are a necessary but insufficiently evocative set of concerns for a transformational politics in the closing years of this century. The politics of radical change in these years will belong to those who can successfully articulate the postmodern—or antimodern—impulses that are increasingly being unleashed in the world.[33]

In the case of education, until now it has been the Right and the religious fundamentalists who have, for the most part, showed themselves more adept at this task. They have been (for obvious reasons) the more successful and the more ready to assume this kind of language. They have, we believe, been able to step into what we know from our work with teachers and community groups is the discursive emptiness of the present moment, where educational talk is conducted without reference to some prophetic vision of society or human life; a discourse bereft of the mobilizing power that can come only through a moral focus that can link the work of education to the needs, hopes, and possibilities of the larger culture. Such a focus is one that would insist on linking our education concerns, policies, practices, and goals to the question of the quality and character of our personal and communal lives. It would insist that educational questions are always, at the same time, questions about what it means to be human and about how we as humans ought to live together.

NOTES

This chapter has been developed as part of a larger project on the construction of a new public discourse for education undertaken by the author and his colleague David E. Purpel.

1. The assertion of "totalizing" political thinking and its inherent dangers has been central to the critique of Marxism by both postmodern and feminist writers. See, for example, David Kolb, *The Critique of Pure Modernity* (Chicago: University of Chicago Press, 1987); Jean-François Lyotard, *The Postmodern Condition* (Minneapolis: University of Minnesota Press, 1984); Michel Foucault, *Power/Knowledge:*

Selected Interviews and Other Writings, 1972–77. (New York: Pantheon, 1980); Linda Nicholson (ed.), *Feminism/Postmodernism* (New York: Routledge, 1990).

2. Alvin Gouldner, *The Two Marxisms* (New York: Seabury Press, 1990); Martin Jay; *Marxism and Totality* (Berkeley: University of California Press, 1984); Russell Jacoby; *Dialectic of Defeat* (Cambridge: Cambridge University Press, 1981).

3. A growing concern with the emphasis on "difference" in Left political thinking at the expense of a notion of community is found in a number of writers. See, for example, Marshall Berman, "Why Modernism Still Matters," *Tikkun*, January/February, 1987; Barry Kanpol, *Towards a Theory and Practice of Teacher Cultural Politics: Continuing the Postmodern Debate* (Norwood, NJ: Ablex, 1992); Wendy Kohli, "Postmodernism, Critical Theory and the 'New' Pedagogues: What's at Stake in the Discourse?" *Education and Society*, 9(1) (1991): 39–46 (special issue edited by Peter McLaren); Suzanne Moore, "Gender, Post Modern Style," *Marxism Today*, May 1990.

4. See, for example, Steven Cormor, *Postmodern Culture* (New York: Basil Blackwell, 1989); David Kolb, *Postmodernism Publication* (Chicago: University of Chicago Press, 1990); Douglas Kellner, *Jean Baudrillard: From Marxism to Postmodernism and Beyond* (Oxford: Polity Press, 1988).

5. Fritjof Capra and Charlene Spretnal, *Green Politics* (New York: E. P. Dutton, 1984); Carl Boggs, *Social Movements and Political Power* (Philadelphia: Temple University Press, 1986).

6. Rudolf Bahro, *The Alternatives in Eastern Europe* (London: NLB, 1978).

7. See, for example, Frances Fox Piven and Richard A. Cloward, *The New Class War* (New York: Pantheon, 1982); Boggs, *Social Movements and Political Power*; Jürgen Habermas, *Legitimation Crisis* (Boston: Beacon Press, 1975); Richard Flacks, *Making History: The Radical Tradition in American Life* (New York: Columbia University Press, 1988).

8. Douglas Kellner, *Critical Theory: Marxism and Modernity* (Baltimore: Johns Hopkins University Press, 1989).

9. See, for example, H. Svi Shapiro, *Between Capitalism and Democracy: Education Policy and the Crisis of the Welfare State* (Westport, CT: Greenwood Press, 1990); also, Stanley Aronowitz and Henry A. Giroux, *Education Still under Siege* (Westport, CT: Bergin & Garvey, 1994); Ira Shore, *Culture Wars* (Boston: Routledge, 1986).

10. Michael Lerner, "A New Paradigm for Liberals: The Primacy of Ethics and Emotions," *Tikkun*, 2(1) (1987): 22–28, 132–138.

11. Ibid., pp. 24–25.

12. See ibid.; also see Christopher Lasch, "What's Wrong With the Right," *Tikkun*, 1(1) (1986): 23–29; and Robert Bellah et al., *Habits of the Heart* (Berkeley: University of California Press, 1985).

13. For an analysis of the question of social agency in the quest for radical school reform, see Svi Shapiro, "Beyond the Sociology of Education: Culture, Politics, and the Promise of Educational Change," *Educational Theory*, 38(4) (Fall 1988): 415–430; also see Geoff Whitty, *Sociology and School Knowledge* (London: Methuen, 1985).

14. There is now a large literature that attempts to address this issue. See, for example, the work of Stanley Aronowitz, *The Crisis in Historical Materialism* (Minneapolis: University of Minnesota Press, 1990); Stuart Hall, *The Hard Road to Re-*

newal (London: Verso, 1988); Raymond Williams, *The Year 2000* (New York: Pantheon Books, 1983).

15. R. Todd Erkel, "The Birth of a Movement," *Networker* May/June 1990, pp. 26–35.

16. Sharon Welch, *Communities of Resistance and Solidarity* (New York: Orbis Press, 1985).

17. Foucault, *Power/Knowledge*. See also Nancy Hartsock, "Foucault on Power: A Theory for Women," in Nicholson, *Feminism/Postmodernism*.

18. The list of authors who have contributed to our view of the ethical and spiritual crisis of the nation is a long one. It includes Cornel West, Michael Harrington, Robert Bellah, Barbara Ehrenreich, Theodore Roszack, Matthew Fox, Beverly Harrison, Maya Angelou, Michael Lerner, Philip Slater, Richard Sennett, Sharon Welch, Dorothy Soelle, Harvey Cox, Peter Clecak, and Sallie McPhague, among others.

19. This criticism must not be interpreted in a personalized manner. In no sense is this statement meant to invalidate the overall powerful and important work of critical educational theorists that has been, and continues to be, done. It concerns only the accessibility of what has been written and the need for a discourse about schools that can go beyond the limited constituencies that are now its primary audience.

20. Among these, Michael Lerner, Cornel West, Dorothy Soelle, Isaac Balbus, Stuart Hall, Douglas Kellner, Stanley Aronowitz, Sheila Rowbottom, Andrew Gorz, Murray Bookchin, Jean Cohell, Terry Eagleton, bell hooks, and others.

21. See, for example, Sharon Welch, *A Feminist Ethic of Risk* (Minneapolis: Fortress Press, 1990); Beverly Harrison, *Making the Connections* (Boston: Beacon Press, 1985); Matthew Fox, *A Spirituality Named Compassion* (Minneapolis: Winston Press, 1979).

22. See, for example, Andre Gorz, *Ecology as Politics* (Boston: South End Press, 1980); Murray Bookchin, *The Modern Crisis* (Philadelphia: New Society Publishers, 1986); Petra Kelly, *Fighting for Hope* (Boston: South End Press, 1984).

23. See, for example, *Marxism Today*, October 1988 special edition on "New Times"; also see Alvin Toffler, *Powershift* (New York: Bantam Books, 1990).

24. See, for example, Peter Gabel, "Creationism and the Spirit of Nature," *Tikkun*, 2(5) (1987): 55–63; Michael Harrington, *The Politics at God's Funeral* (New York: Holt, Rinehart and Winston, 1983); Harvey Cox, *Religion in the Secular City* (New York: Simon and Schuster, 1984); see also the work of Marion Woodman, Theodore Roszack, or Fritjob Capra.

25. See, for example, Isaac D. Balbus, *Marxism and Domination* (Princeton, NJ: Princeton University Press, 1982); see also Terry Eagleton, *The Ideology of the Aesthetic* (Oxford: Basil Blackwell, 1990).

26. See, for example, the work in this country of Sharon Welch, Beverly Harrison, Dorothy Soelle, Matthew Fox, Walter Breuggeman, Starhawk, and Judith Plaskow.

27. This is perhaps best reflected in the wave of admiration for the work of the French guru of postmodern social theory, Jean Baudrillard, with its cynical, self-indulgent assertion of the meaninglessness of social and political struggle. For an excellent discussion of the phenomenon, see Kellner, *Jean Baudrillard*.

28. Of course, it is this that is embodied in the fearful conservatism of intellectuals like Alan Bloom, Daniel Bell, E. D. Hirsch, William Bennett, and others.

29. See, for example, Stuart Hall, "Blue Election, Election Blues," *Marxism Today*, July 1987, pp. 30–35.

30. See, for example, Brian Simon, "Lessons in Elitism," *Marxism Today*, September 1987, pp. 12–17.

31. See, for example, H. Svi Shapiro, "Educational Theory and Recent Political Discourse: A New Agenda for the Left?" *Teachers College Record*, 89 (2) (Winter 1987).

32. Ernest Laclau and Chantal Mouffe, *Hegemony and Socialist Strategy: Towards a Radical Democratic Politics.* (London: Verso, 1985); see also Samuel Bowles and Herbert Gintin, *Democracy and Capitalism* (New York: Basic Books, 1986).

33. See, for example, Cox, *Religion in the Secular City.*

2

Radical Democracy, the Politics of Difference, and Education

Michael Peters

Are the democracies that govern the world's richest countries capable of solving the problems that communism has failed to solve? That is the question.

Norberto Bobbio, 1991

On the eve of the twenty-first century, amid the upheavals the world is witnessing, the task of rethinking democratic politics is more urgent than ever. For those who refuse to see "really existing" liberal democratic capitalism at the "end of history," radical democracy is the only alternative.

Chantal Mouffe, 1992

THE MARKETIZATION OF DEMOCRACY

At the same time as historical communism in Eastern Europe was disintegrating in a series of popular uprisings that quickly gained force after 1989, the declining capitalist economies of the United States and Britain approached the end of the first decade of "reform" designed to restore market liberalism in a fierce repudiation of Keynesian policies that had been dedicated to the establishment of the welfare state and the elimination of mass unemployment. At the very moment when people in communist states began, en masse, to articulate the urgent demand for democracy at great human cost, the principles of liberal democracy under the new Right had become even more firmly identified with the defense of private property and the capitalist economy in a rejuvenation of economic liberalism that severely compromised the ideal of equality and reduced the notion of freedom to a narrowly individualistic concept based on consumer rights.

In countries like Britain, the United States, Australia, and New Zealand, the push to establish a fully privatized market society has meant an historic entrenchment of the connection between the political project of liberal democracy and economic liberalism with, accordingly, less hope of rehabilitating notions of citizenship and community as the basis for a more participatory and pluralistic democracy. With the subordination of both the state and civic society to the market, the nature of democracy has undergone profound changes. There has been a move away from normatively regulated parliamentary processes to systems of informal bargaining and contracting where the state operates, increasingly independent of its electoral support, in support of big business. There has been a strong separation of administration from public opinion and democratic participation and, increasingly, the traditional ethos of service that used to characterize public administration has been replaced by the "new managerialism" based on private-sector models. Government has been entrusted to a public policy elite, to government ministers and their expert advisers, who do not allow themselves to be influenced or captured by political considerations represented by the vested interests of the wider public.

With the introduction of the new information technologies, a new media-based mode of electoral politics has emerged based on intensive public opinion polling and the techniques of mass marketing. In the age of telepolitics, democracy has become a pure spectacle. On this model, which developed under the sway of rational choice theorists, the structural parallel between the political and economic systems is almost complete: political parties have become entrepreneurs in a profit-seeking economy; professional media consultants use policies as part of the packaging to sell candidates in the political marketplace; voters, modeled on the assumptions of *homo economicus*, have become passive individual consumers.

The effects of these changes have been to privatize public opinion, to reduce the need to consult, to subordinate policy issues to matters of political style, to compromise standards of public accountability to grassroots membership, to minimize the potential for active participation in the political process, and to greatly increase the opportunities for the manipulation of public opinion. In short, democracy has become commodified with the revival and ascendancy of economic liberalism at the cost of the project of political liberalism; civil society and the state have become subordinated to the market.

Nowhere is this more true than in the sphere of public education. Education was conceived and shaped as, perhaps, the most important social democratic institution of the welfare state, concerned, above all, with the promotion of equality of opportunity and with the question of social integration. On the one hand, it was seen as the primary means for establishing a meritocracy. On the other hand, it was seen as a way of pursuing the goals of social democracy. As one of the most important forms of government intervention, public education in postwar liberal democratic states served to socialize individuals into the larger society and provided the major avenue for intergenerational mobility. Of all state institutions it was the one that instilled some faith in the ideals of democracy. As the central legitimating institution it held out the possibility for fundamental change and hope for the future. In some respects the separation between economic and political liberalism was clearest in the realm of state-funded education. Criticisms, of course, were made: public education, like the welfare state in general, had been overly paternalistic, bureaucratic, and centralized; the ideology of equality of opportunity served to mask how schools reproduce the dominant social relations of the larger society. These criticisms were made in the service of the egalitarian dream, to deepen the political commitment to the ideals of social democracy. They also offered a set of strategies, both philosophical and practical, whereby those who have been systematically excluded from the public sphere of education could begin the process of claiming their democratic rights.

These strategies made some headway in the late 1960s and 1970s as the notion of rights was developed and instantiated in legalistic conceptions of equal employment and educational opportunities and in the idea of affirmative action. Some gains in person rights were made during this period, but the liberal conception was still strongly tied to a Kantian version that, while it avoided a propertarian interpretation, was still committed to highly individualistic and rationalistic assumptions that it adopted from and shared with neoclassical economic theory. It shared, for instance, the principle of methodological individualism: the assumption that rationality is exclusively an attribute of individual actors. Such a view militated against the recognition of collective rights, of rights that could be justifiably predicated of social and cultural groups on the basis of their shared political identities. At the point when political theorists were beginning to articulate an alternative account of citizenship based on the politics of difference—an account that recognized and affirmed group differences—and the new social movements implicitly appealed to a conception of social justice based on group rights, the whole discourse of citizenship was officially abandoned as neoliberals substituted the market for the polity as a distributive mechanism. In essence, the neoliberal restructuring of public education led to forms of deregulation and privatization whereby market principles replaced political principles and, accordingly, the sovereignty of the consumer replaced that of the citizen.

What has been a curious and, indeed, an ironic characteristic of the debate concerning the role of the state is that neoliberals should echo classic left-wing criticisms. They have readily seized left-wing arguments concerning a reappraisal of the welfare state. These arguments have not, however, been advanced as a basis either to improve the conditions of those groups structurally disadvantaged, or for a rethinking of more effective and feasible alternatives to the bureaucratic welfare state. Rather they have been used as a set of arguments from which to infer *political* conclusions for the reduction of the role of the state, for a reprivatization of the public sphere and for a reduction of welfare interventionism.

THE POSSIBILITIES OF RADICAL DEMOCRACY

Noberto Bobbio (1987, 1990) has consistently argued that it is only through a deepening of the liberal democratic tradition that socialist goals can be achieved (although he favors the liberal idea of representative democracy over more participatory forms). Chantal Mouffe (1988, 1992) concurs, arguing that it is not possible to find more radical principles for organizing society than those of freedom and equality: they have provided the symbolic resources to wage democratic struggles in the past and democratic advances have occurred as new groups have claimed rights on the basis of them. The notion of radical democracy is simply a recognition of this state of affairs. It is, at the same time, a deepening and radicalization of the modern democratic tradition through immanent critique, using all the symbolic resources of that tradition, to bring about a reconciliation between the professed ideals and their realization in practice.

For Mouffe such a reconciliation depends upon a reformulation of the liberal tradition. It depends, in the first instance, upon breaking the connection between the political project of liberal democracy and economic liberalism so as to free modern democracy from its highly rationalistic and individualistic premises, while rehabilitating the notions of citizenship and community as the basis for a more participatory and pluralistic conception. Radical democracy thus defined, Mouffe argues, is the only hope for the renewal of the left-wing project. Yet this deceptively simple outline of the project for radical democracy leaves unanswered a vitally important question: How is it possible to rehabilitate notions of community and citizenship without succumbing to an ideology of individualism or falling back on some notion of an organic sociocultural unity? In other words, how is it possible to reinvent notions of citizenship and community that recognize the increasing degree of differentiation characterizing pluralistic societies in the West without privileging either the liberal notion of individual or the Marxist notion of class?

The two arms of this question concerning the crucial issue of political identity and agency in increasingly pluralistic societies have been taken up in separate but related debates. On the one hand, communitarians have critiqued the individualism underlying liberalism and in recent political theorizing liberal thinkers have begun to confront the challenge of the communitarian critique through the strategy of reforming the core presuppositions of liberalism to provide an expanded account of the individual subject. On the other hand, poststructuralist thinkers have raised an important set of objections against those who seek to develop a notion of radical democracy based on a universal conception of community, appealing to an organic sociocultural unity.

My argument is that the project to reform liberalism and the project of radical democracy based on a notion of community, whether defined in universal or historical contingent terms, have been unsuccessful precisely to the extent that they have ignored the poststructuralist critique of subject-centered reason and the historical importance of the new social movements. Both liberal and communitarians, for instance, are tied into a basic opposition characteristic of the binary logic of modernism: they each privilege one term or concept that the other seeks to deny. The former, committed to an ideology of individualism, privileges the individual in universal and historical terms as the ultimate unit of analysis. Both Kantian and market liberals share an emphasis on rationality as the exclusive predicate of individual actors, but where Kantian liberals provide a procedural interpretation of Kant's concept of autonomy and his notion of the categorical imperative to emphasize formal rights, market liberals draw on the behavioral postulate of *homo economicus*, arguing that people should be treated as "rational utility-maximizers" in all of their behavior.

Communitarians, by contrast, claim that liberal theory is excessively individualistic and not sufficiently historically and culturally sensitive. Liberal theory, on this account, misunderstands claims to rights. Rights are not to be treated as transcendent principles but rather as historical and contingent features of liberal communities. Communitarians deny methodological individualism, arguing that rationality can be predicated also of institutions and political cultures. On this view, the political community is not merely an aggregate of individuals but rather constitutive of what it is to be a human being. We are what and who we are by virtue of our membership in a community of shared values and meanings. Communitarians, while more historically sensitive, are wedded to a notion of community that is privileged over and against the notion of the individual in an appeal to an organic unity.

Iris Young (1990, p. 228) has effectively argued that contemporary discussion sets up an exhaustive dichotomy in a set of binary oppositions: individualism/community, separated self/shared self, private/public. Yet the terms "individualism" and "community" share a common logic that permits them to define each other negatively.

Each entails a denial of difference and a desire to bring multiplicity and heterogeneity into unity, though in opposing ways. Liberal individualism denies difference by positing the self as a solid, self-sufficient unity, not defined by anything or anyone other than itself. Its formalistic ethic of rights also denies difference by bringing all such separated individuals under a common measure of rights. Proponents of community, on the other hand, deny difference by positing fusion rather than separation as the social ideal. They conceive the social subject as a relation of unity or mutuality composed by identification and symmetry among individuals within a totality. Communitarianism represents an urge to see persons in unity with one another in a shared whole. (Young, 1990a, p. 228)

The question of unity is also one that Jean-François Lyotard (1984) explores in relation to Jürgen Habermas' work. Habermas (1985, p. 196) believes that if modernity has failed, it has done so by allowing the splintering of the totality of life, or unity of experience, into "a pluralization of diverging universes of discourse." His answer to this "specifically modern experience" is to seek a relinking of modern culture with an everyday praxis through "clarifying a concept of communicative rationality that escapes the snares of Western logocentrism." The version of radical democracy formulated in terms of the Habermasian problematic is, therefore, a universalistic one appealing to a notion of unity. Further, it is one that is defended on the basis of transcendental arguments grounded in an evolutionary conception of moral development. Habermas dreams of a kind of radical democracy, based on the ideal of transparent communication, where validity claims are discursively redeemable at the level of discourse and the force of pure argumentation reigns without the possibility of coercion or domination.

Lyotard's (1984, pp. 72–73) question is to determine what sort of unity Habermas has in mind:

Is the aim of the project of modernity the constitution of sociocultural unity within which all elements of daily life and of thought take their places as in an organic whole? Or does the passage that has to be charted between heterogeneous language games—those of cognition, of ethics, of politics—belong to a different order from that? And if so, would it be capable of effecting a real synthesis between them?

The first hypothesis, of Hegelian inspiration, does not challenge the notion of a dialectically totalizing *experience*; the second is closer to the spirit of Kant's *Critique of Judgment*; but must be submitted to that severe reexamination of the thought of the Enlightenment, on the idea of a unitary end of history and of a subject.

The notion of the unity of experience as expressed in the appeal to an organic whole or a sociocultural unity exemplified in the liberal discourse of "one nation, one culture" is the foundation of the dominant conceptions of democracy, including its radical Left-Hegelian variant. Advocates of this view prescribe one set of democratic norms and defend them either in terms of a universalist philosophy based on Enlightenment reason (Habermas), or, jettisoning the epistemological project of self-foundation, in terms of a more pragmatic and openly ethnocentric strategy—the institutions and practices that characterize North Atlantic democracies simply are the best that have evolved to date (Richard Rorty).

The problem of the "Other" in liberal democracies has obvious historical roots going back beyond the establishment of the modern nation-state. The modern origins of one distinctive form of the problem, in political terms, dates from the first European contact with indigenous races and cultures of the New World and in the process of colonization that followed. Its intellectual origins are evident in theories of the development of the nation-state and in associated theories of race. The problem also clearly surfaces in anthropological literature and in European evaluations of primitive or traditional cultures and rationalities.

The specifically modern variant of the problem of the Other, especially as it has appeared in the policy discourses of liberal democracies since World War II, has been dominated by an assimilationalist ideal—an ideal that lies close to the heart of liberal ideology and helps define the liberal vision of society—liberal ideology expressing an assimilationalist ideal aimed at creating a nation-state in which one culture and language was dominant. The one nation, one culture conception is based on a set of ideals and values that depict the liberal vision of a modern democracy—a common national culture in which all individuals, freed from their ethnic origins and their traditional cultural beliefs, can participate fully in a modern, technological society. Cultural pluralism and the traditionalism of ethnic minority groups, on this view, are seen as inconsistent or at odds with the demands of modern society: they promote group rights over individual rights, regarding the group rather than the individual as primary; they stress historic prejudices based on we-they attitudes; they also lead to the Balkanization of the nation-state. The traditionalism of these other cultures, the liberal assimilationalist argues, therefore exacerbates rather than diminishes inequality, stratification based on group ethnicity, and cultural conflict.

Modern liberal discourse in its conception of citizenship has systematically excluded groups historically defined as Other. It has effectively achieved this end by promoting an idea of civic community that is both homogeneous and monocultural—the aggregate of free, rational, and autonomous individuals. This universalist and rational construction of the individual as citizen "brackets out particularity, difference, and the vicissitudes of embodiment": "the *res publica* in the liberal vision cannot assume substantive features precisely because it brackets out all that belongs to the substantive social life of individuals. Like the market it admits only the formally commensurable features of individual lives" (Yeatman, 1992, p. 5).

On this basis the liberal civic ideal excludes not just the cultural Other but all minorities who do not or cannot exhibit the universal characteristics of the formal ideal. As Yeatman (1992) has demonstrated so well, the ontological approach to citizenship of liberal discourse, which dictates that civic community originates in a shared order of being as the foundation of *one* group with a bounded and coherent identity, is at odds with the "contemporary politics of voice and representation." Such a politics, Yeatman (1992, p. 3) argues, "opens up the group itself to its internal lines of dissent and contested domination, and to its own historically specific contradictions, ambiguities, ambivalences, 'forgettings' and repressions." She points out that liberal discourse shares the assimilative ideal with the other dominant discourses of modern citizenship. The republican discourse sets up a vision of a substantive civic community based on the regulative ideal of a participatory and dialogical reason, which is monocultural and intolerant of a plurality of differences. The republican ideal postulates a public that comes into being through reason, a rational consensus that assimilates substantive cultural differences and denies the heterogeneity of social life. The welfare state discourse of citizenship shares similar faults.

[It is] predicated on a dualism of independence and dependency. It comes out of the same complex of values as the modern republican and liberal discourses of citizenship. They all identify the modal citizen with the formal individuality of the rationally-oriented, freely contracting subject. For such an identification to work, all that is substantively needy about our lives, which makes us interdependent with each other, has to be bracketed out. Again the welfare state discourse invents an other on whom this interdependency conceptualized as dependency is projected: women, who thereby become associated with all who are substantively needy (husbands, children, elderly parents, disabled relatives, etc.). (Yeatman, 1992, p. 6)

With the communitarian critique of liberalism we have learned to be suspicious of the universal and rationalistic pretensions underlying abstract individualism, which both abstracts individuals from their social and cultural contexts and disregards the role of social relationships and community in constituting the very identity and nature of human beings. We have come to realize that the individuals of neoliberalism, posited as rational utility-maximizers and theorized to form communities based fundamentally on competition, covertly screen out gender and cultural values. Neoliberalism thereby promotes an ideal of community that subscribes to an instrumental conception of social relations, based on calculated self-interest. Most importantly, perhaps, we are beginning to understand that modern liberal thought rests on individualistic *male* values that originate in the false universalization of a particularistic, sociohistorical, eurocentric conception of being. From the perspective of feminist communitarianism,

highly individuated selves have been viewed as a problem. They are seen as incapable of human attachments based on mutuality and trust, unresponsive to human needs, approaching social relationships merely as rationally self-interested utility maximizers, thriving on separation and competition, and creating social institutions which tolerate, even legitimize violence and aggression. (Friedman, 1989, p. 280)

As educators, negotiating our practice within the confines of increasingly privatized, market societies, we are having to relearn the social, cultural, and institutional consequences of living under an ideology of individualism. Yet at the same time, as Friedman (1989) argues, communitarian philosophy disregards gender-related problems of community. It is clear that traditional communities are and have been highly oppressive for women, ascribing them subservient roles on the basis of a primitive division of labor and denying them status as fully fledged members of the community. The same argument applies to other minorities and their exclusion from the polity. While communitarian philosophy has a relevant and significant critique to make of liberalism, it is guilty of substituting one universalistic notion, that of the social self, for another, the individual self (see Peters and Marshall, 1993). In this way, communitarians falsely romanticize the notion of community, privileging unity over difference. The notion of community based on the universal idea of the social self can be undesirably utopian and politically problematic in several ways. As Young (1986, p. 2) argues,

it fails to see that alienation and violence are not only a function of mediation of social relations but can and do exist in face-to-face relations. It implausibly proposes a society without a city. It fails to address the political questions of the relations among face-to-face communities.

The ideal of community, finally, totalizes and detemporalizes the conception of social life by setting up an opposition between authentic and inauthentic social relations.

Elsewhere, Young (1990, p. 234) restates her original objection in unambiguous terms: simply, the ideal of community that values and enforces homogeneity often operates to exclude or oppress those seen as different. This objection, succinctly stated, of course, works just as effectively against those attempts to reform liberalism to make it compatible with an expanded view of the individual so as to accommodate the communitarian critique (e.g., Gutmann, 1985, 1989). An expanded or reformed liberalism that attempts to combine community with a commitment to basic liberal values, moreover, suffers a number of obstacles. First, it must jettison its highly universalistic and rationalistic pretensions in its construction of the citizen as individual to take on board the criticism of being insufficiently historical in its orientation. In so doing, political liberalism must distance itself, at this critically historical juncture, from the assumption of *homo economicus* that underlies neo-liberalism. While this might be possible at the level of theory, it seems to me both unlikely and improbable at the level of practice. To this extent, while I am sympathetic to Mouffe's position, I also remain skeptical of its intermediate historical possibilities. Second, having effected a marriage between the abstract individualism of liberalism and the notion of community (assuming such a project might be carried through), any reformed project still faces those criticisms aimed at communitarian theory. In this respect, a reformed liberalism still faces the poststructural critique of subject-centered reason, out of which the demand for a politics of difference emerges.

THE POLITICS OF DIFFERENCE

The case for a politics of difference and a notion of participatory or radical democracy based upon it, while still in its infancy, is developed strongly in the work of Iris Marion Young (1990, 1992), and those who follow her basic orientation (e.g., Yeatman, 1992). It has also been developed, independently, in the work of Chantal Mouffe (1988, 1992) and Fred Dallmayr (1986). All of these authors draw their inspiration for a notion of politics based on the meaning of difference from French poststructuralists: Jacques Derrida, Gilles Deleuze, Michel Foucault, J. F. Lyotard, and Julia Kristeva.

Young's (1990, p. 7) starting point is the historical importance of the new social movements. Her aim is to express "some of the claims about justice and injustice implicit in the politics of these movements" that lead her to question and displace the distributive paradigm of justice that motivates liberal theory. By contrast, Young argues that a conception of justice should begin with concepts of domination and oppression and she elaborates a family of five concepts: exploitation, marginalization, powerlessness, cultural imperialism, and violence. As she explains: "Distributive injustices may contribute to or result from these forms of oppression, but none is reducible to distribution and all involve social structures and relations beyond distribution" (p. 9). Young (pp. 6, 7) seeks to elaborate "a heterogeneous public that acknowledges and affirms group difference," in part, by appropriating the postmodernist critique of "unifying discourse to analyze and criticize such concepts as impartiality, the general good, and community." Yeatman (1992, pp. 3–4) argues that a politics of difference, following this line of argument, involves a nonontological approach to citizenship. It must be, she asserts, an identity politics.

Here an openly contested politics of voice and representation makes it very difficult to sustain ontological orientations for it becomes very evident that any one of them is in a highly contested relation to others. More significantly, it becomes evident also that these ontological orientations are internally contested, and that their "being" is more a creature of contingent history than it is of some pre-historical point of being. By bringing out how all constructions of homogeneous community or identity depend on systemic exclusions, on domination, these internal contestations make it all the more difficult to forget the forgetting of those who are bothered by assertions of self and group identity.

Young (1992) shows how the ideology of group difference as Otherness exhibits a logic of identity such that it represses difference—the particularity and heterogeneity of group experience—by asserting a unity that actually generates dichotomies of the included and the excluded. Social groups thus conceived are seen as noninterrelational, as mutually exclusive, as creating clear borders that mark one group off from another. The deconstruction of the logic of identity reveals how the binary oppositions generated by it, in fact, require one another for their assertion. A politics of difference, by contrast, unfreezes fixed identities, recognizing that they are both relational and contextual: "A politics that treats difference as variation and specificity, rather than as exclusive opposition, aims for a society and polity where there is social equality among explicitly differentiated groups who conceive themselves as dwelling together without exclusions" (Young, 1992, p. 19).

Mouffe's work approaches the notion of radical democracy perhaps more directly than Young's, but it also demands a nonessentialist perspective and similarly draws on the postmodernist critique of subjectivism. Mouffe, in collaboration with Ernesto Laclau (1985), produced the standard left-wing interpretation of radical democracy in the 1980s—a socialist reformulation that, like Habermas, pursues the "unfulfilled project of modernity," but, unlike Habermas, does not require the Enlightenment project of epistemological self-foundations. Mouffe (1988, p. 34) explains that the challenge to rationalism and humanism does not imply for her the abandonment of the political project of modernity: the deepening of the commitment to the achievement of equality and freedom. It does, however, require that the project for democracy "takes account of the full breadth and specificity of the democratic struggles in our times." This is the point where Mouffe (1988, p. 35) combines the poststructuralist critique with an analysis of the new social movements in much the same way as Young does.

To be capable of thinking politics today and understanding the nature of these new struggles and the diversity of social relations that the democratic revolution has yet to encompass, it is indispensable to develop a theory of the subject as a decentered, detotalized agent, a subject constructed at the point of intersection of a multiplicity of subject positions between which there exists no a priori or necessary relation and whose articulation is the result of hegemonic practices. New perspectives for political action are said to emerge from recognizing that identities are never fixed or definitively established: openness and ambiguity characterize the way different subject positions are articulated.

Radical democracy becomes a new political philosophy, for it provides the new common sense that has the potential to transform the identity of different groups in ways that avoid the homogeneous unities of notions of the individual or of class, and the exclusions that are predicated upon them. This is a claim that Mouffe (1992, p. 10) repeats in a recent work: "pluralism can only be formulated within a problematic that conceives of the social agent not as a unitary subject but as the articulation of an ensemble of subject positions, constructed within specific discourses and always precariously and temporarily sutured at the intersection of those subject positions." Yet at the same time she emphasizes the limits of pluralism, which means that not all differences can be accepted. A radical-democratic project, she argues, must be distinguished from other forms of postmodern politics that valorize all differences. For pluralism to be made compatible with the struggle against inequality, "one must be able to discriminate between differences that exist but should not exist, and differences that do not exist but should exist" (p. 13). If such criteria cannot be provided by either traditional liberal pluralists or postmodern celebrations of difference, as she maintains, where are they to come from? Her answer is given in the barest of terms. She reinvokes a notion of consensus—a framework of institutions and practices comprising democratic society—within which pluralism can exist. To this extent, while recognizing new forms of pluralism, Mouffe is more committed than either Young or Yeatman to the political project of liberalism.

Fred Dallmayr's (1986) paper examines the changing historical connotations of democracy and criticizes those conceptions that link advances in democracy to the unfolding logic of modernity. In the final section of his paper, which is of central interest here, Dallmayr postulates a postmodern democracy that rests upon a new and ontologically grounded kind of pluralism said to differ from both preliberal and liberal versions. It is a pluralism "which is predicated neither on status or other ascriptive factors nor on class or utilitarian interests, and which may be called a "practical-ontological" type since it relies on concrete life experiences or practical modes of life (Dallmayr, 1986, p. 163).

He indicates that the notion of a postmodern pluralist polity is foreshadowed in Martin Heidegger's notion of co-being (*Mitsein*) and also in Heidegger's comments on appropriation (*Ereignis*), although he does not expand on this observation. Thus, while Dallmayr argues a similar case to Young and Mouffe, he can be distinguished from both the former by emphasizing an ontological pluralism (though this may amount to a terminological nicety), and the latter by emphasizing such a pluralism may be considered postliberal in some sense.

Dallmayr (p. 160) wants to question the assumption of linear continuity and also "the equation of Western rationality with the apex of human and social-political development." In this sense, Dallmayr's position would seem to have reasonable grounds given that in pluralistic liberal democratic societies we have witnessed the reassertion and cultural renaissance of those groups traditionally defined as the Other, which have disputed the very canons of Western rationality that, in the past, legitimated their systematic exclusion. Poststructuralist modes of thought question traditional logocentric rationality and have an erosive effect on prevailing teleological perspectives. Heidegger's discussion of the question of the meaning of being displaces the notion of history as a smoothly unfolding teleology; Foucault's investigation of modes of objectification that transform human beings into subjects decenters the paradigm of consciousness; Deleuze's (and Derrida's) notion of difference provides grounds for questioning the modern philosophy of representation.

THE POLITICS OF IDENTITY

Elsewhere I have maintained that there is a relation between the postmodern critique of reason and the rise of the new social movements: that much postmodern discourse emerged out of the development of the new social movements (Peters, 1991). I interpreted the growth of what Habermas (1981) has called "new social movements," by which he means "subinstitutional, extra-parliamentary forms of protest" originating in the 1960s and developing thereafter, as the historical means by which Marxism as the master discourse of liberation has been stripped of its overtly rationalistic and scientistic elements that it inherited from the Enlightenment.

Marxism taught us the valuable lesson that we make history but under conditions that are not of our own choosing. This was the first moment of the critique of the subject. While Marxism championed the collective subject in terms of the priority of class, equally it insisted that the subject was always inserted in existing social practices and that groups and individuals can never be the sole origin or authors of those practices. As Stuart Hall (1991, p. 43) remarks: "That is a profound historical decentering in terms of social practice." Many of the incipient social movements—those based around the philosophy of decolonization and feminism—drew their inspiration from the Marxist critique, sometimes combined with the Freudian critique, which also disturbed the stable language of identity by emphasizing the importance of unconscious processes in the formation of the self.

Within the old identity politics of the 1960s, social movements introduced some theoretical refinements, splitting and questioning the priority of class as the leading collective subject whose goal was emancipation. There was greater recognition, in particular, of race and gender as specifying in a non-reductive way lines of oppression. In an important sense these social categories depended, in their early stages, on essentialist readings: it marked them out in contrast to the other dominant modernist readings of political identity—those of class, and of nation. Where the notion of class permanently broke apart the idea of a homogeneous collective unity of nation, those of race and gender led to a greater understanding of an internal social differentiation. Yet these social movements still subscribed to the old logic of identity as stable and homogeneous categories, "which could be spoken about almost as if they were singular actors . . . right but which . . . placed, positioned, stabilized, and allowed us to understand and read, . . . the imperatives of the . . . self: the great collective social identities of class, of race, of nation, of gender, and of the West" (Hall, 1991, p. 14).

The poststructuralist critique of the subject and of reason was instrumental in unsettling the modernist discourse of identity, in taking the process several stages further. It problematized the category of the individual as the last vestige of a rationalistic liberalism that has privileged the Cogito—the self-identical and fully transparent thinking subject, the origin and ground of action—as *the* universal subject against which all irrational others are defined. It carried out this critique in a way that problematized not only the unity of the subject but also that of any group, which, on the basis of an alleged shared experience, may have been thought of as a unity or singular actor.

It must be remembered that despite differences with their predecessors, the French poststructuralists can be interpreted as continuing the enterprise of the critique of the subject through a series of reflections on Hegel. Judith Butler (1987, p. 175), for instance, understands the twentieth-century history of Hegelianism in France in terms of two constitutive moments: "the specification of the subject in terms of finitude, corporeal boundaries, and temporarility" evident in the work of J. P. Sartre and Emanuel Levinas, among others; and "the splitting (Jacques), displacement (Derrida), and eventual death (Foucault, Deleuze) of the Hegelian subject."

Butler (p. 185) plots the growing instability of the subject in the work of Alexandre Kojéve, Jean Hyppolite and Sartre, and summarizes the progression of French thought as a series of reflections on Hegel's anthropcentrism.

While the subject in Hegel is projected and then recovered, in Sartre it is projected endlessly without recovery, but nevertheless *knows itself* in its estrangement and so remains a unitary consciousness, reflexively self-identical. In the psychoanalytic structuralism of Lacan and in the Nietzschean writings of Deleuze and Foucault, the subject is once again understood as a projected unity, but this projection *disguises* and falsifies the multiplicitous disunity constitutive of experience, whether conceived as libidinal forces, the will-to-power, or the strategies of power/discourse.

In postmodern critical theory, which underwrites the new politics of identity, the subject is no longer seen as a unitary, rational ego—as it has been historically produced and self-reproduced under the influences of the liberal human sciences—rather, it is seen as occupying different subject positions within discursive practices that are produced by the power/knowledge relations of particular discourses. As such the subject exists in process, only as a partial, and sometimes nonrational voice occupying multiple sites or positions that might themselves be contradictory (see Peters and Marshall, 1991). As Stuart Hall (1991, p. 15) comments:

[The] great collective social identities have not disappeared . . . .But the fact is that none of them is . . . in either the social, historical or epistemological place where they were in our conceptualizations of the world in the recent past. They cannot any longer be thought in the same homogeneous form. We are as attentive to their inner differences, . . . contradictions, . . . segmentations and . . . fragmentations as we are to their already-completed homogeneity . . . .They do not operate like totalities. If they have a relationship to our identities, cultural and individual, they do not any longer have that suturing, structuring, or stabilizing force.

NARRATIVE OF CHANGING POLITICAL IDENTITIES

Let me retell briefly two stories of changing identities. The first is that of Stuart Hall's learning to be black and what happened to black identity as a matter of cultural politics in Britain. The second is that of Steven Seidman's unlearning to be a gay subject. The moral they point to is similar in certain respects.

Stuart Hall (1991) recounts how he was born into a Jamaican family yet he never thought of himself as black at that time. He first heard the term uttered in the wake of the Civil Rights movement and it was only after the cultural revolution based around the reggae style of Bob Marley in 1970s Jamaica that "black" people there recognized themselves as black. As a Jamaican immigrant, Hall, like other people from the Caribbean settling in Britain, learned to identify as black in the antiracist struggles of the 1970s, centered around black community resistance. The point is that black was "created as a political category in a certain historical moment" yet at the same time "the question of Black, in Britain, also has its silences" (pp. 54, 56)—the silencing of all that the term black concealed: the different cultural experiences of Caribbeans, East Africans, of Asian people of color (Indians, Pakistanis, Bangladeshis, etc.), of black people who did not identify with the collective subject; the gender and class dimensions that also positioned individuals and groups. Hall (p. 57) asks himself the question "what is it like to live, by attempting to valorize and defeat the marginalization of the variety of Black subjects and to really begin to discover the lost histories . . . of Black experiences, while at the same time recognizing the end of any essential Black subject?" And he gives the following answer:

It is the politics of recognizing that all of us are composed of multiple social identities. . . . That we are all complexly constructed through different categories, of different antagonisms, and these may have the effect of locating us socially in multiple positions of marginality and subordination, but which do not yet operate . . . in exactly the same way . . . has to be a struggle which is conducted positionally.

Such struggles conducted as wars of position are difficult. They have no rules and no one knows definitely how to play these political games. As Hall (p. 59) suggests, there are no political guarantees already inscribed in any one particular identity and yet, in his view the "notion of a politics which, as it were, increasingly is able to address people through . . . multiple identities . . . is the only political game that the locals have left . . . ."

Steven Seidman's (1991, p. 180) story revolves around how his identification as a gay activist led him to take the postmodernist turn.

He indicated how the human sciences had produced a discourse on homosexual identity and helped to develop an elaborate apparatus of homosexual oppression: it justified incarceration, curative therapies, legal criminalization, medical surveillance, and control. As a powerful practical-moral social force, science had created a sexual regime of identities in terms of the master categories of heterosexual/homosexual:

Its power lay not only in its capacity to rationalize the exclusion of same-sex desire from moral legitimacy or to rationalize the denial of civil rights or claims to social inclusion. In addition, through its cultural and institutional authority, science could inscribe in our bodies and minds a sexual/social regime—one that made desire into an identity, one that made choice of sexual object into a master category of sexual identity, one that made sexual/social identities mutually exclusive, one that purified a heterosexual life while polluting a homosexual life. (p. 181)

Seidman, however, was led to abandon the modernist interpretation of this struggle as one of gay liberation—as the emancipation of the homosexual subject. He was also led to abandon modernist assumptions about the duality of knowledge and power; the link between science, truth, and social progress, an essential unified subject; and the course of history as the grand narrative of its emancipation. To be certain, the construction of the gay subject and his or her liberation had definite social and political value in the 1970s: it had been useful in shaping desire and behavior; it helped create social bonds and became the basis of political mobilization. Yet at the same time, he realized, the gay subject was not a transhistorical or historically emergent entity. Behind the universal claims to speak for all homosexually inclined people were a set of values that excluded or marginalized many who described themselves as gay: lesbians, bisexuals, and others of nonconventional sexual/lifestyle choices. The construction of the gay subject legitimated homosexuality simply by inverting the heterosexual/homosexual duality, leaving unchallenged the underlying binary logic, and thereby, reinforcing the dominant sexual regime that defined sexual desire and identity by choice of sexual object. Further, this essentialist construction promoted a narrowly focused interest-group politics that reflected normative constructions of gay identity built around projected ideals of body type, dress, and lifestyle based on white, middle-class values (p. 182).

Seidman recounts how such an essentialist ethnically closed model of homosexuality may have been necessary in the 1970s for political purposes, but by the 1980s when the gay community came under intense attacks by antigay crusaders, the model had outlived its usefulness. Seidman (p. 183) writes:

The early 1980s simultaneously saw the rise of coalition politics in the gay community and the rise of social constructionism. Framing gay identity as an emerging socio-historical event, as an unstable, contestable institutional/discursive production and strategy, provided gays with a rationale to . . . see themselves as having multiple identities, recognizing . . . contradictory positions of social power and oppression, and seeing their own fight for sexual/social empowerment as connected to struggles around gender, race, ethnicity, class and so on.

Seidman, like Hall, through telling part of his own adult life history, is elaborating, in personal terms, the basis of a new politics of identity that he explores in more theoretical terms by examining the links between the new social movements, postmodernism, and democratic pluralism—a position he identifies with the later work of Foucault (1980), of Lyotard (1984), of many postmodern feminists and constructionist gay theorists. This is not to say that Hall and Seidman adopt similar political positions, but they do, at least, concur in recognizing the need for a new understanding of identity based on the politics of difference.

CONCLUSION

Historically, new political identities have established themselves in relation to a set of differences treated as essential or fixed characteristics and upon this basis conferred privileges, rights, and responsibilities. At the same time, these differences have constituted the Other, sanctioning and legitimating various forms of discrimination, oppression, and violence.

On the Left, the social movements that emerged in the 1960s have now reached a new stage of political maturity built on the recognition that the process of fixing differences as Otherness has led to the reproduction of those very forms of oppression they were trying to combat. The process of identity formation is now seen as a contingent and relational construction; a political process that takes place in complex settings. The new politics of identity, founded on more understanding of difference, provides the basis for building new intersubjectivities and solidarities, and offers the hope of reinventing through struggle the promise of participatory democracy. That promise and its emancipatory goal remains one of the central purposes of education and educational theory. The politics of difference emerges as the new desideratum for understanding the complex nature of oppression in education and the way in which multiple and contradictory subjectivities and identities are socially constructed at the intersections of race, gender, and class, among other configurations. It also offers the prospect of rehabilitating the use of the concept of citizenship from the minimal notion of consumer rights to which it has collapsed under the New Right, and provides both grounds and strategies for a greater democratization of the state.

REFERENCES

Banks, James (1986). "Multicultural Education: Development, Paradigms and Goals." In James Banks and James Lynch (eds.), *Multicultural Education in Western Societies*. London: Holt, Rhinehart and Winston.

Bobbio, Norberto (1987). *The Future of Democracy*, trans. R. Griffin, ed. R. Bellamy. Cambridge: Polity Press.

———. (1990). *Liberalism and Democracy*, trans. M. Ryle and K. Soper. London: Verso.

———. (1991). "The Upturned Utopia." In Robin Blackburn (ed.), *After the Fall: The Failure of Communism*. London: Verso: 3–5.

Butler, Judith (1987). *Subjects of Desire: Hegelian Reflections in Twentieth Century France*. New York: Columbia University Press.

Dallmayr, Fred (1986). "Democracy and Postmodernism," *Human Studies*, 10(1): 143–170.

Foucault, Michel (1980). *Power/Knowledge: Selected Interviews and Other Writings, 1972–77*. Ed. and trans. C. Gordon. Brigton, Sussex: Harvester Press.

Friedman, Marilyn (1989). "Feminism and Modern Friendship: Dislocating the Community." *Ethics*, 99: 275–290.

Gutmann, Amy (1985). "Communitarian Critics of Liberalism." *Philosophy and Public Affairs*, 14: 308–322.

———. (1987). *Democratic Education*. Princeton, NJ: Princeton University Press.

Habermas, Jürgen (1981). "New Social Movements." *Telos*, 49 (Fall): 33–37.

———. (1985). "Questions and Counterquestions." In Richard Bernstein (ed.), *Habermas and Modernity*. Cambridge: Polity Press.

Hall, Stuart (1991). "Old and New Identities, Old and New Ethnicities." In Anthony King (ed.), *Culture, Globalisation and the World System: Contemporary Conditions for the Representation of Identity*. London: Macmillan: 41–68.

Laclau, Ernesto and Mouffe, Chantal (1985). *Hegemony and Socialist Strategy: Towards a Radical Democratic Politics*. London: Verso.

Lyotard, Jean-François (1984). *The Postmodern Condition: A Report on Knowledge*, trans. G. Bennington and B. Massumi. Manchester: Manchester University Press.

Mouffe, Chantal (1988). "Radical Democracy: Modern or Postmodern?." In Andrew Ross (ed.), *Universal Abandon? The Politics of Postmodernism*. Minneapolis: University of Minnesota Press: 52–45.

———. (1992). "Democratic Politics Today." In Chantal Mouffe (ed.), *Dimensions of Radical Democracy: Pluralism, Citizenship, Community*. London: Verso: 1–14.

Peters, Michael (1991). "Postmodernism: The Critique of Reason and the Rise of the New Social Movements." *Sites: A Journal for Radical Perspectives on Culture*, 24: 142–160.

Peters, Michael and Marshall, James (1991). "Education and Empowerment: Postmodernism and the Critique of Humanism." *Education and Society* (Peter McClaren (ed.), 9(2): 123–134.

———. (1993). "Beyond the Philosophy of the Subject: Liberalism and the Critique of Individualism," *Educational Philosophy and Theory*, 25(1): 19–39.

Rorty, Richard (1991). "Postmodernist Bourgeois Liberalism." In *Objectivity, Relativism and Truth*. Cambridge: Cambridge University Press.

Seidman, Steven (1991). "Postmodern Anxiety: The Politics of Epistemology." *Sociological Theory*, 92: 180–190.

Yeatman, Anna (1992). "Minorities and the Politics of Difference." *Political Theory Newsletter*, Special Issue, Symposium on The Politics of Difference, Moira Gatens and Anna Yeatman (eds.), 4(1): 1–10.

Young, Iris Marion (1986). "The Ideal of Community and the Politics of Difference." *Social Theory and Practice*, 12(1) (Spring): 1–26.

———. (1990). *Justice and the Politics of Difference*. Princeton, NJ: Princeton University Press.

———. (1992). "Together in Difference: Transforming the Logic of Group Political Conflict." *Political Theory Newsletter*, Special Issue, Symposium on The Politics of Difference, Moira Gatens and Anna Yeatman (eds.), 4(1): 11–26.

3

The Fringe Dwellers: African American Women Scholars in the Postmodern Era

Beverly M. Gordon

INTRODUCTION

While the postmodern era has been characterized as witnessing a decline in and challenge to the influence of Western Anglo domination and hegemony across the global community by the non-Anglo, non-Western majority of the world population, it has also been observed that within intellectual and popular cultural circles, both the dominant critical pedagogic and feminist perspectives and critiques subordinate race to class and gender issues. People of color face at least two interesting sites of opposition: one within the dominant modernist discourse and position (current political and social configurations, the powers that be, etc.), and the second within the postmodernist discourse that employs discourses of difference, some versions of which exclude voices and representation of those Others who have been historically excluded from the dominant societal discourse. Instead of asking why African American writings and theorizing are absent from the dominant narratives, one might ask what the mechanisms are that make these voices mute.

In the politics of representation, what is it that can legitimate and justify the dominant narratives that speak for, interpret, and understand the voices of the Other? In defining critical postmodernism, Henry Giroux "dethrones" European tradition as "the" measure of historical, cultural, and political truth (1992, p. 122). Elsewhere I raised a somewhat different question as to why American educational theorists went to the European theater for the conceptual systems within which they ground their critical theorizing, when there existed here in the American experience conceptual systems of social critique that preceded by at least two decades Felix Weiler's conception of the Frankfurt Institute (Gordon, 1985). The raising of and response to such a question seems to have been lost, marginalized, or ignored in the contemporary feminist and to a lesser extent critical discourses of intellectual theory, and, as such, supports the need for challenges to the scientific hegemony of the academy's dominant narratives of what constitutes reliability and validity and proof in inquiry.

While there are various definitions of postmodern, Cornel West (1985, p. 88) has pointed to one initial aspect of postmodernism: namely, the so-called First World (that is, Euro-Anglo-American) reflection on the decline of European cultural dominance and the rise of the United States as the predominant military, political, and cultural power that is "parochial and provincial." The academic and popular components of postmodernism come from a revolt against the domesticated, diluted modernism of museums, the academy, architectural forms, and literary circles. More specifically for this present discussion, within the academy the postmodern discourse has focused on difference, marginality, and Otherness; the relationship between popular culture and resistance; and the push toward inclusion, diversity, and heterogeneity. This discourse, however, is far removed from the realities that confront people of color, the poor, and others living their daily lives over the edge and on the fringes of American society. The reality of daily life on the fringes of society flies in the face of the deconstructionist and postmodernist arguments "that there is no concrete political or economic reality aside from our imaginative texts and narratives" (D. King, 1992: p. 38).

In an eye-opening way, in looking at African American social issues, Debra King (1992) illuminates that black women have been positioned in a blind spot of sorts, within the dominant discourse on the African American community, while the main and preponderant attention has been focused on black males. King raises what Sylvia Wynter (1991, p. 37) would describe as "perfectly scientific questions" by asking:

What does this particular construction illuminate or obscure about African American life and social issues? To what extent does this construction, implicitly or explicitly, place African American women and men in competition against and conflict with one another? In whose interest is it to define Black men as . . . the number one problem?

Instead of asking how the ruling class keeps voices and perspectives silent, we ask how ruling-class structures perpetuate the oppression of a population. King demonstrates that from the outset, the interpretive frameworks of the ruling class are, at the very least, unreliable, because of how the questions are structured and the way in which a population is conceptualized. In other words, trying to resolve social issues while employing a half-scientific/half-narrative structure that studies only one-half of the African American community's population (black males) and renders invisible the other half of the community (black females) produces curious if not inaccurate constructions of the African American community at large as well as social issues related to it (D. King, 1992). Moreover, the prescriptions and policies based on such faculty constructions exacerbate the problems instead of constructing meaningful solutions for the advancement and well-being of the African American community. The persistent continuity of implementing erroneous policies and prescriptions has sinister implications. The constructed invisibility or marginalizing of black women within the context of understanding the African American community will adversely change how black social issues are constructed. Solutions must come from examination of the totality of the community with all of its intricate weaving of the idiosyncrasies, differences, and commonalities into a complex *kente*-cloth.

This effort is not only to challenge white middle-class feminist narrative and position by pointing out its own propensity toward domination. If this discussion was only another impositional stance, I would also fall into this trap. Instead, this effort will try to articulate a position that speaks to difference and multilayered discourses and narratives that support competing ideologies. The purpose and direction of this current discussion of the voice, theory, criticism, and perspective in the works of African American women intellectuals and scholars is at least twofold. This exploration is an initial effort to illuminate the endogenous cultural knowledge produced by women of the African diaspora in the Americas; the "inscribed" situations and conditions in which it was generated; and the inherent meanings of this work for African American women, the whole of their community, and the whole of humanity.

AFRICAN AMERICAN WOMEN'S *LIEUX DE MÉMOIRE*

Black feminist thought consists of specialized knowledge created by African American women that clarifies a standpoint of and for black women. For Patricia Hill Collins (1990), black feminist thought consists of "those experiences and ideas shared by African American women that provide a unique angle of vision on self, community and society—and theories that interpret these experiences" (p. 22). In a word, black feminist thought "encompasses theoretical interpretations of black women's reality by those who live it" (p. 22). As such, the voice and perspective of women of the African diaspora throughout the world across time is more than voice under siege and subjugated perspectives. The black woman's narrative is, if not the oldest, one of the oldest narratives produced by women since antiquity.

Not only is Margaret Busby's (1992) monumental and triumphant anthology of the writings of some 400 African women throughout the millennia—*Daughters of Africa*—the definitive statement of the African woman's voice and representation throughout history; but her words in the acknowledgements, "Apologies—To all those excellent writers I have had to leave out" (p. xxvii) speak to worlds of voices yet to be discovered and rediscovered. From the verses of Queen Hatshepsut (1501–1447 B.C.) to contemporary women of the African diaspora in Germany, Scotland, England, Jamaica, Zimbabwe, Russia, Brazil, Mali, the United States, and so on, there is no question that women of the African diaspora have a long history of voice and representation. Their narratives articulate ideology, love, philosophy, theology, and spirituality, as well as resistance and possibility.

In the historical epoch of Africans and their relations with Euro-Americans, the history of African American women speaks to struggle for freedom, rights, equity, and sexual autonomy, as well as to social critique, the articulation of alternative modes of meaning and being, institution building, and the like. History is replete with stories known and unknown about African American women who dedicated their life work to the advancement of African American people. As demonstrated in the works of numerous African American women scholars (e.g., Giddings, 1984; Washington, 1987; Lerner, 1973; Carby, 1987), in response to their cultural hegemonic image and status constructed from the ravages of slavery, African American women waged struggles to define and situate themselves, as well as their communities, as constituent elements and partial creators and re-creators of American society. Historically, African American women have made enormous sacrifices and contributions to the New World. Indeed, contemporary theory, criticism, and perspective are grounded in historical antecedents.

Since the seventeenth century, as Africans first arrived in the Americas, they struggled and fought against the brutality and inhumane treatment of American slavery. The socially constructed views and status of African women relative to Western science and narrative knowledge reflected the nature of their status in the social structure and the hierarchy of power in the New World, while commonsense socially constructed views of Africans rarely mention the autobiographies, culture, religion, and history that Africans brought with them to the New World. Africans did not arrive tabulae rasae. What they brought with them from Africa transformed them, their reality, and indeed the American experience:

African environments of memory shifted gradually from the conscious to the subliminal. Personal images were lost: and ancestral memory began its retreat into the collective unconscious, to be transferred to succeeding generations as a corpus of skills, rituals, and habits rather than immediate and specific visions of lost home and kin. African lieux de memoire replaced autobiographical memory. (Bethel, 1992, p. 827)

While both African men and women were dehumanized as part of their oppressed state, black women's oppression differed from men's because of the issue of sex and sexual politics. African women were conceptualized not only as laborers but also as breeders. In their struggle to thwart their own sexual exploitation by whites and, more importantly, to avoid bringing children into the hideous world of slavery, they participated in rebellions, acts of sabotage, and escapes; they joined maroon societies; and they used birth-control methods, self-induced abortions, and even "reluctant acts of infanticide" (Davis, 1983, p. 205; Washington, 1987; Giddings, 1984).

During the period directly after the Civil War and Emancipation, from 1865 to 1868, African American women and their husbands attempted to establish a "traditional" family structure wherein the freedmen worked and their wives attended to their homes and families, instead of participating as part of the labor force working in the fields. The result was a significant loss in the available labor force and, subsequently, a corresponding loss of profit in the agriculture business throughout Georgia, Alabama, South Carolina, and Mississippi. As might have been expected, whites took immediate punitive measures, such as reducing pay to black workers in an attempt to force black women back into the workforce. Tensions with whites coupled with extreme economic hardships resulted in, among other things, the rise of black domestic violence. Frances Ellen Harper (1825–1911)—a public speaker, newspaper editor, teacher, poet and lecturer—reported on and preached against domestic violence (Carby, 1987). In 1867, before the American Equal Rights Association (an organization to promote black and woman suffrage founded by Susan B. Anthony, Elizabeth Cady Stanton, and Frederick Douglass), Harper endorsed Frederick Douglass' support of the Fifteenth Amendment, in opposition to Sojourner Truth, who sided with the white feminists in not supporting the amendment (Carby, 1987; Giddings, 1984). Harper is one example of the writers and social activists of nineteenth-century African American women who critiqued, challenged, and influenced American life as well as its social and political institutions. These challenges came through the creation of their own institutions, organizations, and activism that contributed to the struggle of the race for social justice and a better life in American society.

The nineteenth century has revealed itself as an interesting transformative movement in the history of African Americans, during which many African American women challenged dominant social structures and narratives and created institutions to serve the African American community. In northern cities like New York, Philadelphia, and Boston were found small middle-class communities of African Americans comprised of merchants, business people, educators, publishers, and militant abolitionists. Within these and other communities were African American women who made great contributions to their communities.

Maria Stewart (1803–79), a "freeborn" New Englander, was the first

African American woman political writer, activist, and teacher. During her political career in Boston, Stewart published three speeches in William Lloyd Garrison's *Liberator*, gave four public speeches, and published a political essay. After leaving Boston she taught in Baltimore, New York, and Brooklyn. During the Civil War she moved to Washington, DC and continued teaching. Later she was appointed matron of the Freedmen's Hospital (now Howard University Hospital) (Richardson, 1987; Loewenberg and Bogin, 1976). Stewart is, of course, only one example of the many African American women who before, during, and after the Civil War advanced themselves and their community.

Businesswoman Madame C. J. Walker was the first black woman millionaire, who made her money in the black hairdressing and products business; and Maggie L. Walker, with the support of the Independent Order of St. Luke (a mutual benefit society), was appointed president of St. Luke's Bank in Richmond, the first African American woman bank president (Brown, 1989). Like other accomplished women, both of these women were considered leaders of the communities, served in numerous civic activities, and were members of the famous national Black Club movement beginning in the late eighteenth century. The National Federation of Afro-American Women united thirty-six black women's organizations in a dozen states. In 1896, through her vanguard efforts as leader of the National League of Colored Women in Washington, DC, Mary Church Terrell united the federation and the league into the National Association of Colored Women (NACW), "a watershed in the history of Black women" (Giddings, 1984: 95).

There were some commonalities between black women's and white women's clubs, such as the unquestioning belief in the "superiority of middle-class values or way of life" and women's influential role in the home and the belief that the family was a "microscosm and corner stone of society" (Giddings, 1984:95). However, for African American women, clubs and organizations were the mechanisms through which they could receive recognition for their social and political work, while, for white women, the impetus for their formation of clubs was generated from their own sense of frustration from having been excluded from the clubs, organizations, and activities of their white male counterparts only because they were women, even though they had the same education and qualifications as men. For African American women aware of their ties to the larger black community, their frustration came because of race.

In essence, the focus of the club movement was the commitment of African American women to service a community suffering under the physical and intellectual deprivation of a legacy of bondage and subjugation throughout the nineteenth century. The issues of greatest concern were health, education, and the interrelationships of morality, family, community, and society—morality being the nexus connecting the other issues. Giddings

(1984) points out that the middle-class values of African American women were tantamount to a race-conscious mission. There are obvious problems with such a perspective: it does not take into account a critique of blaming the victim; it copies and emulates a problematic model in that these leading women perceived themselves as "living examples" for a rank-and-file membership that consisted mainly of working-class women, most of whom lacked the education, influence, visibility, and acceptability within white women's circles or white society. Nevertheless, they were trying to confront the challenges and dangers of their time. What they saw was the hope, promise, sorrow, and tragedy of the aftermath of human bondage and degradation. These women not only witnessed this, but they themselves experienced racism and gender bias, while their white counterparts experienced gender bias only, since neither race nor class were issues for them.

Black women leaders like Mary Church Terrell (1863–1954) sought through the club movement to focus specifically on black women as a group, believing that the black community was judged in large measure by the values, morals, ethics, and position of black women—hence the NACW motto: "Lifting as we climb." Terrell was one of the best-educated and wealthiest women of her time. Mary Church graduated from Oberlin College in 1884 at the head of her class. She taught school in Washington, DC, where she married Robert Terrell, a Harvard graduate and attorney who was eventually appointed as a municipal judge. During the 1890s, two tragic incidents galvanized her activism. In 1892 she lost a life friend, Thomas Moore, when he and his two business partners were lynched in Memphis, and then she lost her firstborn child in a poorly equipped segregated hospital. Terrell became nationally known for her suffragist and activist work in black civic activities and political organizations as well as being appointed to several civic positions, such as serving on the Washington, DC Board of Education (Lerner, 1973, p. 206).

Some time after the death of her friend, she read the words of a black woman columnist and cofounder of the black Memphis newspaper, *Free Speech*. The editorial by Ida B. Wells-Barnett read in part, "The city of Memphis has demonstrated that neither character nor standing avails the Negro if he dares to protect himself against the white man or become his rival" (Giddings, 1984, p. 19). A family friend, the abolitionist Frederick Douglass, introduced Terrell to Wells-Barnett in 1893, which initiated their decades-long association with each other.

Ida B. Wells-Barnett (1862–1931), a journalist, political activist, and suffragist, was best known for her antilynching campaign and for organizing the first political club for black women, the Alpha Suffragist Club in Chicago, which actively engaged in city, state, and national political activities, such as supporting black candidates for elected positions. Unlike Mary Church Terrell, who was born of privilege, Ida Wells-Barnett was one of eight children of slave parents. Her earliest memory of school was the freedmen's school she first attended. At fifteen years of age, due to the death by yellow fever of her parents and younger brother, she had to leave college and support her siblings, which she did by lying about her age and securing a teaching position, which she held for two years. In 1884 she moved to Memphis, continued teaching, and attended classes at Fisk University. During this time she wrote articles for black newspapers under the pen name "Iola," but was eventually fired from her teaching job in 1891 because she exposed the inadequate school facilities of black children. The journalist coverage and editorials that Wells-Barnett published on the unjustified March 9, 1982, lynching of Thomas Moore, Calvin McDowell, and Henry Steward was the turning point in her life. They were co-owners of a successful business, People's Grocery, and the "target of White resentment" (Giddings, 1984, p. 17), which subsequently cost them their lives by brutal mutilation and hanging. Echoing Thomas Moore's last words before the mob killed him and his partners—"Tell my people to go west . . . There is no justice for them here" (Giddings, 1984, p. 17)—Wells-Barnett called for the black citizens of Memphis to move West, and they did. So many African Americans within the Memphis community left that the white business community, which was dependent upon black customers, suffered greatly. Many businesses went into, or were close to, bankruptcy. As a result of her activism, her business was destroyed and she was threatened with murder if she returned to Memphis. Wells-Barnett began her own personal crusade against lynching through her writings, lectures, and organizations and was ready to protect herself against aggressive racist attack. She purchased a pistol, determined to "sell my life as dearly as possible." Wells told her community, "When the white man . . . knows he runs as great a risk of biting the dust every time his Afro-American victim does, he will have greater respect for Afro-American life" (quoted in Giddings, 1983, p. 20). Wells believed that lynching was an integral part of racial oppression motivated by economics and politics. She eventually became chair of the Anti-lynching Bureau of the National Afro-American Council. She was also influential in the growth and development of the black women's club movements and was critical of, and conflicted with, black leaders who accommodated whites. Although a founding member of the NAACP, she eventually withdrew from its activities because she advocated a "more militantly race-consciousness leadership" (Lerner, 1973, p. 198).

Other women primarily dedicated to the education of the black community also engaged in the club movement and the struggle for suffrage, such as Charlotte Forten Grimke (1873–1914), Craft Laney (1854–1933), Frances (Fannie) Jackson Coppin (1837–1913), Anna Julia Cooper (1858–1964), Charlotte Hawkins Brown (1882–1961), and Mary McCloud Bethune (1875–1955). While several of these women created educational institutions, all were educators whose work and goals were, in part, interrelated with the social activism and advancement of the community at large.

They participated in various organizations in an effort to educate African American people, as well as to organize the community for political action (Lerner, 1973; Giddings, 1984; Lowenberg and Bogin, 1976).

In some regards, the "Lifting as we climb" efforts of these early pioneers were tainted by the middle-class aspirations of the organization leadership to espouse white, middle-class values and attitudes, especially in relation to the rank-and-file membership of these Negro women's organizations, composed of working-class women (Lerner, 1973). However, that many of these early leaders who carried political and cultural currency in a society that socially constructed the category of race were fair-skinned with straight hair does not negate their efforts.

Obviously, the aforementioned women represent a few of the many leaders and do not begin to tell the stories of the nameless thousands across the country whose contributions to their communities will never be recorded. These women were concerned with the social, political, and economic issues, as well as the pejorative controlling sexual issues, that structured black women's oppression and the relationships between black men and women, the family, and the community in its entirety.

In analyzing the work of these intellectual, business, and activist women, we see that their strengths came from their ability to build and sustain academic, business, cultural, and civic institutions. These women reflected their positions in that they were concerned with black women as constituting an essential part of the whole community. In a word, they conceptualized black women as markers, and standard-bearers by which the whole of the community would be judged. Their perspectives (albeit Eurocentric and middle-class) and operant theoretical frameworks (albeit similar to those of the talented tenth in which they situated themselves as leaders) were generated out of their lived experiences, and provided them "a unique angle of vision of self, community, and society" through which they interpreted their experiences and acted upon them. Their visions were humanistic, and their work was premised on the survival of the community as an entity. While African American women have contributed their voices across time and disciplines, since the time of the African diaspora, they have focused much voice, theorizing, and criticism on the struggle to defeat Western Eurocentric American cultural hegemony, domination, and subjugation, as well as to articulate their own conception of being in the world, rather than accept a configuration imposed by the dominant culture.

The black suffrage movement seems to be the most prominent and telling historical carryover to today's struggle for political rights. African American men and women struggled to gain the right to vote against the racism of white men and the expedient political perspectives of white women. The struggle for black suffrage sets the tone and historical context from which to view the conflicting interests of black and white women. At the turn of the century, the major struggle they waged with black men was for a black suffrage movement.

SPEAKING THE UNSPOKEN OUT LOUD: THE TENSION BETWEEN BLACK WOMEN AND WHITE WOMEN

The following exchange between Frederick Douglass and Susan B. Anthony occurred on May 12, 1869, at an American Equal Rights Association (AERA) meeting in New York City's Steinway Hall. Because women had been excluded in the guarantees of the Fifteenth Amendment, Susan B. Anthony and Elizabeth Cady Stanton fought against the convention's endorsement of its ratification.

Mr. Douglas: I do not see how anyone can pretend that there is the same urgency in giving the ballot to women as to the negro. With us, the matter is a question of life and death. It is a matter of existence, at least, in fifteen states of the Union. When women, because they are women, are hunted down through the cities of New York and New Orleans; when they are dragged from their houses and hung upon lamp-posts: . . . when their children are not allowed to enter schools; then they will have urgency to obtain the ballot equal to our own. (Great applause.)

A Voice: Is that not all true about black women?

Mr. Douglas: Yes, yes, yes, it is true of the black woman, but not because she is a woman but because she is black. (Applause.)

Miss Anthony: If you will not give the whole loaf of justice and suffrage to an entire people, give it to the most intelligent first. (Applause.) If intelligence, justice, and moralities are to be placed in the government, then let the question of women be brought first and that of the negro last. (Applause.) . . . Mr. Douglas talks about the wrongs of the negro; how he is hunted down, . . . but with all the wrongs and outrages that he today suffers, he would not exchange his sex or take the place of Elizabeth Cady Stanton. (Laughter and applause.) . . .

Mr. Douglas: Will you allow me—

Miss Anthony: Yes, anything; we are in for a fight to-day. (Great laughter and applause.)

Mr. Douglas: I want to know if granting you the right of suffrage will change the nature of our sexes. (Great Laughter.) (Blassingame and McKivigan, 1979, pp. 216–217)

Douglass' resolution to the AERA convention in support of the Fifteenth Amendment was not adopted, but the most important result of this raucous convention meeting was the eventual split in the Woman Suffrage movement, resulting in two groups: the National Woman Suffrage Association

and the American Woman Suffrage Association (Blassingame and Mc-
Kivigan, 1979, p. 214).

When the Susan B. Anthony one-dollar coin flopped, it was no surprise
that African Americans, particularly African American women, were undis-
mayed, if not relieved. Despite Anthony's abolitionist background, some of
her behaviors were racist, and openly so toward black suffrage. The following is a salient example of the activities of two of the better-known nineteenth-century feminists, Elizabeth Cady Stanton and Susan B. Anthony:

> Stanton and Anthony took the further step of opposing feminism to Black suffrage.
> . . . They argued that white women, educated and virtuous, were more deserving of
> the vote than the ex-slaves. On the other hand, they attempted to build feminism
> on the basis of white women's racism. At times, Stanton even fueled white women's
> sexual fears of Black men to rouse them against Black suffrage and for their own
> enfranchisement. (DuBois, 1981, p. 92)

While there were differences and even conflicts between black men and
women, the struggle for suffrage was the one issue that coalesced them in
their struggle for the right to vote. This cause placed the black community
at odds with white feminists, whose position on the issue of suffrage was
one of *expediency*, which, in essence, was their attempt to close ranks with
white men on this issue (Giddings, 1984). White feminists reasoned that if
only one group was to get the vote, they would try to position themselves
in the best way they could in an effort to influence white men. White women
were all too clear that they wanted a decision in their favor, even at the
expense of black men and women. While African American women like
Frances Ellen Harper expressed their concerns at white women's forums that
the criterion for voting should be based on character, not race, education,
or class, and Ida Wells-Barnett expressed her concerns directly to Susan B.
Anthony, the white Woman Suffrage Movement, led by Anthony and Stanton, held fast to its "women first" position. In fact, at the turn of the
century, the suffragists began to embrace a new contingent of white
women—namely, southern white women, who also wanted the vote and
willingly joined with northern white women under the common-expedient
principle of white woman suffrage as a means to ensure white domination
and supremacy over African Americans. In 1893, for example, in a politically
expedient move to gain the support of the southern white women's contingency, the National American Women's Suffrage Association (NAWSA)
took the position on voting eligibility that educational requirements were a
prerequisite for voting that "would ensure permanent supremacy for the
native-born White portion of the population" (Giddings, 1984, p. 124).
Another example of the concessions made to the southern white suffragists
occurred at the 1903 NAWSA convention, when the membership was per-
suaded to allow NAWSA state affiliates to set their own membership criteria,

in essence allowing the southern affiliates to practice racial exclusionary politics without being censured by other suffragists.

Needless to say, clashes between black and white women suffragists occurred. One of the more interesting incidents occurred at the 1913 suffrage march in Washington, DC. Two Negro women's groups—one from Washington, DC led by Mary Church Terrell, and one from Chicago led by Ida Wells-Barnett—were scheduled to march; but for the sake of expediency, they were relegated to a "segregated" section. Apparently, Wells-Barnett did not take the news well, and disappeared from her group prior to the beginning of the march and reappeared in the crowd along the march route, stepped into the segregated white suffrage contingent line, and "marched as she pleased" (Giddings, 1984, p. 128).

Contemporary women's organizations and the institutionalization of women's studies have over the years resulted in meaningful and substantive efforts in raising American consciousness toward multiple and complex issues confronting women and has done much to illuminate and incorporate women in the mainstream. However, when I confront such statements pronouncing that feminism is "embedded in popular practice which seeks to transform the world" (Lather, 1991, p. 27), my initial response is: Where do these feminists and their supporters situate the historical and contemporary theorizing and work of African American women (and men for that matter)? As pointed out earlier, African American women activists and scholars have historically sought to transform the world for themselves and for their communities, and finally also for the dominant (white) community at large, while white women sought to advance themselves, expediently dismissing black men and women. Contemporary feminism, like Marxism, is a discourse of opposition; but both feminism and Marxism relegate race to a liminal category. While it is is true, as Lather points out, that women of color have been resistant to feminist theory that embraces gender relations as the primary form of oppression, it is not completely accurate. As she states for women of color, theorizing was generated out of a need for survival— but survival of what? Survival of racism. Beyond issues of survival, women of color also desire to articulate their own authentic worldview and perspectives from politics to theology and popular culture. More than likely, even the most ardent black feminist would agree that her perspective is different from white feminists, because it is unique to the African American experience. Likewise, the experience and perspective of the dominant narratives of white feminists are unique to them and different from African American women (as well as other women of color and class and educational distinctions), because the socially constructed category of race distinguishes them from other women of color; and this distinction is what contextualizes them in Western societies like the United States.

My concern is that when contemporary feminist literature does refer to women of color, although it acknowledges some tensions, it seldom deals with, or confronts, the critiques given by black women, particularly those who are neither radical feminists nor lesbians, nor express disdain toward their fathers, brothers, and other black men. The critique is that quite apart from feminist theory's being for a middle-class white woman audience, its negation of race gives the advantage to those women (white women) who are not disadvantaged by race. Contemporary white feminists' theory has not reconciled itself with its historical past so as to transcend these issues or at least adjust itself to them.

Within the current social, economic, and political climate, a look at the professions is revealing as to the conditions, tensions, and position of black women in relation to white women and males and black males. In her work *Black Women and White Women in the Professions*, Natalie Sokoloff, (1992, pp. 100–102) demonstrates that from 1960 to 1980, while there has been some employment gains for black women in the elite and nonelite male professions, gender-neutral professions, and female professions, this has not been the "double advantage" that is believed within the dominant society:

it is abundantly clear that in the elite male professions, Black women made no discernible moves toward parity with white men: in 1980 as in 1960, Black women were tragically and very severely underrepresented. . . .

Thus, despite Black women's high rate of increase as doctors, lawyers, psychologists, and the like, and despite whatever access they were able to achieve over time, Black women did not begin to challenge white male control of these coveted positions. Nor did they catch up with white women, who reached parity with white men in several of the nonelite male professions.

The underlying issue was—and still is—the vested interests and the resulting conflicts between African Americans and white women. Compounding these conflicts in the 1970s and 1980s, strains between African American men and women, the issue of black woman femininity or the lack thereof, and female domination and black male emasculation as a rationality for black male sexual attraction to white women added fuel to the fire. Moreover, the belief, rightly or wrongly, that successful black men marry white women— allegedly because they share the same values and lifestyles—is, for African American women, a call to war.

Is the primacy of race or the primacy of gender the real question between African American and white women? Race, gender, class, sexuality, and economics are the component and substantive issues. For black women, racism is the nexus around which issues of gender politics, economics, and social class revolve. For white feminists, sexism is of primary importance. But something else may be underlying, something unspoken. While sympathetic to neo-Marxist analysis (e.g., Sarup, 1986; Apple, 1990), I, along with most other African Americans, have experienced the tension between race and

class. The issues of race and racism and the race/gender dichotomy in relation to multiple levels of discrimination are deep rooted within all of our
psyches. And as we have seen, while black women as well as white feminists
have historically confronted these discriminatory issues, the antagonisms,
albeit socially and politically constructed, center around a difficult and "unspoken" issue—race—specifically with regard to "whiteness" and its resulting ability to influence power and control. While white feminists speak of
building coalitions and alliances with African American and other women
of color, white women are still the wives, lovers, sisters, mothers, and daughters of the white male patriarchy that wields the power and control to discriminate (against people) for their own vested interest; and white women,
as the wives, lovers, mothers, and daughters of the white male power structure, have profited from the oppression of people of color.

The unspoken issue is that white women have their ace card—*the race
card*. Would white women forgo their race card in order to forge alliances
and coalitions with women of color? Could white women forgo their racial
advantage to forge alliances and coalitions? In trying to obtain their own
goals, "race" as a currency allows white women some extra leverage over
women (and men) of color, but at whose expense and for how long? If the
idea of coalition is going to work, then white women are going to have to
come to the table on equal footing with the other women of color; in other
words, they will have to share and share discernibly so. This becomes increasingly difficult because, as economist Julianne Malveaux (1990) observed, white women are intricately tied to the white male patriarchy.

White women are the mothers, daughters, sisters, and wives of the patri-
archs who have also institutionalized racial discrimination against black people. Black women experience an economic oppression that has a basis in
both race and gender. For white women to assume an alliance between
themselves and black women without taking matters of race and family (and,
thus black men) into consideration is a mistake. Too frequently this mistake
characterizes feminist theory, scholarship, activism, and policy development
(Malveaux, 1990, p. 229, as cited in Sokoloff, 1992, p. 133).

The dominant narrative voices within white feminism are going to have
to become reconciled: the oppression of black women as well as other
women of color by the triad of race, economic class, and gender; that white
middle-class feminist ethnocentrism's share in the ideology negates or, at
the very least, marginalizes the experiences of women of color; and white
women's own complicity in, and perpetuation of, the economic, social, and
political oppression of women of color (Brand, 1987; Nain, 1991; Graham,
1991; Cox, 1990; Garcia, 1989; Brewer, 1989).

While there are African American women who are not interested in, or
committed to, feminist perspectives (white or black) for forming coalitions,
it should be noted that there are efforts to explore possibilities, contemporary alliances, and tensions between black and white feminist perspectives.

In an early treatment, *Common Differences: Conflicts in Black and White Feminist Perspective*, Gloria Joseph and Jill Lewis (1981) attempted to explore the contrasting and collaborative perspectives in social, political, and sexual relationships between black and white men and women. Authoring alternating chapters, Joseph and Lewis attempt to focus on the historical and cultural differences, as well as the struggle for equality and freedom from oppression from the perspective of black and white women, by focusing on three areas: black women's and white women's liberation, mothers and daughters, and sexuality and sex attitudes. According to Joseph, job opportunities, day care, sterilization abuse, abortion rights, and sexual harassment and abuse are common issues of concern for black and white women. Yet these issues, more often than not, have different meanings as they relate to the lives of different women and are, in many instances, more critical for black women than for white. For example, abortion rights is only a piece of the larger struggle for adequate health care for African Americans. Black women do not have the "privilege" of focusing on single issues but must, instead, advocate change on a much more inclusive scale. This is equally true in the areas of employment and sexual harassment. Joseph puts forward the belief that despite the necessity for black women to be committed to black liberation, this commitment should not result in their alienation from the women's movement. Instead, black women should strive to expand the mainstream feminist movement to acknowledge the history of the black women's experience.

Joseph and Lewis afford an opportunity to gain an increased awareness of issues that are of significance to women, their relationship to the feminist paradigm, and the perspectives that black and white women bring to the feminist arena. However, for me, the implications of this work seem to be prescribing an "infusion model"—that is, expanding white feminist paradigms and literature to acknowledge and include the history and perspective of black women. This is an outrageous as the February 1993 decision of the National Baseball Owners League to require Marge Schott, the owner of the Cincinnati Reds baseball team, to attend multicultural courses to make her more aware of, and sensitive to, racial and ethnic prejudice in an effort to change her racist behavior. It remains to be seen whether such an infusion model will have any lasting impact on, or will promote, a reconceptualization of dominant (white) feminist narratives. As will be seen, for black women scholars, it is not so much an issue of infusion as an issue of a new way of seeing.

CONTEMPORARY AFRICAN AMERICAN WOMEN'S SCHOLARSHIP

At this juncture, the question becomes: What is the relationship to this history and this cultural knowledge (interpretive frameworks) generated by

African American women? One way of conceptualizing the nexus between history and the perspective, criticism, and theorizing of black women generated out of the endogenous experiences and informed sources for contemporary black women scholars is through Elizabeth Rauh Bethel's (1992) *lieux de mémoire*. African Americans incorporated these *lieux de mémoire* "into a consciously constructed history which revised and challenged the assumptions of inherent racial inferiority and the moral rightness of racial subordination implicit in the Euro-American cultural tradition" (p. 828). Africans arrived in the Americas with their languages, religions, theory values, cultural norms, and so on. While the elders died and their original world eventually faded with them, the sum total of the experiences and knowledge were passed down and now manifest themselves in worldviews, community norms, perspectives, and so on.

Bethel's words signify the influence of Africa on the descendants of the African diaspora in the Americas. They also remind me of the influence of Africanisms on the shaping of knowledge in the master narratives of "traditional canonical American literature," in spite of the taken-for-granted assumptions of patriarchal historians, literary critics, and writers (Morrison, 1992). Toni Morrison uses the term *Africanism* "for the denotative and connotative blackness that African peoples have come to signify, as well as the entire range of views, assumptions, readings and misreadings that accompany Eurocentric learning about these people." She continues:

As a disabling virus within literary discourse, Africanism has become, in the Eurocentric tradition that American education favors, both a way of talking about and a way of policing matters of class, sexual license, and repression, formations and exercises of power, and mediations on ethics and accountability. Through the simple expedient of demonizing and reifying the range of color on a palette, African Africanism makes it possible to say and not say, to inscribe and erase, to escape and engage, to act out and act on, to historicize and render timeless. It provides a way of contemplating chaos and civilization, desire and fear and a mechanism for testing the problems and blessing of freedom. (pp. 6–7)

From Morrison's vantage point, the entire

body politic, the Constitution, and the entire history of the [American] culture [as well as conceptions of] individualism, masculinity, social engagement versus historical isolation; acute and ambiguous moral problematics; the thematics of innocence coupled with an obsession with figuration of death and hell—are not in fact responses to a dark, abiding, signing Africanist presence. (p. 5)

Hazel Carby's (1987, p. 17) *Reconstructing Womanhood* focuses on how African American women scholars produced their cultural knowledge and cultural artifacts "within the social relations that inscribed them." Carby's contention that white women used race and class as ideological sites from which to advance their subordinated status within the white patriarchal structure speaks in parallel worlds to the positions of expediency that white women took during the struggle for suffrage. Moreover, by conceptualizing "whiteness" as a racial category, she clarifies the historical and contemporary advantage that "race" has given white women over women of color.

Thus it is with the theorizing, epistemology, and conceptual frameworks and issues of validity and reliability in the works of contemporary African American women scholars. While the works of Giddings, Lerner, Washington, and so on provide a magnificent history and historiography of the works of African American women intellectuals, contemporary African American women scholars such as Patricia Hill Collins, Vivian Gordon, Toni Morrison, Hazel Carby, Alice Walker, Angela Davis, and bell hooks provide theory, criticisms, and perspectives that echo these *lieux de mémoire* through the culturally, historically, and politically informed positions of their work.

Patricia Hill Collins' (1990) *Black Feminist Thought* has delineated clearly the perspective, theoretical constructs, and Afrocentric nature of black feminist thought. Collins puts forward the idea that African American women intellectuals employ an "outsider-within" stance through which we critique the process of oppression. This view allows us to look with very different and new eyes, as it were, at dominant society, mainstream feminism, and black scholarship. This view allows us clearly to see contradictions between ideologies of womanhood and the devalued status of black women. The oppression of black women has been structured through the exploitation of labor, the denial of their political rights and privileges, and the socially constructed and perpetuated controlling images of black women that originated during the era of slavery. As African American women, we are outsiders who participate, but do not hold full membership, in the black male community, the white male community, or the white feminist community. Collins suggests that any changes in this permanent marginal status require us to reclaim the black feminist intellectual tradition by discovering, reinterpreting, and analyzing the literary and intellectual works and societal deeds of black women from an Afrocentric feminist standpoint. Moreover, she makes the case that black feminist thought goes beyond race, gender, and class to include other social relationships of domination that revolve around religion, ethnicity, sexual orientation, and ageism. The Afrocentric feminist perspective would employ three dimensions: concrete experience as a criterion of meaning, the use of dialogue in assessing knowledge claims, and an ethic of caring and concern for the totality of the entire black community. In such a humanist vision of community, black men and women are nurtured in order to confront oppressive social institutions. The perspective is not just a focus on women and women's issues and an ethic of personal accountability (Collins, 1990).

According to Collins, the theoretical framework of black feminist thought in which the Afrocentric perspective is inherent sees race, class, and gender as interlocking systems of oppression. Within this framework the dominant narratives of feminist—particularly white feminist—theory is problematized by revealing new ways of knowing. As concrete experiences are a criterion of meaning, then such meaning must be validated by ordinary African American women. An important feature of issues of validity and reliability within black feminist thought is that such thought is accepted by the community of Black women scholars. Black feminist thought addresses the ongoing epistemological debates in feminist theory and in the sociology of knowledge concerning ways of assessing "truth." Such thought challenges the nature of proof and scientific validations of Eurocentric masculine political and epistemological requirements that African American and other scholars are confronted with in the academy. Finally, this theoretical framework embraces social change as a change in individual consciousness coupled with the social transformation of political and economic institutions. In other words, individuals define their jobs as institutional transformation. This is especially relevant to those African American women scholars and other African American women leaders who are in positions to create real change in various ways. As indicated in the work of the National Association of Colored Women, formed in 1896, whose motto was "Lifting as we climb," self-help and service to the community reveal a long memory within the African American women's consciousness, as well as in organizations, societies, and social movements (Lerner, 1973; Giddings, 1984).

Of course, when speaking of voice and agenda, we must surely acknowledge the multirepresentationality of black women's voices. Just as there are multiple perspectives, values, lifestyles, and so on among white women, so there are among African American women intellectuals and scholars. The voice of black women is not by any means monolithic. Clearly, there are various voices and perspectives reflecting similar—as well as competing and even contradictory—views. For example, while the issues of family relations and service are seen throughout much of the literature as recurrent themes of strength and support within black families, the writings of bell hooks, (1984, 1991 [hooks and West]) seems to take exception to this, particularly family service in regard to her own family's dysfunctionality in her lived experience. Another example was the controversy surrounding the movie *The Color Purple*, based on Alice Walker's book, because of how black males were vilified and portrayed as the antithesis or enemy. Other voices include those of black lesbians and black women in interracial relations. Such views, perspectives, and lifestyles are not in and of themselves the issue. The issue is whether those who ascribe to and control the dominant narratives and discourses (i.e., whites) accept these perspectives as *the* perspective of black community, instead of the perspective of different African American women generated from their own lived experiences—particularly if the perspective appears to be the damnation of, or expressed hatred toward, black males. Acknowledgment of these voices may not be in the forefront of black intellectual thought; but it is an issue that will surely need to be reckoned with in African American scholarly, popular-cultural, intellectual, and activist circles.

There are more voices. The voice of Vivian Gordon (1987), for example, seems to me to bring an Afrocentric woman's perspective that makes the overall well-being of the whole community (male and female) the primary issue. Gordon makes the case that coalitions between black and white women are, at the very least, historically situated and issue-specific, as I have tried to point out. Her thesis is that a coalition with white women by its very nature negates, or at least jeopardizes, building stronger bonds with black males here in the Americas, as well as developing alliances and coalitions with the African continent.

Within the literature, there are also those African American women scholars who embrace an Afrocentric or black studies perspective. One example of this is also found in the work of Vivian Gordon (1987). In *Black Women, Feminism and Black Liberation: Which Way* she puts forward a perspective in which the primary issues center on an Afrocentric axis of race, economics, relationships between women and men, and community well-being. She articulates a manifesto of sorts—a way of seeing the world and participating in it. To this end, she makes some interesting arguments that confirm the writings of African American women scholars, as well as arguments that are known by African American women scholars through the lived experience, the way of knowing that, as Collins reminds us, challenges the nature of proof and scientific validations. Race is the primary issue, but Gordon does not want the issues of race and sex to fragmentize thinking. The oppression experienced by black and white women is very different, because it is oppression based on gender-specific issues. Black women are oppressed by the trilogy of racism, sexism, and economics. Not only do white women participate in the oppression of black women, but women's studies traditionally portrays black women through pathology models; and in the "presentation of Black women, the perspective which usually dominates is that of the radical feminist and the radical feminist lesbian who certainly present valid issues of oppression, but who do not represent the primary experiences of the pluralistic majority of Black women" (V. Gordon, p. 15). Gordon identifies the seven issues that she argues are the major concerns to Black women. In rank order, they are education, employment, family (home and motherhood), housing (including health and crime), perceptions of self and role, leadership, and women's liberation (pp. 51–52). The essence of her message is that racism is the primary issue confronting African Americans. While sexism in black men emanates from their lack of power due to racism, resulting in "misdirected hostilities" of black men toward black women in the form of domestic violence and rape, such tensions would be diminished when the effects of racism diminished. Black liberation "represents freedom from sexism and racism and embraces a Black female/male co-partnership

in struggle and love" (p. 46). From Gordon's perspective, building coalitions with white women will be detrimental not only to African American
women but to the African American community at large: "That a Black
woman's coalition with a White woman dominated movement centered
around an Eurocentric focus holds the potential for an isolation of Black
women from the promised rewards of the coalition as well as an isolation
from their historic identity and efforts in behalf of the liberation of the
African American community" (p. 1).

Much of the contemporary theory, criticism, and perspective referenced
in the dominant literature comes from literature and literary criticism and
popular culture. Henry Giroux's (1992) discussion of the marginalization
of African American feminist writers Hazel Carby, bell hooks, June Jordan,
Audre Lorde, and Michele Wallace entitled "Afro-American Feminist Writers and the Discourse of Possibility" points, again, to universal echoes from
a long historical memory that focuses on the politics of resistance, solidarity,
and possibility. Moreover, he argues that the dominant forms of "multicultural education" do not critique how the "white" race functions as an
historical and social construction. As will be seen, his ideas are similar to
those of Sylvia Wynter (1992a), who argues the necessity of breaking up
the current definitions of multicultural education because it is constructed
as an infusion model, whereas what is needed is a recreation or reinvention
of the master narrative.

For Giroux, the black feminist literary writers reflect the politics of resistance, solidarity, critique, and possibility. They theorize voice with regard
to race, class, and gender; and in doing so black feminist writers produce,
and engage in, the discourse of difference. Giroux acknowledges that black
feminist writers employ alternative forms of knowledge construction in their
works, which consist of personal narratives, experiences, and life histories.
Most important for Giroux is that the theory of the politics-of-difference
discourse of black feminists includes their critique of the normative codes
and relations in the dominant society, a critique of white feminist notions
of different and identity politics wherein race is subordinated to sex, and a
reconstruction of difference through the development of narrative forms.

Beyond being somewhat guilty of presenting a narrow perspective of the
works of African American women scholars that Vivian Gordon (1987)
spoke against, Giroux, unfortunately, fails to address some issues. One is the
influence of Africanisms on the construction of forms of knowledge (Holloway, 1990; Morrison, 1992). Another is the multiplicity of black women's
voices and representation in education pertaining to issues of race, gender,
class, community, and family, particularly in conjunction with black men
(King and Wilson, 1990; Ladson-Billings and Henry, 1990; Hollins and
Spencer, 1990, B. Gordon, 1990, 1993; J. King, 1992b; Henry, 1992;
Wynter, 1992a & b; Foster, 1990; Nelson, 1990; Perkins, 1990; Lee et al.,
1990). These voices represent various disciplines and ideology; and while

black women authors and literary writers have made powerful statements, there are black women scholars in all disciplines (education, law, film, communications, medicine, etc.) addressing the issues that must be raised and acted upon within the black community at large. Specifically, Giroux's analysis neglects to situate any of the writings of contemporary African American women in education or black studies, which also struggle with issues of representation and voice within educational discourse. To his credit, Giroux is one of very few white scholars (male or female) to look seriously at the contributions to social theorizing and the generation of alternative narratives that this body of endogenous knowledge—generated from the history of the diaspora of Africans in the Americas—has made within and beyond the black community. Such scholars within the fields of education and black studies also critique the normative codes and relations within society, critiquing white feminist notions and developing alternative models that recreate and reinvent voice and representation of African Americans.

THE BLACK STUDIES CULTURAL MODEL

So far, I have not focused on the theory, criticism, or perspective of black women's voices on issues within the field of education. The discussion will now focus on an example of current work of black women scholars that makes problematic the regimes of truth operating within dominant narratives that constitute school curriculum.

Ironically enough, much of the postmodern discourse focuses on issues of otherness and marginality; and while feminist scholarship has made inroads into this discourse, there is little serious engagement with the works of black women scholars. Many examples of the marginalized view of the Other and Otherness can be found. In the curriculum field, a salient example of the marginalized voice can be readily seen in issues surrounding whose knowledge will be disseminated in the preparation of both students and teachers. A particularly cogent example was the textbook adoption controversy in California (I. King, 1992b; Wynter, 1992b; B. Gordon, 1992). What follows is a summarizing essay of some of the writings and lectures of Sylvia Wynter (B. Gordon, 1992).

In her critique of the California textbook adoption controversy, Wynter (1992b) conceptualizes it as an epistemological struggle between those who challenge the Anglo-Euro-American master narrative within the book context and those who embrace the master narrative of the Anglo-Euro-American canon, which depicts America as a country of immigrants. As reflected in the 1893 Report of the Committee of Ten on Secondary Education and, particularly, the 1895 Report of the Committee of Fifteen on Elementary Education, both written by the National Education Association, the curriculum decisions made by educators, the knowledge and material selected to be taught, constituted, consciously or not, the principle of Western anglicized Euro-American canon, which in turn canonized "whiteness" in the dominant narratives disseminated in the schools and in the very fiber of American literature, as Morrison (1992) has demonstrated.

For Wynter, this challenge to the anglicized Euro-American canon—"the regime of truth," as it were—comes from employing a black studies cultural model generated from the particular perspective of the African American reality. This reality is the result of Africans bringing with them, and preserving, African conceptualizations and ways of thought and living—this argument being the same as was made by Bethel (1992). These conceptualizations transformed Judeo-Christianity into an Afro-Judeo-Christian popular culture; as such, this popular culture is known throughout the world and represents what Wynter considers to be the first emerging universal culture.[1]

Wynter's black studies cultural model challenges the American master narrative to change from the canonization of whiteness to a global cultural narrative in which human beings are viewed as symbolically kin related. America is emerging as the first *world* civilization, something that Wynter argues is unique and new in world history. As the twenty-first century approaches, bringing with it global transformations and realignments of allegiance and power, particularly within the Third World, the pertinent question is: Will America reinvent itself into the democratic egalitarian society or remain as it was originally invented—a hierarchical society based on a structure of domination and subjugation? For Wynter, the stakes are high: the planetary environment is at risk of being destroyed because of the logic of the collective behaviors of individual groups and the way Western culture views science and humankind.

Wynter (1990), in "America as a 'World,' " argues that in Western culture, science is constituted with half scientific knowledge and half narrative knowledge. More precisely, she proposes that the narrative-knowledge side of science in Western society views humans as naturally evolved organisms. Wynter counters this view by proposing that humanness constitutes more than a biological genetically preprogrammed organism. Humans are preprogrammed to be human, but their humanness "comes into being when humans initiate a cultural system that is a moral and ethical system coded in the [founding] narrative" (Wynter, 1991). Humanness comes into being simultaneously with culture through representation and discourse. In other words, humanness, (i.e., humans coming into being—the human *being*) occurs simultaneously with culture. What separates humankind from other animals is that humans regulate their behavior through discourse, language, and meaning.

This is the prerequisite for Wynter's thesis that "race" is the cultural canon of the United States and other Western nations. The underpinning is that whiteness is constructed as the highest level among the biogenetically evolved natural organisms and that native people (in this instance, the Africans) are the lowest and least evolved species, with gradations of human-ness in between. The one culture of America is race-based, and this "race" base is part of the founding master narrative.

Wynter's black studies cultural model is predicated upon this image of humanness, one that focuses on how models of being and models of hu-manness are instituted in society. In articulating the challenge that black scholars are confronted with at the dawn of the twenty-first century, she parallels the role of contemporary black scholars to other great moments in time: the thirteenth and fifteenth centuries, when lay humanist intellectuals struggled against the intellectual hegemony of the clergy and church over the people. These lay intellectuals challenged the "regimes of truth" by deconstructing intellectual knowledge (i.e., the scientific and narrative knowledge), which ultimately led to the end of the church's hegemony over knowledge and the secularization of human beings. The contemporary chal-lenge for black scholars is the deconstruction of the body of knowledge within the academy and the reinvention of the Unum[2] that reflects this vision of humanity and the emergent universal popular culture.

One might begin by asking scientific questions, such as: What are the rules governing the production of knowledge that regulate human behavior? With regard to understanding the function of curriculum, and, more spe-cifically, the function of curricular knowledge found in school knowledge. Wynter argues that the canon upon which the textbook is based is the Eu-rocentric male founding narrative, the very nature of which is antithetical to nonwhites (i.e., it demotivates black students and secures certain societal role allocations at the levels of race, class, and gender). The question here is "What must be the 'regime of truth' operating in school curriculum that manages to produce [and reproduce], regularly and precisely, the racial strat-ification between and among groups we see in [American] society?" (Wyn-ter, 1991). Her call, therefore, is to change the system of symbolic representation (the Unum) in order to change the school curriculum, and ultimately American society. The challenge now is for America to reinvent itself as a world civilization by reinventing the rewriting the Unum in a way that conceives of humankind as symbolically kin-related rather than genet-ically bonded and separated. For Wynter, black studies, being diaspora lit-eracy, is scientific knowledge.

The thesis put forward by Wynter, in many ways, epitomizes the per-spectives, theory, criticism, and voice of many of the women presented in this discussion. The *lieux de mémoire* of black women are manifested through their currents of thought, politics of resistance, and commitment to study African American women within their own rights, and as an essen-tial feature of understanding the totality of the African American community at large. Conversely, there are obviously points of contention and tensions within African American women's intellectual, scholarly, and popular dis-course. However, my point is that *lieux de mémoire* transcend time, and that the universals operating therein manifest themselves in recognizable codes of conduct and meanings that connect. Thus, phrases from "Lifting as we climb" to "Girlfriend, I heard that!" speak to worlds of understandings and meanings even when heard for the first time.

FINAL THOUGHTS, FUTURE ISSUES

As the twenty-first century approaches, there are many compelling sites of struggle where African American women must continue to increase their involvement. These sites range from local communities and urban and suburban public schools to engagement with the international community. In light of two recent developments—(1) lifting the ban on distributing contraceptive information by the Office of World Population Management for international population control, by the Clinton administration; and (2) a recent proposal put forward by Donald Schaefer, governor of Maryland, to make the use of implanted birth-control devices for teenage mothers (the majority of whom are African Americans) a condition for receiving local and state assistance, and also to perform vasectomies on male prisoners (a majority of whom are African Americans) as a condition of parole—the monitoring issues and policies surrounding sexuality and reproductive rights in both urban centers and the Third World take on new urgency. Related to this, as mentioned by Vivian Gordon (1987), is the need for African Americans to nurture relationships and build coalitions with Third World people, particularly Africans and people of the African diaspora throughout the global community. As the threat of the Soviet Union and the spread of communism declines, U.S. attention has shifted to the Third World. The nature and tenor of such attention also merits monitoring (Childs, 1991).

White middle-class feminism—represented not only in literature, but also through social actions and behavior—may need to transform itself or perhaps transcend to a humanist position—which is inclusive of the entire community, not just women. The position of exclusivity inevitably becomes a dominant, masculine, controlling narrative, the one that feminists are supposed to be challenging as controlling power. I do not mean a disconnected humanism as the concept of the individual ("Humanism: Autonomous individualism, self-directive, natural rights, shape, potentially fully conscious, refusal to accept limits. Socio-political human, producer" [Lather, 1991, p. 160]), but a humanism connected to the collective and personal as an autonomous being related to the community in the sense of: We are therefore I am—I am therefore we are: humanism, as a way of seeing, as a totality of vision, instead of experiencing "the artificial fragmentation that is so common to Western and Western-influenced societies [which] has resulted in the separation of beauty and art, the separation between politics and history, of economics and ethics, and of our individual selves from ourselves as citizen, worker, mother—whatever role we perform" (Hamilton, 1992, p. 434).

Patti Lather's (1991) conception of feminist research argues for doing research in a different way. The narrative component within Lather's methodology is reminiscent of Collins' assertion of employing the concrete experience as a criterion of meaning and the use of dialogue in assessing knowledge claims; that is, as a position of Otherness, there is a natural need to critique the dominant narratives and power structures, which are the white, male, elite structures. What comes to the fore is that race, gender, family, and such sexual concepts as patriarchy, family, and reproduction have very different and even contradictory meanings for white women and African American women and other women of color. Moreover, that white women are in power relations as oppressors of black women and men—power by virtue of race—raises the obvious issue that dominant feminist theory is still ethnocentric.

I have reservations about a black-white women's coalition. Historically speaking, as previously seen, black women and white women see the world in very different ways. While there are issue-specific points of overlapping interests, race and class positionality and interests are tensions that result in real-life consequences (Sokoloff, 1992). Moreover, it is not at all clear to me that, in general, coalitions between African American women and white women can be constructed, first, because the socially constructed hierarchical positions of both are unequal and disproportionately out of balance; and second, because of the danger that such coalitions could result in unanticipated (detrimental) implications for the black community at large and most surely would exacerbate African American male-female relationships, subsequently tearing at the African American community *kente*-cloth fabric.

For example, in contemporary society, African American and white women have similar concerns over the issue of child care. As more white middle-class and upper-middle-class women are entering the job market and getting on career ladders, the issue of child care has become the focus of national debate and the beginning of the passage of federal legislation, such as the Family Leave Bill, signed into legislation by President Bill Clinton in January 1993. Yet, historically speaking, it is only recently that both groups are on the same side, needing the same thing—child care. In the not too distant past, and even today, domestic workers (most of whom were black) took care of the children of the white middle-class women, who seemingly were not too concerned about who was taking care of the children of their "girl," while this "girl" was attending to their children. African American (and other women of color, as well as poor white) domestic and child-care worker exploitation occurs because of the undervaluing of such work. The 1993 failed nomination of attorney Zoe Baird for U.S. attorney general, as well as examples in literary criticism (Morrison, 1992) and the previously discussed historical accounts (Giddings, Lerner, Washington, Loewenberg and Bogin) speak to this issue.

In light of this and other historical baggage, when I overhear women who consider themselves feminists refer to their domestic worker and/or child-care provider as their "girl," I question the relationship between what dominant feminist narratives mean and how these feminists see and position themselves with the constituent Other. Such issues need to be discussed before one can begin to speak about commonalities, much less coalitions. White women have historically participated in, and still continue to participate in, the sexual and racial oppression of African American and other women of color under the guise of expediency (Giddings, 1984).

Mindful of Carby's (1987, p. 17) assertion that "the terrain of language is the terrain of power," and numerous conversations with friends is sorting out some of the issues discussed in this chapter, I have become cautious about embracing the language of feminists, because it is austensibly a language controlled and dominated by white women. And, from my vantage point, whoever controls the language, conceptual structures, and meanings ultimately controls the narratives and discourses. Black woman are not hostile toward white women and white feminist narratives. We, nonetheless, realize that there are points of tensions—conflicting vested interests—between these groups of women; and at such junctures white women, be they radical feminists or conservative Republicans, can and do use the race card, consciously or not, to their advantage. White women have not come clean on the issue of using "race-as-white" privilege, to use Giddings' terms, for political expediency and power.

Through our own voices, perspectives, theorizing, and criticisms, black women scholars are recreating or reconstructing spheres of meaning by challenging the assumptions of cultural and political discourse of both theory and the common, everyday terrain of life. Clearly, we have our work cut out for us.

NOTES

1. For example, people around the world know about gospel, blues, and jazz. In a somewhat related vein, Houston A. Baker, Jr. (1984) talks about the contribution of African American blues, ideology, and literature to popular "vernacular" American culture.

2. Unum, from *E pluribus unum*.

REFERENCES

Apple, Michael (1990). *Ideology and Curriculum*, 2nd ed. New York: Routledge.
Baker, H. A. Jr. (1984). *Blues, Ideology and Afro-American Literature—A Vernacular Theory*. Chicago: University of Chicago Press.

Bethel, Elizabeth Rauh (1992). "Images of Hayti: The Construction of an Afro-American *Lieu de Mémoire.*" *Callaloo,* 15(3): 827–841.

Blassingame, John W. and McKivigan, John R. (eds.) (1979). *The Frederick Douglass Papers.* Series One: *Speeches, Debates, and Interviews.* Volume 4: 1864–80. New Haven, CT: Yale University Press.

Brand, Dionne (1987). "Black Women and Work: The Impact of Racially Constructed Gender Roles on the Sexual Division of Labour." Part One. *Fireweed,* 25 (Fall): 28–37.

Brewer, Rose M. (1989). "Black Women and Feminist Sociology: The Emerging Perspective." *American Sociologist,* 20(1) (Spring): 57–70.

Brown, Elsa Barkley (1989). "Womanist Consciousness: Maggie Lena Walker and the Independent Order of Saint Luke." *Signs,* 14(3) (Spring): 610–633.

Busby, Margaret (ed.) (1992). *Daughters of Africa. An International Anthology of Words and Writings by Women of African Descent: From the Ancient Egyptian to the Present.* New York: Pantheon Books.

Carby, Hazel V. (1987). *Reconstructing Womanhood. The Emergence of the Afro-American Woman Novelist.* New York: Oxford University Press.

Childs, John Brown (1991). "Notes on the Gulf War, Racism and African American Social Thought." *Journal of Urban and Cultural Studies,* 2(1): 81–92.

Collins, Patricia Hill (1990). *Black Feminist Thought: Knowledge, Consciousness and the Politics of Empowerment.* New York: Routledge, Chapman and Hall.

Cox, Cherise (1990). "Anything Less Is Not Feminism: Racial Difference and the W.M.W.M. (White Middle-class Women's Movement). *Law and Critique,* 1(2) (Autumn): 237–248.

Davis, Angela (1983). *Women, Race and Class.* New York: Vintage Books.

DuBois, Ellen Carol (1981). *Elizabeth Cady Stanton, Susan B. Anthony: Correspondence, Writings, Speeches.* New York: Schocken Books.

Evans, Mari (1970). *I Am a Black Woman.* New York: William Morrow.

Foster, Michele (1990). "The Politics of Race: Through the Eyes of African American Teachers." *Journal of Education,* Special Issue: History and Voice in African American Pedagogy, 172(3): 123–141.

Garcia, Alma M. (1989). "The Development of Chicana Feminist Discourse, 1970–1980." *Gender and Society,* 3(2) (June): 217–238.

Giddings, Paula (1984). *When and Where I Enter: The Impact of Black Women on Race and Sex in America.* New York: Bantam Books.

Giroux, Henry (1992). *Border Crossings: Cultural Workers and the Politics of Education.* New York: Routledge, Chapman & Hall.

Gitlin, Todd (1989). "Postmodernism Defined, at Last!" *Utne Reader,* July/August, pp. 52–61.

Gordon, Beverly (1985). "Toward Emancipation in Citizenship Education: The Case of African American Cultural Knowledge." *Theory and Research in Social Education,* 12(4): 1–23.

———. (1990). "The Necessity of African American Epistemology for Educational Theory and Practice." *Journal of Education,* Special Issue: History and Voice in African American Pedagogy, 172(3): 88–106.

———. (1992). "Reconstructing Curriculum Discourse: Alternative Narratives for Teachers and Students." Symposium: New Challenges to "the Regimes of

Truth." Towards a New Intellectual Order. Presented at the American Educational Research Association meeting, April 1992, San Francisco.

——. (1993). "African American Cultural Knowledge and Liberatory Education. Dilemmas, Problems and Potentials in a Postmodern American Society." *Urban Education*, 27(4): 448–470.

Gordon, Vivian (1987). *Black Women, Feminism and Black Liberation: Which Way?* Chicago: Third World Press.

Graham, Hilary (1991). "The Concept of Caring in Feminist Research: The Case of Domestic Service." *Sociology*, 25(1) (February): 61–78.

Grimshaw, Anna (ed.) (1992). *The C.L.R. James Reader*. Oxford: Blackwell.

Hamilton, Cynthia (1992). "A Way of Seeing: Culture as Political Expression in the Works of C.L.R. James." *Journal of Black Studies*, 22(3), 429–443.

Henry, Annette (1992). "African Canadian Women Teachers' Activism: Recreating Communities of Caring and Resistance." *Journal of Negro Education*, 61(3): 392–404.

Hollins, E. R. and Spencer, K. (1990). "Restructuring Schools for Cultural Inclusion: Changing the Schooling Process for African American Youngsters." *Journal of Education*, 172(2): 89–100.

Holloway, Joseph, (ed.) (1990). *Africanisms in American Culture*. Bloomington: Indiana University Press.

hooks, bell (1984). *Feminist Theory from Margin to Center*. Boston: South End Press.

hooks, bell and West, Cornel (1991). *Breaking Bread: Insurgent Black Intellectual Life*. Boston: South End Press.

Hull, Gloria, Bell, Patricia Scott, and Smith, Barbara (eds.) (1982). *All the Women Are White, All the Blacks Are Men, But Some of Us Are Brave*. New York: The Feminist Press at CUNY.

Joseph, Gloria I., and Lewis, Jill (1981). *Common Differences—Conflicts in Black and White Feminist Perspectives*. Boston: South End Press.

King, Debra (1992). "Unraveling Fabric, Missing the Beat: Class and Gender in Afro-American Social Issues." *The Black Scholar*, 22(3): 36–44.

King, Joyce (1992a). "Diaspora Literacy and Consciousness in the Struggle Against Miseducation in the Black Community." *Journal of Negro Education*, 61(3): 317–340.

——. (1992b). "The Middle Passage Revisited: Diaspora Literacy and Consciousness in the Struggle Against "Miseducation" in the Black Community." Symposium: New Challenges to "the Regimes of Truth." Towards a New Intellectual Order. Presented at the American Educational Research Association meeting, April 1992, San Francisco, CA.

King, J. E. and Wilson, T. L. (1990). "Being the Soul-freeing Substance: A Legacy of Hope in Afro Humanity." *Journal of Education*, 172(2): 9–27.

Ladson-Billings, G., and Henry, A. (1990). "Blurring the Borders: Voices of African Liberatory Pedagogy in the United States and Canada." *Journal of Education*, 172(2): 72–88.

Lather, Patti (1991). *Getting Smart. Feminist Research and Pedagogy with/in the Postmodern*. New York: Routledge.

Lee, C., Lomotey, K. and Shujaa, M. (1990). "How Shall We Sing Our Sacred Song in a Strange Land? The Dilemma of Double Consciousness and the Complexities of an African-centered Pedagogy." *Journal of Education*, 172(2): 45–62.

Lerner, Gerda (ed.) (1973). *Black Women in White America: A Documentary History.* New York: Vintage Books.

Loewenberg, Bert James and Bogin, Ruth (eds.) (1976). *Black Women in Nineteenth-Century American Life: Their Words, Their Thoughts, Their Feelings.* University Park: Pennsylvania State University Press.

Malveaux, Julianne (1990). "Gender Difference and Beyond: An Economic Perspective on Diversity and Commonality among Women. In Deborah L. Rhode (ed.), *Theoretical Perspectives on Sexual Difference.* New Haven, CT: Yale University Press, pp. 226–238.

Morrison, Toni (1992). *Playing in the Dark—Whiteness and the Literary Imagination.* Cambridge, MA: Harvard University Press.

Nain, Gemma Tang (1991). "Black Women, Sexism and Racism: Black or Antiracist Feminism." *Feminist Review*, 37 (Spring): 1–22.

Nelson, Linda Williamson (1990). "Code Switching in the Oral Life Narratives of African-American Women: Challenges to Linguistic Hegemony." *Journal of Education*, 172(3): 142–155.

Perkins, Linda M. (1990). The National Association of College Women: Vanguard of Black Women's Leadership in Education, 1923–1954." *Journal of Education*, Special Issue: History and Voice in African American Pedagogy, 172(3): 65–75.

Richardson, Marilyn (ed.) (1987). *Marcia Stewart, America's First Black Woman Political Writer—Essays and Speeches.* Bloomington: Indiana University Press.

Sarup, Madan (1986). *The Politics of Multiracial Education.* London: Routledge and Kegan Paul.

Sokoloff, Natalie J. (1992). *Black Women and White Women in the Professions.* New York: Routledge, Chapman and Hall.

Sterling, Dorothy (ed.) (1984). *We Are Your Sisters: Black Women in the Nineteenth Century.* New York: W. W. Norton.

Walker, Alice (1983). *In Search of Our Mothers' Gardens: Womanist Prose.* San Diego: Harcourt Brace Jovanovich.

Wall, Cheryl (ed.) (1989). *Changing Our Own Words: Essays on Criticism, Theory and Writing by Black Women.* New Brunswick, NJ: Rutgers University Press.

Wallace, Michele (1990). *Invisibility Blues—From Pop to Theory.* London: Verso Press.

Washington, Mary Helen (ed.) (1987). *Invented Lives: Narratives of Black Women, 1860–1960.* New York: Anchor Press.

West, Cornel (1985). "The Dilemma of the Black Intellectual." *Cultural Critique*, 1: 109–124.

———. (1989). "Black Culture and Postmodernism." In B. Kurger and P. Mariana (eds.), *Remaking History.* Seattle: Bay Press, pp. 87–96.

Williamson Nelson, Linda (1990). "Code Switching in the Oral Life Narratives of African American Women: Challenges to Linguistic Hegemony." *Journal of Education.* Special Issue: History and Voice in African American Pedagogy, 172(3): pp. 142–155.

Wynter, Sylvia (1990). "America as a 'World': A Black Studies Perspective and 'Cultural Model' Framework." Presented in a letter to California State Board of Education Members, September.

———. (1991). "Diaspora Literacy and the Black Studies Perspective in Curriculum Change." Seminar. Santa Clara University, July 27. Invited Speaker.

———. (1992a). "Re-thinking Aesthetics: Notes toward a Deciphering Practice." In M. Cham (Ed.), *Ex-iles: Essays on Caribbean Cinema*. Trenton, NJ: Africa World Press, pp. 237–279.

———. (1992b). "The Challenge to Our Episteme: The Case of the California Textbook Controversy." Symposium: New Challenges to "the Regimes of Truth." Towards a New Intellectual Order. Presented at American Educational Research Association meeting, April 1992, San Francisco.

4

Multicultural Education and Postmodernism: Movement Toward a Dialogue

Carl A. Grant and Judyth M. Sachs

INTRODUCTION

Multicultural education developed in the United States, the United Kingdom, Canada, and Australia during the 1970s as an educational concept and process to help galvanize and articulate the competing social and political interests of diverse ethnic and cultural groups (e.g., blacks, women). Issues such as equality of opportunity, gender equity, ethnic identity and cultural diversity, and cultural pluralism provided the theoretical and conceptual platform on which multicultural education rested, and was developed to be implemented into educational institutions. Its implementation in schools as policy and pedagogic practice has taken a variety of forms in the above contexts. Similarly, its impetus in the above countries has been motivated by different initiatives. Given the different historical, material, and ideological conditions and motivating initiatives existing in the United States, the United Kingdom, and Australia, it is not surprising that the conceptualization and practice of multicultural education differs significantly in its emphasis (Lynch, 1986; Sleeter, 1989).

In this chapter we argue that postmodern theory can contribute to understanding the complexities of education for a multicultural society (i.e., multicultural education). In order to do this, we will review recent theoretical literature concerning multicultural education. We assert that much of this literature is concerned with "a normative politics of cultural difference" in the form of practical concerns for teachers and administrators. Such an

orientation renders silent or ignores the development of the critical perspective of multicultural education.

Drawing on current debates within postmodernist and poststructuralist
theory, we propose a discussion on multicultural education that will help to
illuminate the changes taking place in contemporary culture. As Featherstone (1988, p. 208) suggests, these can be understood in terms of changes
in the everyday practices and experiences of different groups "who may be
using regimes of signification in different ways and developing new means
of orientation and identity structures." In this chapter our intent is twofold:
First, we are concerned with identifying the nature and scope of current
multicultural education practice. Second, given the silences and omissions
evident in much of the mainstream literature, we propose a discussion of
multicultural education and postmodernism that may serve to open up lines
of communication between proponents of these two paradigms and their
concerns about issues of metanarratives regarding race, gender, class, and
other areas of oppression. Liberal rhetoric, we maintain, is often concerned
with focusing on specific interventions, such as educational programs for
culturally different groups, while not being concerned with structural inequities as they exist in society that help reinforce social and economic dis-
advantage. Such perspectives omit two theoretically important concepts—
discourse and culture. In this chapter these concepts provide the basis for
our discussion of postmodernism and multicultural education.

POSTMODERNISM: A USEFUL LENS FOR
EDUCATORS OF MULTICULTURAL EDUCATION?

The postmodernist debate poses in a dramatic way the issue of competing
paradigms for social theory and the need to choose paradigms that are most
theoretically and practicably applicable to social conditions in the present
era (Kellner, 1988, p. 267). West (1987, p. 27) tells us that "the postmodernism debate is principally a battle over how we conceive of culture
and, most importantly, how we interpret the current crisis in our society
and muster resources to alleviate it." Its project is to move beyond all totalizing discourses and to be incredulous of what Lyotard (1984) called
metanarratives. For Lyotard the postmodern condition is one in which
"grand narratives of legitimation" are no longer credible. Postmodernism
recognizes that canons are socially constructed and always will need to be
reconstructed through dialogues among and between various communities.
The strength of postmodernism is that it simultaneously holds out possibilities for the revival and widening of a cultural politics and for its neutrali-
zation (Connor, 1989, p. 224). Postmodernism is concerned with
rethinking culture and the power relations embodied not only in cultural
representations but also material practices. For multicultural education this
is particularly important. First, because it offers another lens through which

to analyze and interrogate the literature on school practice and the distribution of culture and power in society. Second, the treatment of difference and Otherness is central to any investigation or understanding of the dynamics of social change, and postmodernism can contribute to how multicultural educators engage in this discussion. For example, "difference theory" versus "deficit theory" has for decades been a part of the multicultural debate. How teachers perceive their students greatly determines how they work with them. Nieto (1992, p. 79), an advocate of multicultural education, recently posited:

If students are perceived as to be "deficient," the educational environment will reflect a no-nonsense, back-to-basics, drill orientation. However, if they are perceived as intelligent and motivated young people with an interest in the world around them, the educational environment will tend to reflect an intellectually stimulating and academically challenging orientation.

Postmodernism and its "suspiciousness . . . [of the] ways in which we subordinate, exclude, and marginalize" (Giroux, 1988, p. 24) can serve to illuminate and reinforce the argument that multicultural educators make to mainstream educators regarding their hard-to-release doubts about the academic ability of students of color, especially African American and Hispanic students.

We share Hebdige's (1988) qualified view that the term "postmodernism," while characterized by much abstract theoretical debate and to some extent a degree of incoherence, is so wide-ranging that it must describe something. We maintain that for multicultural educators, postmodernism provides another lens through which to examine everyday experiences and the role common sense has in the constitution of ethnic, racial, socioeconomic, and gender difference as a focus of power in society. It also can lead to a more comprehensive study of the various subject positions that individuals inhabit, since "one is not just one thing" (Spivak, 1990, p. 60).

Central to postmodernism and poststructuralism is the investigation of power and how power relations are played out among various groups, whether they be gender, ethnic, cultural, or sexual identities. Theoretically it helps us to analyze mechanisms of power locally, focusing on contextualizing notions of power-in-use, and, as Lather (1991, p. 156) states, "to explore the meanings of difference and the possibilities for struggling against multiple oppressive formations simultaneously."

An implication of postmodernism is to redefine the strategies of critique and to challenge the criterion of critique that has been used to legitimate the policies and practices of Western society. Giroux (1991, p. 23) argues:

As a form of cultural criticism, postmodernism has challenged a number of assumptions central to the discourse of modernism. These include modernism's reliance on metaphysical notions of the subject, its advocacy of science, technology, and rationality as the foundation for equating change with progress, its ethnocentric equation of history with the triumphs of European civilization, and its globalizing view that the industrialized Western countries constitute [quoting Richard, 1987/1988, p. 6] "a legitimate center—a unique and superior position from which to establish control and to determine hierarchies."

An additional implication of postmodernism, Popkewitz (1992) explains, is how language constructs "self" and "other" and can marginalize and/or colonialize.

Detractors of postmodern and poststructural theory have been critical of its subjectivism and relativism, which often border on nihilism. We are concerned with "a critical theory which is committed to emancipation from all forms of oppression, as well as to freedom, happiness and a rational ordering of society" (Kellner, 1990, p. 12).

In practice the role of the postmodern critic is to contest hegemonic discourses. This requires a detailed, scholarly comprehension of one's own location within the field of discourse and cultural practice (Bove, 1986). Accordingly there is a need to

pay full attention to the social and institutional context of textuality in order to address the power relations of everyday life. Social meanings are produced within social institutions and practices in which individuals, who are shaped by these institutions, are agents of change, rather than its authors, change which may either serve hegemonic interests or challenge existing power relations. (Weedon, 1987, p. 25)

This practice is important and in agreement with many multicultural educationists for it forecasts the need for educators to reposition themselves as "critical intellectuals [who] must understand the historical specificity of the cultural practices of their own period with an eye to bringing their own practice and discourse in line with other oppositional forces in a society struggling against hegemonic manipulation" (Bove, 1986, p. 7). The specificities of this and strategies for teachers will be presented later in this chapter.

MULTICULTURAL EDUCATION

Earlier we argued that much of the multicultural education literature is concerned with the implementation of practical solutions derived from a liberal tradition to provide solutions for specific social and educational problems. Grant, Sleeter, and Anderson (1986) after a review and analysis of sixty-nine books written on multicultural education from four countries—Australia, 3; Canada, 3; England, 9; and the United States, 54—reported that most of this multicultural literature was written for classroom teachers.

Importantly, teachers were seen as the primary agent of change. Grant and Sleeter's (1985) review and analysis of 200 journal articles on multicultural education from seven countries (Australia, Canada, England, Indonesia, Scotland, Sweden, and the United States) produced similar results. In particular the results showed that most of these articles were very short (about five pages), with little if any discussion of power, and the majority of them advocated an assimilationist approach. Also these reviews and another by Sleeter and Grant (1987) revealed that the multicultural education literature does not show a tight correspondence between ideas and practice, nor does it provide a thorough discussion of the theoretical framework in relationship to proposed approaches or goals. Furthermore, while there are suggested multicultural education goals for several educational areas, including curricula, instruction, and school policy, most school practices are often limited to curricula. The curricula, as Gay (1979, 1988) and Hernandez (1989) among others have argued, are not ethnically pluralistic and culturally relevant, especially for students of color.

Additionally, in the literature and in everyday discourse (similar to postmodernism) the term "multicultural education" takes on numerous meanings, leading to conceptual confusion and ambiguity (Gibson, 1976; Banks, 1977; Grant, 1977; Gay, 1983; Gollnick and Chinn, 1983; Pratte, 1983). For example, Gibson (1976) identified four meanings or approaches educators took to multicultural education: (1) education of the culturally different, or benevolent multiculturalism, which seeks to incorporate culturally different students more effectively into mainstream culture and society; (2) education about cultural difference, which teaches all students about cultural differences in an effort to promote better cross-cultural understanding; (3) education for cultural pluralism, which seeks to preserve ethnic cultures and increase the power of ethnic minority groups; and (4) bicultural education, which seeks to prepare students to operate successfully in two different cultures.

Important to this discussion of multicultural education and postmodernism is to note that an increasing number of multicultural educators (Banks, 1991; Ladson-Billings, 1991; Gay, 1988; Gollnick and Chinn, 1993; Grant and Sleeter, 1985; Nieto, 1992) are arguing that multicultural education should prepare students to deal with race, class, and gender oppression in society, and to take charge of their life circumstances. For example, Sleeter and Grant (1988, p. 176) argue:

Education that is Multicultural and Social Reconstructionist deals . . . with oppression and social structural inequality based on race, social class, gender, and disability. It prepares future citizens (students) to reconstruct society so that it better serves the interests of all groups and especially those who are of color, poor, female, and/or disabled.

Having provided a synopsis of the multicultural educational literature, our task as cultural critics is to examine the ideas identified earlier as the conceptual touchstones of postmodernism and apply them to the area of multicultural education. The first of these concepts is "discourse."

DISCOURSE

Drawing on the work of Foucault (1978), the concept of discourse can be used to discuss multicultural education. Discourse provides the basis for understanding what people say, think, and do, but also, as Ball (1990) argues, who can speak, when, and with what authority. This concept helps us to understand and interrogate the relationship between power and knowledge. Knowledge and power are inseparable to the extent that forms of power are situated, constituted, and distributed within knowledge. For multicultural education this is significant because it provides the opportunity to further examine which discourses deny access to institutional structures that the dominant groups take for granted.

These discourses may well be imbedded within both overt and hidden curricula, the structure of language required in schools, or the commonsense knowledge that people use in their everyday interactions inside and outside of schools. In all contexts "any discourse concerns itself with certain objects and puts forward certain concepts at the expense of others" (Macdonell, 1986, p. 3). Having recognized that discourses provide for certain possibilities of thought, the project of multicultural education then becomes one of identifying which discourses are constituted as legitimate and which are excluded. In practice, Foucault argues that we must make allowances for the discourses that can be instruments and effects of power, but also hindrances, stumbling blocks, points of resistances and starting points for opposing strategies (Foucault, 1978). The oppositional strategy for multicultural education means giving both teachers and students a legitimate voice to contest and critique educational policy and practice. It requires that teachers and students develop the confidence and competence to speak what has previously been unspoken, to identify sources of individual and collective oppression, and to work to eliminate them. In policy and practice the focus of multicultural education would be on developing a discourse that illuminates a greater understanding of the self and the multiple ascribed characteristics (ethnicity, gender, socioeconomic status) that are used to define oneself, both by others and by oneself, understanding how institutions work, their histories of exploitation and repression. It further means, as Shapiro (1991, p. 114) argues, "the classroom becomes the site not merely of an individual's apprehension of his or her own experience, but a place where there is a collective reinterpretation of our lived world. There is, in other words, the making of a communal culture that opposes that which is hegemonic." The use of the postmodern lens would help to validate the urgency and need that proponents of multicultural education have to point out how language structures who people are (e.g., at-risk, disadvantaged, dominated group, culturally deprived). Also, the postmodern lens would support the need and be of assistance in the search by proponents of multicultural education for a language that critiques, facilitates the discussion of and between the diverse groups in the country, articulates a vocabulary of empowerment, and makes clearer discussion of educational programs and practices. For example, teachers because of personal and organizational constraints often find it expedient to adopt the language (e.g., latchkey kid, single-parent home, Head Start, bussed-in students, color-blind teaching) and the implicit meanings that it carries, that is given to them by social scientists and administrators, with very little means and structure for critique. Without this language of critique, teachers become less able to participate in the deconstruction of these socially constructed "meanings" and thereby become marginalized and deskilled in the education of their students. Other issues relating to cleavages in the distribution of power that dominant groups take for granted and that some oppressed people may not consider to serve as a barrier to oneself would also constitute areas of study.

With an understanding of discourse, students of color and other marginalized groups will not only learn about their own histories, they also will be provided with the opportunity to examine how discourses emerge to suit the interests of particular groups and deny other groups. Welch (1985 [quoted in Shapiro, 1991, p. 121]) declares: "It is oppressive to free people if their own history and culture do not serve as the primary source of the definitions of their freedom." Discourses and meanings arise out of struggle "in which what is at stake is ultimately quite a lot more than either words or discourses" (Macdonell, 1986, p. 51). At stake are not only the life chances and lives of nondominant groups, but also the rights and privileges that accompany equal and equitable participation. Additionally, some discourses may be seen not only to deny, or provide access, or say who can or cannot speak, or say when or where one may speak, and with what authority, but rather they may be seen as "neutral." This idea of neutral discourses must also be examined. For many unassuming teachers, especially preservice teachers, discourse as it is presented in textbooks and other curricular material is thought to be neutral and the teachers' teaching position is also thought to be neutral. For example, two questions asked by one of the authors to the students in an Introduction to Education class—"Is K-12 education neutral?" and "To what extent do you believe that your K-12 teachers took a neutral position while teaching?"—present interesting results and give emphasis to our discussion. For more than fifteen years, most preservice teachers in that class (twenty students out an average class size of twenty-six) have reported that K-12 education is neutral, and that for the most part their K-12 teachers took a neutral position while teaching. Most of these students had not developed their own awareness of the persuasiveness of schooling, nor were they familiar with the thesis of Bourdieu and Passeron (1979 [1964]), who argued that schools are not socially neutral institutions but reflect the experience of the dominant class. A postmodern lens would enrich this discussion by raising questions about neutral as even a position that a teacher could take. In other words, when a teacher takes a neutral position or offers a neutral discourse, he or she is merely presenting a perspective. And all discourses (including a so-called neutral one) are merely perspectives (Poster, 1984, in Shapiro, 1991, p. 117).

Finally, a postmodern lens will help proponents of multicultural education to better understand how educational words are changed, manipulated, and deployed and come to be what Popkewitz (1991) describes as the language of regulation as a "means of control." Popkewitz (p. 199) points out how language use in educational reform standards can seem to represent and convey socially accepted interests, which upon a closer critique are misleading. He explains that the language of reform standards is cast as the rhetoric of schooling, which addresses learning competencies, and measurement:

The universal language [of schooling] homogenizes social distinctions and conflicts by casting them as procedural categories. Policy is articulated through an instrumental language that makes the problems seem administrative in focus and universal in application. The rationality of reform pays no attention to new goals but takes for granted the goals of the existing institutional relations. Human ends are no longer conceived as ends in themselves or as subjects of philosophic discourse . . . This provides significance to what is specified, but at the same time, creates silence about the social arrangements implicit in the organization of schooling. The assumption is that there is a common school for all and equity is only a matter of equalizing the effectiveness of "delivery systems."

Multicultural education supported by a postmodern perspective would increase the number of critics, sharpen the critique, and better inform teachers that the discourse of multicultural education that they choose to espouse in their classrooms will bring with it a particular ideology regarding classroom policy and practice, power and knowledge, and view of the world.

The dominant discourses of schooling incorporate values, priorities, experiences, and ideas that play out and make natural inequalities of outcome and opportunity. For example, "at-risk" has become a part of the education vocabulary in practically every part of the school culture (e.g., policy, practice, informal conversation). Administrators, teachers, parents, community members, and even students use "at-risk" as a synonym to refer to students in Chapter I programs, students who live at or below the poverty level, students of color, especially Hispanic and African Americans. Recently, a school where one of the authors regularly visits requested volunteers to work with middle school at-risk students, who were below grade level in reading achievement. A potential female volunteer was asked during the screening interview to become a tutor: "What credentials, skills or knowledge do you have that qualify you to work with underachievers in reading?" The potential volunteer responded, without being informed who the students were, "Black children live next door to me and we get along very well."

Knowledge and discourses become the sites for struggle between dominant and subordinate groups. In theoretical terms this is a significant point, for as Ball (1990, p. 18) reminds us: "Meanings thus are not from language but from institutional practices, from power relations, from social position. Words and concepts change their meaning and their effects as they are deployed within different discourses." As illustrated earlier, we noted that "multicultural education" lacks conceptual clarity. This has enabled critics and dissenters of multicultural education (who have social and political positions of power to use their influence to gain access to the popular and professional media and to selectively choose the definition of multicultural education they want to criticize and to structure the nature of the discourse regarding its meaning) to have political and social value and importance. For example, Diane Ravitch (1990, p. A44), at present the assistant to the secretary of Education, recently wrote: "The real issue on campus and in the classroom is not whether there will be multiculturalism, but what kind of multiculturalism will there be." Ravich is against "particularism"—that is, multicultural education that is defined as Afrocentric or Hispanocentric. Similarly, Arthur Schlesinger, Jr. (1991, p. 2) in *The Disuniting of American: Reflections on a Multicultural Society* posits:

Instead of a transformative nation with an identity all its own, America increasingly sees itself as preservative of old identities. Instead of a nation composed of individuals making their own free choices, America increasingly sees itself as composed of groups more or less indelible in their ethnic character. The national ideal had once been *e pluribus unum*. Are we now to belittle *unum* and glorify *pluribus*? Will the center hold? or will the melting pot yield to the Tower of Babel?

The project then of multicultural education is to ensure that all students have a knowledge of the apparatus, formal and informal, structures and discourses that oppress them. Accordingly, they need to have access to knowledge of more than one discourse and the recognition that meaning is plural allows for a measure of choice on the part of the individual and even where choice is not available, resistance is possible (Weedon 1987, p. 106). Furthermore, it requires a rethinking and re-examination of the form and content of curriculum. Questions such as whose knowledge is taught, whose cultures and languages and so on become a legitimate part of educational praxis. This means that students' "habitus" (Bourdieu, 1977) as well as their experience outside of schools is seen as a legitimate form of knowledge and as such has a place within the formal school curriculum. With regard to "habitus" an analysis and examination can be made of those who occupy similar positions in social and historical space, and who tend to possess a certain sense of place, including categories of perception that provide a common sense understanding of the world, especially, what is natural or even imaginable. (Bottomley, 1992, p. 211)

Discourse, knowledge, and power are complementary concepts that enable us to understand and interpret the complexities and dynamics of contemporary life. A further dimension needs to be added to our understanding of the symbolic aspects of everyday life—the dimension of culture. This concept is important for the purposes of this chapter for as Pettman (1992, p. 126) argues, "Culture isn't just a disguise or a mobilizing or containing strategy. Cultural expectations do inform our ways of being, knowing and understanding." As previously suggested, access to dominant cultural capital is crucial to getting on in either America or Australia.

CULTURE

"Culture," a powerful analytic concept in the social sciences, is often one of the most neglected concepts in multicultural education (Sachs, 1986). For the purposes of our argument here, "culture is highly political in its representation and reinforcement of structures of power" (Pettman, 1992, p. 119). Nevertheless, despite this important political point, much educational literature has downplayed the concept to incorporate normative characteristics of behavior, group and individual lifestyles, or essentialized and reified it as "the total way of life of any group." It reflects as well our vested disciplinary interests in characterizing "exotic otherness" (Keesing, 1990). It is worth quoting Keesing at length regarding the consequences of this:

In pervading popular thought, anthropology's concept of culture has been applied to complex, contemporary ways of life—"Greek culture," "Chinese culture"—as well as exotic "primitive" ones in the TV documentaries. Ironically, with our all-inclusive conception of "culture," as it has passed into popular discourse have gone our habits of talk that reify, personify and essentialize. (p. 48)

The essentializing (e.g., the primacy of the Western canon) and popularizing of culture fails to apprehend that culture varies in status from society to society and group to group, and that there are variations in its invocation and its very meaning. The work of Bourdieu and Passeron (1979 [1964]) addressed the point of culture status and variation. They analyzed the impact of culture on the class system and on the relationship between action and social structure. Specifically, and important to our position on multicultural education, we point out that students from the dominant class and possessing high culture begin school with key social and cultural cues, which students from working-class backgrounds do not have and must learn in order to have a successful school experience. E. T. Hall (1976, pp. 1-2) speaks of the variations of culture across societies when he claims that

culture has always been an issue, not only between Europe and Russia, but among the European states as well. The Germans, the French, the Italians, the Spanish, Portuguese, and English, as well as the Scandinavian and Balkan cultures, all have their own identity, language, system of nonverbal communication, material culture, history, and ways of doing things.

The essentializing and popularizing of culture fails to acknowledge that the social distribution of culture is skewed, and that its meaning favors the interests of the dominant groups. Bourdieu and Passeron (1979 [1964]) and other social scientists refer to this as the dominant group having "cultural capital." They conclude that students from the dominant class enter schools with key cultural and social cues and experiences that correspond to the way school practices are conducted, while working-class and minority students have to learn these cues and have middle-class experiences in order to have school success.[1] Legitimacy is given to particular notions of participation, progress, and social identity in a way that transforms cultural struggles to coincide with rules of existing institutional arrangements (Popkewitz, 1988, p. 82).

By using a depoliticized or apolitical concept of culture, the experiences of people of color are effectively silenced insofar as they do not fit in what counts as true, real, and important. What counts as important, and thus worthy of study, is the culture and knowledge of hegemonic groups.

Moving beyond essentialist notions of culture means that we must examine how knowledge and ideas are produced and distributed within groups. For multicultural education this is particularly significant, for as numerous studies on the hidden curriculum have pointed out, knowledge is differentially distributed among different cultural and ethnic groups. S. Hall (1988, p. 44) makes the important point that "The circle of dominant ideas does accumulate the symbolic power to map or classify the world for others; its classifications do acquire not only the constraining power dominance over other modes of thought. . . . It becomes the horizon of the taken-for-granted: what the world is and how it works."

Postmodernism has helped to raise new questions about the terrain of culture as a field of domination and contestation. The historical situatedness, production, and hegemonic force of cultural meanings, in terms of internal structures and cleavages in society, are the focus of study (Keesing, 1990). However, as Giroux (1988) correctly points out, the postmodern problematic of culture and Otherness is not without its ambiguities and problems. There is the danger of affirming difference, simply as an end in itself without acknowledging how difference is formed, erased, and resuscitated within and despite asymmetrical relations in power. Lost here is any understanding of how difference is forged in both domination and opposition (Giroux, 1988, p. 18).

WAYS FORWARD FOR TEACHERS

The challenge for multicultural education then is to identify the symbolic aspects of everyday life as well as the various cultures that constitute contemporary social relations. Giroux (1988, p. 13) gives us some idea of what this means: "We need to understand how the field of the everyday is being reconstituted not simply as a commodity sphere but as a site of contestation that offers new possibilities for engaging the memories, histories and stories of those who offer not simply otherness but an oppositional resistance to various forms of domination." To achieve this, first, we need to provide students with the knowledge and skills to enable them to give a definitive account of how 'culture' is acquired, transmitted and distributed, as well as its meaning and the part it plays in the formation of commonsense knowledge and assumptions that are so important for the maintenance of hegemonic forms of power in our society. Furthermore, students must realize that the acquisition or non-acquisition of certain cultural beliefs, values and experiences can lead to their exclusion or inclusion from certain jobs, resources and high status groups (Lamont and Lareau, 1988).

An important benefit that postmodernism provides for multicultural education is to be found by analyzing the discourses of education and schooling. Such an approach provides students with opportunities to "ask questions about what we have not thought to think, about what is most densely invested in our discourses/practices, about what has been muted, repressed, unheard in our liberatory efforts" (Lather 1991, p. 156). There has been a tendency for teachers to teach about culture in practical and essentialist ways (Sachs, 1989). Much of the literature and day-to-day discussion on multicultural education informs preservice and inservice education of teachers as well as their students that culture should be represented through the three "f's": foods, fairs, festivals; while culture in single-sex schools and in schools for people of color is mainly defined by the celebration of special days or weeks, recognition of certain ethnic heroes and heroines, eliminating biases, and developing acceptance of human difference. In many classrooms culture is presented as something possessed by individuals, learned and ideological insofar as ideologies define the world in terms of idealized subject positions. Culture thus presented is marginalized and the possibility of emancipatory teaching for students from a variety of ethnic and cultural backgrounds is reduced.

Second, Keesing (1990) makes a useful suggestion about how we might proceed by advocating a critical conception of culture. Such a conception would take the production and reproduction of cultural forms as problematic: that is, it would examine the way symbolic production is linked to power and interest (in terms of class, hierarchy, gender, etc.) . . . a critical conception of the cultural would begin with the assumption that in any "community" or "society" there will be multiple, subdominant and partially submerged cultural traditions (again, in relation to power, rank, class, gender, age, etc.), as well as the dominant tradition. (p. 57)

Using this perspective the type of multicultural education we have presented would not only be concerned with the identification of the multiple sources of cultural knowledge and how these are used by various groups, but also how such knowledge is distributed within various communities and institutions. Having done this it is possible for both teachers and students to examine the nature and effects of hegemony, especially as it relates to the educational experience of various cultural groups, whether these be based on race, gender, religion, sexuality, or whatever.

By focusing on the everyday and how this is experienced by various sectorial interests, the multicultural education we envisage, informed by postmodern perspectives on concepts such as discourse and culture, provides powerful ways for students to rethink their own personal and group experiences and strategies for dealing with these. One outcome may well be that ideas such as equity and social justice become the stuff of education, not just abstract peripheral rhetoric favored by bureaucrats and politicians. In such a situation multicultural education may well be a postmodern solution!

CONCLUSION

The title of this chapter suggests that proponents of multicultural education and proponents of postmodernism should enter a discussion, because many of their interests are similar, and they could possibly be of help to one another. For us, preparing for this chapter has shed a new light on old problems. We did not find agreement with all that we read on postmodernism, but we did discover points of agreement and, perhaps more importantly, we found points that beg for a collective discussion. We have tried to offer encouragement for that discussion to take place. By pointing out how the lens of postmodernism could assist multicultural education, we believe if proponents of postmodernism would review the literature on multicultural education they may reach a similar conclusion.

We have noted that an increasing number of proponents of multicultural education are dealing with both theories and practices that promote or sustain race, class, gender, and disability oppression. We further noted that an increasing number of proponents of multicultural education advocate the importance of teaching students how to take charge of their life circumstances. Implicit in the multicultural literature is praising diversity and advocating the affirmation of all groups of color, women (white and of color), people who have disabilities, and people who are poor or live on the margin of the economy. It is from our knowledge and respect for this multicultural population, the problems, issues, and challenges they face, and contributions they make, that we believe proponents of multicultural education can contribute to this discussion. Cornel West (1987) in an article, "Postmodernism and Black America," offers some important words that we can relate to this discussion. He says that

distinctive issues of the postmodern debate surface: the relation of high and popular culture, the effectiveness of opposition in politics and culture, the possibilities of a post-European world. These issues involve the culture and political agency of peoples of color owing to the centrality of race in the U.S. and the decolonization process in the Third World. . . . It is not just racial parochialism that circumscribes postmodernism debate, but the larger political and cultural contexts which permit the parochialism to flourish . . . (p. 27)

Perhaps, even more poignantly, bell hooks' (1990) reflections on postmodernism further address the reason why multiculturalists and postmodernists should begin a dialogue.[2] We quote her at length:

Radical postmodernist practice, most powerfully conceptualized as a "politics of differences," should incorporate the voices of displaced, marginalized, exploited and oppressed black people. It is sadly ironic that the contemporary discourse which talks the most about heterogeneity, the decentered subjects, declaring breakthroughs that allow recognition of Otherness, still directs its critical voice primarily to a specialized audience that shares a common language rooted in the very master narratives it claims to challenge. If radical postmodernist thinking is to have a transformative impact, then a critical break with the notion of "authority" as "mastery over" must not simply be a rhetorical device. It must be reflective in habits of being, including styles of writing as well as chosen subject matter. (p. 25)

We have taken Shapiro's (1991, p. 112) comment seriously: "It is surprising that those concerned with education, with some few exceptions, have failed to join the debate on the meaning and implications of a postmodern culture, philosophy and politics." Similarly, we suggest Sleeter's (1989, p. 69) advice be taken seriously: "Multicultural education in the United States has many insights and theorists needed to strengthen and lead radical challenges to racism through education. Rather than ignoring or dismissing the field, educators on the left should be working with it." Proponents of multicultural education, we believe, would contribute much to the discussion of postmodernism.

NOTES

The authors are very appreciative of the suggestions and encouragement received from several colleagues, especially Ann D. De Vaney, Gloria Ladson-Billings, Thomas S. Popkewitz, and William F. Tate.

1. Although we find Bourdieu's work useful, we disagree with his belief that people of color do not have a "culture" that has value in the marketplace.

2. bell hooks and Cornel West's illuminating comments are posited directly toward African Americans. We believe for the most part that their comments are applicable to other peoples of color, low-income people, and women, and we have used them within that context.

REFERENCES

Ball, S. (1990). *Politics and Policy Making in Education.* London: Routledge.

Banks, J. (1977). "The Implication of Multicultural Education for Teacher Education." In F. H. Klassen and D. M. Gollnick (eds.), *Pluralism and the American Teacher* (pp. 1–34). Washington, DC: AACTE.

———. (1991). "A Curriculum for Empowerment, Action, and Change." In C. E. Sleeter (ed.), *Empowerment Through Multicultural Education* (pp. 125–142). Albany: State University of New York Press.

Bottomley, G. (1992). "Culture, Ethnicity and the Politics/Poetics of Representation." *Australian and New Zealand Journal of Sociology,* 28(2).

Bourdieu, P. (1977). *Outline of a Theory of Practice.* Cambridge: Cambridge University Press.

Bourdieu, P. and Passeron, J. C. (1979[1964]). *The Inheritors: French Students and Their Relation to Culture.* Chicago: University of Chicago Press.

Bove, P. (1986). "The Ineluctability of Difference: Scientific Pluralism and the Critical Intelligence." In J. Arac (ed.), *Postmodernism and Politics.* Minneapolis: University of Minnesota Press.

Connor, S. (1989). *Postmodernist Culture: An Introduction to Theories of the Contemporary.* Oxford: Basil Blackwell.

Featherstone, M. (1988). "In Pursuit of the Post Modern: An Introduction." *Theory, Culture and Society,* 5(2–3): 195–215.

Foucault, M. (1978). "Politics and the Study of Discourse." *Ideology and the Study of Discourse,* 3: 7–26.

Gay, G. (1979). "On Behalf of Children: A Curriculum Design for Multicultural Education in the Elementary School." *Journal of Negro Education,* 48 (3): 324–340.

———. (1983). "Multiethnic Education: Historical Developments and Future Prospects." *Phi Delta Kappan,* 64(8): 560–563.

———. (1988). "Designing Relevant Curricula for Diverse Learners." *Education and Urban Society,* 20 (4): 327–340.

Gibson, M. A. (1976). "Approaches to Multicultural Education in the United States: Some Concepts and Assumptions." *Anthropology and Education Quarterly,* 7: 7–18.

Giroux, H. (1988). "Postmodernism and the Discourse of Educational Criticism." *Journal of Education,* 170(3): 5–30.

Gollnick, D. and Chinn, P. (1983). *Multicultural Education in a Pluralistic Society.* St. Louis: C. V. Mosby.

Grant, C. (1977). "Education That Is Multicultural—Isn't That What We Mean?" *Journal of Teacher Education,* 29 (5): 45–48.

Grant, C. and Sleeter, C. (1985). "The Literature on Multicultural Education: Review and Analysis." *Educational Review,* 37(2): 97–118.

Grant, C., Sleeter, C., and Anderson, J. (1986). "The Literature on Multicultural Education: Review and Analysis II. *Educational Studies,* 12(1): 47–72.

Hall, E. T. (1976). *Beyond Culture.* New York: Doubleday.

Hall, S. (1988). "The Toad in the Garden: Thatcherism among the Theorists." In C. Nelson and L. Grossberg (eds.), *Marxism and the Interpretation of Culture.* Urbana: University of Illinois Press.

Hebdige, D. (1988). *Hiding in the Light: On Images and Things.* London: Comedia.

Hernandez, H. (1989). *Multicultural Education.* Columbus, OH: Merrill.

hooks, b. (1990). *Yearning: Race, Gender, and Cultural Politics.* Boston: South End Press.

Keesing, R. (1990). "Theories of Culture Revisited." *Canberra Anthropology,* 13(2): 46–60.

Kellner, D. (1988). "Postmodernism as Social Theory: Some Challenges and Problems." *Theory, Culture and Society,* 5(2–3): 239–269.

———. (1990). "Critical Theory and the Crisis of Social Theory." *Sociological Perspectives,* 33(1): 11–33.

Ladson-Billings, G. (1991). "Beyond Multicultural Illiteracy." *Journal of Negro Education,* 60(2): 147–157.

Lamont, M. and Lareau, A. (1988). "Cultural Capital: Allusions, Gaps and Glissandos in Recent Theoretical Development." *Sociological Theory,* 6(Fall): 153–168.

Lather, P. (1991). *Getting Smart: Feminist Research and Pedagogy with/in the Postmodern.* London: Routledge.

Lynch, J. (1986). "Multicultural Education in Western Europe." In James Banks and James Lynch (eds.), *Multicultural Education in Western Societies* (pp. 125–152). New York: Praeger.

Lyotard, J. F. (1984). *The Postmodern Condition: A Report on Knowledge,* trans. G. Bennington and B. Massumi. Manchester: Manchester University Press.

Macdonell, D. (1986). *Theories of Discourse,* Oxford: Blackwell.

Nieto S. (1992). *Affirming Diversity.* New York: Longman.

Pettman, J. (1992). *Living in the Margins: Racism, Sexism and Feminism in Australia.* Sydney: Allen and Unwin.

Popkewitz, T. (1988). "Culture, Pedagogy and Power: Issues in the Production of Values and Colonialization." *Boston University Journal of Education,* 170(2): 77–90.

———. (1991). *A Political Sociology of Educational Reform.* New York: Teachers College Press.

———. (1992). personal communication.

Pratte, R. (1983). "Multicultural Education: Four Normative Arguments." *Educational Theory,* 33: 21–32.

Ravitch, D. (1990). "Multiculturalism, Yes, Particularism, No." *The Chronicle of Higher Education,* October 24: A44.

Sachs, J. (1986). "Putting Culture Back into Multicultural Education." *New Community,* 13(2).

———. (1989). "Match or Mismatch: Multicultural Education Policy and Teachers' Conceptions of Culture." *Australian Journal of Education,* 33(1).

Schlesinger, A. Jr., (1991). *The Disuniting of America: Reflections on a Multicultural Society.* Knoxville, TN: Whittle Direct Books.

Shapiro, S. (1991). "The End of Radical Hope? Postmodernism and the Challenge to Critical Pedagogy." *Education and Society,* 9(2): 112–122.

Sleeter, C. E. (1989) "Multicultural Education as a Form of Resistance to Oppression." *Journal of Education,* 171(3): 51–71.

Sleeter C. and Grant, C. (1987). "An Analysis of Multicultural Education in the United States." *Harvard Educational Review,* 57(4): 421–444.

Sleeter, C. E. and Grant, C. A. (1988). *Making Choices for Multicultural Education.* New York: Merrill.

Spivak, G. (1990). *The Postcolonial Critic.* London: Routledge.

Weedon, C. (1987). *Feminist Practice and Post-Structuralist Theory.* Oxford: Basil Blackwell.

West, C. (1987). "Postmodernism and Black America," *Zeta Magazine,* 1(6): 27–29.

5

The Politics of Insurgent Multiculturalism in the Era of the Los Angeles Uprising

Henry A. Giroux

NAMING WHITE SUPREMACY

I want to begin by quoting two teachers, both of whom harbor strong feelings and passions about the issue of multiculturalism and race. The first quote is by the late James Baldwin, the renowned Afro-American writer. The second quote recently appeared in *The Chronicle of Higher Education* and is by Melvin E. Bradford, a former speechwriter for George Wallace and more recently an editorial writer working on behalf of Patrick Buchanan.

If . . . one managed to change the curriculum in all the schools so that [Afro-Americans] learned more about themselves and their real contributions to this culture, you would be liberating not only [Afro-Americans], you'd be liberating white people who know nothing about their own history. And the reason is that if you are compelled to lie about one aspect of anybody's history, you must lie about it all. If you have to lie about my real role here, if you have to pretend that I hoed all that cotton just because I loved you, then you have done something to yourself. You are mad.[1]

I am not a scientific racist. . . . But blacks as a group have been here a long time and, for some reason, making them full members of our society has proven almost impossible. They remain outside. The more privileges black Americans have had, the worse they seem to do. At the core of it is black private life—those things we can't legislate and can't control. . . . I have a deep suspicion that in matters that affect the course of their lives, blacks habitually shoot themselves in the foot.[2]

What these quotes suggest in the most benign sense is that issues concerning multiculturalism are fundamentally about questions of race and identity. A less sanguine analysis reveals what both of these quotes share, but only what Baldwin is willing to name: that multiculturalism is not only about the discourse of alleged others but is also fundamentally about the issue of whiteness as a mark of racial and gender privilege. For example, Baldwin argues that multiculturalism cannot be reduced to an exclusive otherness that references Afro-Americans, Hispanics, Latinos, or other suppressed minorities, as either a problem to be resolved through the call for benevolent assimilation or as a threat to be policed and eliminated. For Baldwin, multiculturalism is primarily about whiteness and its claims to a self-definition that excludes itself from the messy relations of race, ethnicity, power, and identity.

On the other hand, Bradford exemplifies a dominant approach to multiculturalism that serves as a coded legitimation for equating racial, cultural, and ethnic diversity with social chaos, the lowering of standards, and the emergence of an alleged new tribalism that threatens the boundaries of a common culture or national identity. What both of these positions highlight is how differences in power and privilege mediate who speaks, under what conditions, and for whom. In this sense, multiculturalism raises the question of whether people are speaking within or outside a privileged space, and whether such spaces provide the conditions for different groups to listen to each other differently in order to address how the racial economies of privilege and power work in this society.

I want to argue that in the aftermath of the spring 1992 Los Angeles uprising (which occurred after the LA police brutally beat Rodney King during a routine arrest), educators need to rethink the politics of multiculturalism as part of a broader attempt to understand how issues regarding national identity, culture, and ethnicity can be rewritten in order to enable dominant groups to examine, acknowledge, and unlearn their own privilege. In part this demands an approach to multiculturalism that not only addresses "the context of massive black unemployment, overcrowded schools, a lack of recreational facilities, dilapidated housing and racist policing,"[3] but a concerted attempt "to view most racism in this country not as an issue of black lawlessness but primarily as an expression of white 'supremacy.' "[4] More specifically, a critical multiculturalism must shift attention away from an exclusive focus on subordinate groups, especially since such an approach tends to highlight their deficits, to one that examines how racism in its various forms is produced historically, semiotically, and institutionally at various levels of society. This is not meant to suggest that blacks and other subordinate groups do not face problems that need to be addressed. On the contrary, it means that a critical analysis of race must move beyond the discourse of pathology in which whites "confine discussions about race in America to the 'problems' black pose for whites."[5] As Cornel West points out, viewing black people in this manner reveals not only white supremacy as the discursive and institutional face of racism, but it also presents us with the challenge of addressing racial issues not as a dilemma of black people but as a problem endemic to the legacy of internal colonialism rooted in "historical inequalities and longstanding cultural stereotypes."[6]

In opposition to a quaint liberalism, a critical multiculturalism means more than simply acknowledging differences and analyzing stereotypes; more fundamentally, it means understanding, engaging, and transforming the diverse histories, cultural narratives, representations, and institutions that produce racism and other forms of discrimination. As bell hooks points out, for too long white people have imagined that they are invisible to black people. Not only does whiteness in this formulation cease to mark the locations of its own privileges, it reinforces relations in which blacks become invisible in terms of how they name, see, experience, and bear the pain and terror of whiteness. hooks puts it succinctly:

In white supremacist society, white people can "safely" imagine that they are invisible to black people since the power they have historically asserted, and even now collectively assert over black people, accorded them the right to control the black gaze. . . . [And yet] to name that whiteness in the black imagination is often a representation of terror. One must face written histories that erase and deny, that reinvent the past to make the present vision of racial harmony and pluralism more plausible. To bear the burden of memory one must willingly journey to places long uninhabited, searching the debris of history for traces of the unforgettable, all knowledge of which has been suppressed.[7]

It is worth noting that in the aftermath of the recent Los Angeles uprising, many educational commentators have ruled out any discussion about the relationship between race and class and how they are manifested within networks of hierarchy and subordination both in and out of the schools. This particular silence, when coupled with the popular perception that the L.A. uprising can be explained by pointing to those involved as simply thugs, looters, and criminals, makes it clear why the multicultural peril is often seen as a black threat; it also suggests what such a belief shares with the traditionalists' view of the Other as a disruptive outsider. In this scenario, multiculturalism becomes the source of the problem.

In what follows, I want to address the necessity of creating an insurgent multiculturalism as a basis for a new language of educational leadership, one that allows students and others to move between cultures, to travel within zones of cultural difference. At stake here is the need to develop a language that challenges the boundaries of cultural and racial difference as sites of exclusion and discrimination while simultaneously rewriting the script of cultural difference as part of a broader attempt to provide new spaces for expanding and deepening the imperatives of a multicultural and multiracial democracy. In short, I want to address what it means to treat schools and other public sites as border institutions in which teachers, students, and others learn to think and imagine otherwise in order to act otherwise.[8] For it is within such institutions, engaged in daily acts of cultural translation and negotiation, that students and teachers are offered the opportunity to become border crossers, to recognize that schooling is really an introduction to how culture is organized, a demonstration of who is authorized to speak about particular forms of culture, what culture is considered worthy of valorization, and what forms of culture are considered invalid and unworthy of public esteem. Drawing in part upon Homi Bhabha, I want to argue that schools, in part, need to be understood as sites engaged in the "strategic activity of 'authority,' agency," of exercising authority in order "to articulate and regulate incommensurable meanings and identities."[9] Within this perspective, leadership is removed from its exclusive emphasis on management, and it is defined as a form of political and ethical address that weighs cultural differences against the implications they have for practices that disclose rather than mystify, democratize culture rather than shut it down, and provide the conditions for all people to believe that they can take risks and change existing power relations.

WHITE PANIC AND ETHNIC RACE

After the fires went out in Los Angeles, the Bush administration once again reneged on its responsibility to address the problems and demands of democratic public life. In the face of escalating poverty, increasing racism, growing unemployment among minorities, and the failure of an expanding number of Americans to receive adequate health care or education, the Bush administration invoked a wooden morality coupled with a disdain for public life by blaming the nation's ills on the legislation of the Great Society, TV sitcom characters such as Murphy Brown, or the alleged breakdown of family values. Within this scenario, poverty is caused by the poverty of values, racism is seen as a "black" problem (lawlessness), and social decay can be rectified by shoring up the family and the logic and social relations of the alleged free market.

The Bush administration's response to the Los Angeles uprising exemplifies the failure of leadership that was characteristic of the Reagan/Bush eras. Abandoning its responsibility for political and moral leadership, the federal government has reduced its intervention in public life to waging war against Iraq, using taxpayers' money to bail out corrupt bankers, and slashing legislation that would benefit the poor, the homeless, and the disadvantaged. There is a tragic irony at work when a government can raise $500 billion to bail out corrupt bankers and $50 billion to fight a war in Iraq (put in perspective, the combined costs of these adventures exceed the cost of World War II including veterans benefits), while at the same time the same government cuts back food stamp and school lunch programs in a country in which nearly one out of every four children under six live in poverty. But there is more at stake here than simply the failure of moral and political leadership. The breadth and depth of democratic relations are being rolled back at all levels of national and daily life. For example, this is seen in the growing disparity between the rich and poor, the ongoing attacks by the government and courts on civil rights and the welfare system, and the proliferating incidents of racist harassment and violence on college and public school sites.

The retreat from democracy is also evident in the absence of serious talk about how as a nation we might educate existing and future generations of students in the language and practice of moral compassion, critical agency, and public service. The discourse of leadership appears trapped in a terminology in which the estimate of a good society is expressed in indexes that, measure profit margins and the Dow Jones average. Missing in this vocabulary is a way of nourishing and sustaining a popular perception of democracy as something that needs to be constantly struggled for in public arenas such as the schools, churches, and other sites that embody the promise of a multiracial and multicultural democracy.

This current assault on democratic public life has taken a new turn in the last few years. At one level, American conservatives have initiated a long-term project of discrediting and dismantling those institutions, ideologies, and practices that are judged incompatible with the basic ideology of the marketplace. In this instance, a diverse alliance of conservatives and neoliberals has launched a full-fledged and unswervering commitment to the principles of individualism, choice, and the competitive ethic. Accompanying this attempt has been a parallel effort to reprivatize and deregulate schools, health care, the welfare system, and other public services and institutions. The extent to which conservatives have gone to promote this project, one that Stuart Hall has rightly called "regressive modernization,"[10] can be seen in former President Bush's suggestion that Los Angeles sell its international airport to private investors in order to use some of the revenue to rebuild South Central L.A.[11] It is quite remarkable that as the fires were burning in this long-suffering city, the nation's highest elected public official refused to address the smoldering social, economic, and cultural conditions that fueled the uprising. In this discourse, the imperatives of privatization and the profit margin become more important than issues of human suffering and social justice. Of course, this should not be surprising given the radical assaults on all aspects of the public sphere that have been waged during the last decade.

Part of the attempt to rewrite the terms of discourse regarding the meaning and value of public life can be seen in the emergence of a new breed of intellectuals, largely backed by conservative think tanks such as the Madison Group, the Hoover Institute, the Heritage Foundation, and a host of other conservative foundations.[12] With access to enormous cultural resources infused by massive financial backing from the Olin, Scaife, and Smith Richardson foundations, right-wing think tanks have begun to mount mammoth public campaigns to promote their cultural revolution. Many of the major right-wing intellectuals who have helped to shape popular discourse about educational reform in the last decade have received extensive aid from the conservative foundations. These include intellectuals such as Diane Ravitch, Chester Finn, Dinish D'Souza, William Bennett, and Allan Bloom, all of whom have targeted public schools and higher education as two principal spheres of struggle over issues of content, privatization, choice, and difference.[13] In order to understand the model of leadership that these intellectuals provide, it is important to examine how some of their underlying ideological concerns relate to the broader issues of democracy, race, and public accountability.[14]

THE CONSERVATIVE ASSAULT ON DEMOCRACY

For many conservatives, the utopian possibility of cultural democracy has become dangerous at the current historical conjuncture for a number of reasons. First, it encourages a language of critique for understanding and transforming those relations that trap people in networks of hierarchy and exploitation. That is, it provides a normative referent for recognizing and assessing competing political vocabularies, the visions of the future they presuppose, and the social identities and practices they both produce and legitimate. By subordinating the language of management and efficiency to moral and ethical considerations, a critical discourse of democracy keeps alive the importance of democratic values and how they can be institutionalized into practices that animate rather than restrict the discourse of justice, equality, and community. Clearly such a position poses a challenge to right-wing educators whose celebration of choice and the logic of the marketplace abstract freedom from equality and the imperatives of citizenship from its historical grounding in the public institutions of modern society.

In fact, many conservatives such as Lynn Cheney, William Bennett, Herbert Whittle, and Diane Ravitch have been quite aggressive in rewriting the discourse of citizenship *not* as the practice of social responsibility but as a privatized act of altruism, self-help, or philanthropy. It is crucial to recognize that within this language of privatization, the disquieting, disrupting, interrupting difficulties of sexism, crime, youth unemployment, AIDS, and other social problems, and how they bear down on schools, are either ignored or summarily dismissed as individual problems caused, in part, by the people who are victimized by them. Of course, not only does this position ignore the necessity for social criticism in a democratic society, it also erases the moral and political obligation of institutions to both recognize their complicity in creating such problems and in eradicating them. In this scenario, we end up with a vision of leadership in which individuals act in comparative isolation and without any sense of public accountability. This is why many right-wing educators praise the virtues of the competition and choice but rarely talk about how money and power, when unevenly distributed, influence "whether people have the means or the capacity" to make or act on choices that inform their daily lives.[15]

Jonathan Kozol is instructive here in recounting the story of how President Bush told a group of parents in a desperately poor school district in New Jersey that " 'A society that worships money is a society in Peril.' [Kozol responds by asking] Why didn't he say that to the folks in Bloomfield Hills, Michigan or in Great Neck, Long Island? What is the message?"[16] The message, of course, is that power, wealth, and privilege have no bearing on the choices that different groups make, especially if those groups are rich and powerful. Choice in this case serves to rewrite the discourse of freedom within a limited conception of individual needs and desires. What disappears from this view of leadership is the willingness to recognize that the fundamental issues of citizenship, democracy, and public life can neither be understood nor addressed solely within the restricted language of the marketplace or choice. Choice and the market are not the sole conditions of freedom, nor are they adequate to constituting political subjects within the broader discourses of justice, equality, and community. In fact, no understanding of community, citizenship, or public culture is possible without a shared conception of social justice, and yet it is precisely the notion of social justice that is missing in mainstream school reforms. Robert Bellah and his associates have also argued that Americans need a new vocabulary for talking about the problem and future of schooling. They write: "Money and power are necessary as means, but they are not the proper measures of a good society and a good world. We need to talk about our problems and our future with a richer vocabulary than the indices that measure markets and defense systems alone."[17]

It is worth noting that we live at a time when

a Black person in the U.S. is 7.4 times more likely to be imprisoned than a white person, when there are more Black men aged 20–29 who are under control of the criminal justice system than there are black men in college, and one out of every four Black men will go to prison at some point in his life. . . . Furthermore, it costs about $20,000 a year to send a person to prison, about what it would cost to send that person to Harvard."[18]

Additionally, 45 percent of all minority children live in poverty while the dropout rate among minority students has attained truly alarming proportions, reaching as high as 70 percent in some major urban areas. These problems are compounded by an unemployment rate among black youth that is currently 38.4 percent. In the face of these problems, conservatives are aggressively attempting to enact choice legislation that would divert funds away from the public schools to private schools. Against these efforts, it is worth noting, as Peter Dreier, points out, that

since 1980 the federal government has slashed successful urban programs—public works, economic development, health and nutrition, schools, housing, and job training—by more than 70 per cent. . . . In 1980, Federal dollars accounted for 14.3 per cent of city budgets; today, the Federal share is less then 5 per cent. . . . To avert fiscal collapse, many cities have been closing schools, hospitals, police and fire stations; laying off essential employees; reducing such basic services as maintenance of parks and roads; neglecting housing and health codes, and postponing or canceling capital improvements.[19]

Claiming that these problems can be solved by raising test scores, promoting choice, developing a national curriculum, and creating a uniform standard of national literacy is both cruel and mean-spirited. But, of course, this is where the discourse of critical democracy becomes subversive; it makes visible the political and normative considerations that frame such reforms. It also analyzes how the language of excessive individualism and competitiveness serves to make social inequality invisible, and promotes an indifference to human misery, exploitation, and suffering. Moreover, it suggests that the language of excellence and individualism, when abstracted from considerations of equality and social justice, serves to restrict rather than animate the possibilities of democratic public life.

It is becoming increasingly clear that democracy has become a subversive category to those who would subordinate public institutions to the laws of the marketplace and treat cultural difference as the enemy of Western civilization. In part this is exemplified in a recent article in *Education Week* in which Chester Finn attempts to provide a rationale for the privatization of schools and other public institutions by arguing that the concept of the public no longer merits either the attention or the support of the American people. Couched in the bad versus good rhetoric of simplistic binarisms, Finn dismisses public education by arguing that all institutions that attempt to serve the public as a matter of service rather than profit are doomed to fail (i.e., public transportation, public bathrooms, public health, etc.). Like his conservative colleague Allan Bloom, Finn argues that he would rather have " 'you' send your kid to Princeton."[20] Of course, the ubiquitous "you" in this sentence speaks for everyone while failing to mark its own location of privilege. What kind of politics and notion of choice inform the assumption that all parents occupy an equal ground in being able to send their kids to an Ivy League school? More is revealed here than an offensive elitism (not to mention racism). Lacking any sense of specificity, refusing to address how money and power provide the very conditions for exercising choice, Finn uses choice as a code word to suggest that those who are suffering the most in this society simply lack either the intelligence, character, individual initiative, or competitive spirit to pick themselves up and make a successful go of their lives. These are strange words coming from intellectuals who receive massive financial funding from some of the most aggressive, ideologically conservative foundations in the United States.

The second reason that democracy is so threatening to many conservatives is that it provides a rationale for constructing public spheres in which different groups can reclaim their identities and histories as part of an attempt to exercise power and control over their lives, while simultaneously attempting to take part in the political system as true participants rather than as mere consumers.[21] In this context, democracy foretells how cultural difference can be addressed in relation to wider questions of politics, power, membership, participation, and social responsibility.

Most importantly, numerous groups that have been profoundly underrepresented in the social and cultural narratives of the dominant culture have begun to redefine the relationship between culture and politics in order to deepen and extend the basis for a radical democratic society. In this sense, the promise of a critical democracy has mobilized subordinate groups to question how cultural identity and representation are being defined within existing social, cultural, and political institutions. Central to such concerns are questions regarding how the schools and other institutions are actually responding to the changing conditions of a society that will no longer have a white majority by the year 2010.

It is difficult to imagine what is either unpatriotic or threatening about subordinate groups attempting to raise questions such as: "Whose experiences, histories, knowledge, and arts are represented in our educational and cultural institutions? How fully, on whose terms, and with what degree of ongoing, institutionalized participation and power?"[22] Nor in a democratic society should subordinate groups attempting to fashion a pedagogy and politics of inclusion and cultural democracy be derisively labeled as particularistic because they have raised serious questions regarding either how the public school curriculum works to secure particular forms of cultural authority, or how the dynamics of cultural power work to silence and marginalize specific groups of students. This emerging critique of schools and other cultural institutions is based on the assumption that cultural differences are not the enemy of democracy, as E. D. Hirsch and others have argued, but intolerance, structured inequality, and social injustice.[23]

Rather than engage the growing insistence on the part of more and more groups in this country to define themselves around the specificity of class, gender, race, ethnicity, or sexual orientation, conservatives have committed themselves to simply resisting these developments. While conservatives rightly recognize that the struggle over the form and context of public school curriculum is fueled, in part, over anxiety about the issue of national identity, they engage this issue from a largely defensive posture and in doing so lack any understanding of how the curriculum itself is implicated in producing relations of inequality, domination, and oppression. When critical multiculturalists criticize how the curriculum through a process of exclusion and inclusion privileges some groups over others, such critics are summarily dismissed as being political, partisan, and radically anti-American.[24]

Central to the traditionalist view of multiculturalism is a steadfast refusal to rethink the source of "moral truth" in light of the expansion of social, cultural, and political diversity that has come to characterize American life. As new antagonisms have emerged over the purpose and meaning of schooling, curriculum, and the nature of American democracy, conservatives have reasserted their allegiance to a foundation of moral truth based on an orthodoxy that, according to James Davison Hunter, represents.

a commitment on the part of [its] adherents to an external, definable, and transcendent authority. Such an objective and transcendent authority defines, at least in the abstract, a consistent, unchangeable measure of value, purpose, goodness, and identity, both personal and collective. It tells us what is good, what is true, and how we should live, and who we are. It is an authority that is sufficient for all time.[25]

In treating national history in fixed and narrow terms, conservatives relinquish one of the most important defining principles of any democracy—that is, they ignore the necessity of a democratic society to rejuvenate itself by constantly reexamining the strengths and limits of its traditions. In the absence of a critical encounter with the past and a recognition of the importance of cultural diversity, multiculturalism becomes acceptable only if it is reduced to a pedagogy of reverence and transmission rather than a pedagogical practice that puts people in dialogue with each other as part of a broader attempt to fashion a renewed interest in cultural democracy and the creation of engaged and critical citizens.[26] Bhikhu Parekh rightly argues that such a stance defines what he calls demagogic multiculturalism. For Parekh, the traditionalists' refusal of cultural hybridity and differences and the fixity of identity and culture promotes a dangerous type of fundamentalism. He writes:

When a group feels besieged and afraid of losing its past in exchange for a nebulous future, it lacks the courage to critically reinterpret its fundamental principles, lest it opens the door to "excessive" reinterpretation. It then turns its fundamentals into fundamentalism, it declares them inviolate and reduces them to a neat and easily enforceable package of beliefs and rituals.[27]

Parekh's fear of demagogic multiculturalism represents a pedagogical problem as much as it does a political one. The political issue is exemplified in the conservative view that critical multiculturalism with its assertion of multiple identities and diverse cultural traditions represents a threat to democracy. The fatal political transgression committed here lies in the suggestion that social criticism itself is fundamentally at odds with democratic life. Indeed, this is more than mere rhetoric, it is a challenge to the very basic principles that inform a democratic society. Pedagogically, demagogic multiculturalism renders any debate about the relationship between democracy and cultural difference moot. By operating out of a suffocating binarism that pits "us" against "them," conservatives annul the possibility for dialogue, education, understanding, and negotiation. In other words, such a position offers no language for contending with cultures whose boundaries cross over into diverse spheres that are both fluid and saturated with power. How this type of fundamentalism will specifically impact on the schools can be seen in the increased calls for censorship in the schools as well as in the bleaching of the curriculum to exclude or underrepresent the voices and histories of various subordinate groups.

It should be noted that what is at stake here is not simply the balkanization of history and national identity, but the attempt to critically recover the various narratives of struggle and possibility that have for better or worse defined this country's engagement with democracy. Central to the ongoing debates over multiculturalism and the curriculum is the recognition that curriculum has been increasingly linked to an emerging politics of cultural difference, which has raised a number of serious questions about the conditions and forms of authority produced and secured within public schools. More specifically, issues concerning the canon and curriculum have become a contested terrain around questions of representation and the related battle over self-definition and identity.

In spite of the dismissal of multiculturalism and the politics of cultural difference, the conflict over the curriculum cannot be understood merely as an educational problem in the narrow sense of the term, nor can it be dismissed as the ranting of discontented minorities and radical educators. On the contrary, what is at stake in the debate over multiculturalism and curriculum are crucial issues regarding the meaning and purpose of public life, national identity, and cultural democracy. Renato Rosaldo is quite on target in arguing that "these days questions of culture seem to touch a nerve because they quite quickly become anguished questions of identity."[28] Two issues are often overlooked in current public discussions of multiculturalism. On one hand there are the systemic, economic, political, and social conditions that contribute to the domination of many subordinate groups. On the other hand, too little attention is paid to the sundry struggles subordinate groups undertake through the development of counternarratives that make them the subject rather than the object of history.

Instead of responding to the increasing diversity of histories, ethnicities, and cultures complexly layered over time, dominant institutions and discourses appear increasingly indifferent to the alarming poverty, shameful school dropout rate, escalating unemployment, and a host of other problems that accentuate the alienation, inequality, and racial segregation that fuel the sense of desperation, hopelessness, and disempowerment felt by many minorities in this country.

In the aftermath of the Los Angeles uprising, it appears both morally careless and politically irresponsible to define multiculturalism as exclusively disruptive and antithetical to the most fundamental aspects of American democracy. Such a position both fails to explore the potential that multiculturalism has as a critical referent for linking diversity and cultural democracy while simultaneously serving to ignore the social, economic, and political conditions that have spurned the current insurgency among minorities and others around the issue of multiculturalism.

This is not meant to suggest that multiculturalism can be defined in essentialist terms; in fact, in contrast to the notion that multiculturalism is simply dangerous to American society and its public schools, as some traditionalists contend, I would argue that multiculturalism is a complex term that can be defined through a variety of ideological constructs.[29] In fact, I believe that educators need a definition of multiculturalism that offers the possibility for schools to become places where students and teachers can become border crossers engaged in critical and ethical reflection about what it means to bring a wider variety of cultures into dialogue with each other. But if the concept of multiculturalism is to become useful as a pedagogical concept, educators need to redefine it outside of a sectarian traditionalism. They also need to reject any form of multiculturalism in which differences are registered and equally affirmed but at the expense of understanding how such differences both emerge and are related to networks and hierarchies of power, privilege, and domination.

Moreover, in opposition to the liberal emphasis on individual diversity, an insurgent multiculturalism must also address issues regarding group differences and how power relations function to structure racial and ethnic identities. Furthermore, cultural differences cannot be merely affirmed in order to be assimilated into a common culture or policed through economic, political, and social spheres that restrict full citizenship to dominant groups. If multiculturalism is to be linked to a renewed interest in expanding the principles of democracy to wider spheres of application, it must be defined in pedagogical and political terms that embrace it as a referent and practice for civic courage, critical citizenship, and democratic struggle. Bhikhu Parekh offers a definition that appears to avoid both a superficial pluralism and a notion of multiculturalism that is structured in dominance:

Multiculturalism doesn't simply mean numerical plurality of different cultures, but rather a community which is creating, guaranteeing, encouraging spaces within which different communities are able to grow at their own pace. At the same time it means creating a public space in which these communities are able to interact, enrich the existing culture and create a new consensual culture in which they recognize reflections of their own identity.[30]

Multiculturalism, like any other articulating term, is multiaccentual and it takes on a different meaning when situated in a more critical perspective. I believe that an insurgent multiculturalism represents an ideology and a set of pedagogical practices that offer a powerful critique and challenge to the racist, patriarchal, and sexist principles embedded in American society and schooling. Within this discourse, the curriculum is viewed as a hierarchical and representational system that selectively produces knowledge, identities, desires, and values. The notion that curriculum represents knowledge that is objective, value-free, and beneficial to all students is forcefully challenged as it becomes clear that those who benefit from public schooling are generally white, middle-class students whose histories, experiences, language, and knowledge largely conform to dominant cultural codes and practices. More, an insurgent multiculturalism performs a theoretical service by addressing curriculum as a form of cultural politics that demands linking the production and legitimation of classroom knowledge, social identities, and values to considerations of power.

In what follows, I want to suggest some general elements that might inform an insurgent multicultural curriculum. First, a multicultural curriculum must be informed by a new language in which issues of diversity and cultural difference become central to educating students to live in a democratic society. That is, we need a language of politics and pedagogy that is able to speak to cultural differences not as something to be tolerated but as essential to expanding the discourse and practice of democratic life. It is important to note that multiculturalism is not merely an ideological construct, it also refers to the fact that by the year 2010, people of color will be the numerical majority in the United States. This suggests that educators need to develop language, vision, and curriculum in which multiculturalism and democracy become mutually reinforcing categories. Manning Marable has spoken eloquently to this issue and his definition of a multicultural democracy offers important insights for reworking democracy as a pedagogical and cultural practice necessary for what John Dewey once called the creation of an articulate public. Marable is worth quoting at length on this issue:

Multicultural political democracy means that this country was not built by and for only one group—Western Europeans; that our country does not have only one language—English; or only one religion—Christianity; or only one economic philosophy—corporate capitalism. Multicultural democracy means that the leadership within our society should reflect the richness, colors and diversity expressed in the lives of all of our people. Multicultural democracy demands new types of power-sharing and the re-allocation of resources necessary to great economic and social development for those who have been systematically excluded and denied.[31]

Second, as part of an attempt to develop a multicultural and multiracial society consistent with the principles of a democratic society, educators must take account of the fact that men and women of color are disproportionately underrepresented in the cultural and public institutions of this country. Pedagogically this suggests that a multicultural curriculum must provide students with the skills to analyze how various audio, visual, and print texts fashion social identities over time, and how these representations serve to reinforce, challenge, or rewrite dominant moral and political vocabularies that promote stereotypes that degrade people by depriving them of their history, culture, and identity.[32]

This should not suggest that such a pedagogy should solely concentrate on how meanings produce particular stereotypes and the uses to which they are put. Nor should a multicultural politics of representation focus exclusively on recovering and reconstituting the history of subordinate groups. While such approaches are essential to giving up the quest for a pure historical tradition, it is imperative that a multicultural curriculum also focus on dominant, white institutions and histories in order to interrogate them in terms of both their injustices and their contributions for humanity.

Of course, more is at stake here than avoiding the romanticizing of minority voices, or the inclusion of Western traditions in the curriculum. Multiculturalism in this sense is about making whiteness visible as a racial category; that is, it points to the necessity of providing white students with the cultural memories that enable them to recognize the historically and socially constructed nature of their own identities. In part, this approach to multiculturalism as a cultural politics provides white students with self-definitions upon which they can recognize whether they are speaking from within or outside privileged spaces and how power works within and across differences to legitimate some voices and dismantle others.

Bob Suzuki further extends the pedagogical importance of making whiteness visible as an ethnic category. In teaching a course on racism to college students, he discovered that for many white students their ethnic experiences and histories had been erased. By helping them to recover and interrogate their own histories, he found that the white students "could relate more empathetically to the problems of people of color and become more open to understanding their experiences and perspectives."[33] I would further extend Suzuki's important point by arguing that as crucial as it is to get white students to listen emphatically to students of color, it is also crucial that they come to understand that multiculturalism is also about understanding how dominant institutions provide the context of massive black unemployment, segregated schools, racist violence, and run-down housing. An insurgent multicultural curriculum must shift attention away from an exclusive focus on subordinate groups, especially since such an approach tends to highlight their deficits, to one that examines how racism in its various forms is produced historically, semiotically, and institutionally in various levels of dominant, white culture. Multiculturalism means analyzing not just stereotypes but also how institutions produce racism and other forms of discrimination.

Third, a multicultural curriculum must address how to articulate a relationship between unity and difference that moves beyond simplistic binarisms. That is, rather than defining multiculturalism against unity or simply for difference, it is crucial for educators to develop a unity-in-difference position in which new forms of democratic representation, participation, and citizenship provide a forum for creating unity without denying the particular, the multiple, and the specific. In this instance the interrelationship of different cultures and identities becomes a borderland, a site of crossing, negotiation, translation, and dialogue. At stake here is the production of a notion of border pedagogy in which the intersection of culture and identity produces self-definitions that enable teachers and students to authorize a sense of critical agency. Border pedagogy points to a self/other relationship in which identity is fixed as neither Other nor the same; instead it is both and, hence, defined within multiple literacies that become a referent, critique, and practice of cultural translation, a recognition of no possibility of fixed, final, or monologically authoritative meaning that exists outside of history, power, and ideology. Within this pedagogical cartography, teachers must be given the opportunity to cross ideological and political borders as a way of clarifying their own moral vision, as a way of enabling counterdiscourses, and, as Roger Simon points out, as a way of getting students "beyond the world they already know in order to challenge and provoke their inquiry and challenge of their existing views of the way things are and should be."[34]

Border literacy calls for pedagogical conditions in which "differences are recognized, exchanged and mixed in identities that break down but are not lost, that connect but remain diverse."[35] A border pedagogy suggests a literacy forged in the practices of imagination, narrative, and performance; a literacy that insists on an open-endedness, an incompleteness, and an uncertainty about the politics of one's own location. This is not a literacy that pretends to be amorphous or merely self-reflexive, but one that engages the important question of how to deal with the fact of reflexivity, how to strategize about it in the interests of diverse theoretical and pedagogical projects dedicated to creating a multicultural and multiracial democracy.

Underlying this notion of border pedagogy and literacy is neither the logic of assimilation (the melting pot), nor the imperative to create cultural hierarchies, but the attempt to expand the possibilities for different groups to enter into dialogue in order to further understand the richness of their differences and the value of what they share in common. Jeffrey Weeks speaks to this issue well:

We may not be able to find, indeed we should not seek, a single way of life that would satisfy us all. That does not mean we cannot agree on common political ends:

the construction of what can best be described as "a community of communities," to achieve a maximum political unity without denying differences.[36]

Fourth, an insurgent multiculturalism must challenge the task of merely representing cultural differences in the curriculum; it must also educate students to the necessity for linking a justice of multiplicity to struggles over real material conditions that structure everyday life. In part, this means understanding how structural imbalances in power produce real limits on the capacity of subordinate groups to exercise a sense of agency and struggle. It also means analyzing specific class, race, gender, and other issues as social problems rooted in real material and institutional factors that produce specific forms of inequality and oppression. This would necessitate a multicultural curriculum that produces a language that deals with social problems in historical and relational terms, and uncovers how the dynamics of power work to promote domination within both the school and the wider society.

Finally, a multicultural curriculum must not simply be imposed on a community and school. It is imperative that as a power-sensitive discourse a multicultural curriculum refigures relations between the school, teachers, students, and the wider community. In this case, schools must be willing to draw upon the resources of the community, include members of the community in making fundamental decisions about what is taught, who is hired, and how the school can become an integral part of the society it serves. Teachers need to be educated to be border crossers, to explore zones of cultural difference by moving in and out of the resources, histories, and narratives that provide different students with a sense of identity, place, and possibility.[37] This does not suggest that educators become tourists traveling to exotic lands; on the contrary, it points to the need for them to enter into negotiation and dialogue around issues of nationality, difference, and identity so as to be able to fashion a more ethical and democratic set of pedagogical relations between themselves and their students while simultaneously allowing students to speak, listen, and learn differently within pedagogical spaces that are safe, affirming, questioning, and enabling. In this instance, a curriculum for a multicultural and multiracial society provides the conditions for students to think and act otherwise, to imagine beyond the given, and to critically embrace their identities as a source of agency and possibility.

NOTES

This chapter is a revised version of an article originally published, under the same title, in *The Journal of the Midwest Modern Language Association,* 26(1) (Spring 1993): 12–30. It has been used here with permission.

1. James Baldwin, "A Talk to Teachers," in Rick Simonson and Scott Walker (eds.), *Multicultural Literacy: Opening the American Mind* (St. Paul: Graywolf Press, 1988), p. 8.

2. Melvin E. Bradford quoted in Katherine S. Mangan, "6th Generation Texan Takes on 'Trendy Nonsense,' " *The Chronicle of Higher Education,* July 8, 1992, p. A5.

3. Alan O'Connor, "Just Plain Home Cookin," *Borderlines,* 20/21 (Winter 1991): 58.

4. Marcia Tucker, " 'Who's On First?' Issues of Cultural Equity in Today's Museums," in Carol Becker et al., *Different Voices* (New York: Association of Art Museum Directors, 1992), p. 11.

5. Cornel West, "Learning to Talk about Race," *The New York Times Magazine,* Section 6 (August 2, 1992), p. 24.

6. Ibid.

7. bell hooks, *Black Looks: Race and Representation* (Boston: South End Press, 1992), pp. 168, 172.

8. The notion of imagining otherwise in order to act otherwise is taken from Richard Kearney, *The Wake of Imagination* (Minneapolis: University of Minnesota Press, 1988), p. 370.

9. "The Postcolonial Critics: Homi Bhabha," interviewed by David Bennett and Terry Collits, *Arena,* No. 96 (1991): 50–51.

10. Stuart Hall, "And Not a Shot Fired," *Marxism Today,* December 1991, p. 10.

11. Larry D. Hatfield and Dexter Waugh, "Right Wing's Smart Bombs," *San Francisco Examiner,* May 24, 1992, p. A10.

12. For a brief but informative view of right-wing think tanks, see Lawrence Soley, "Right Thinking Conservative Think Tanks," *Dissent,* Summer 1991, pp. 418–420. For a history of these groups, see Russ Bellant, *Old Nazis, the New Right, and the Republican Party* (Boston: South End Press, 1991).

13. For the connection between right-wing foundations and a number of prominent educators such as Diane Ravitch, Chester Finn, Charlotte Crabtree, Allan Bloom, and others, see Dexter Waugh and Larry Hatfield, "Rightest Groups Pushing School Reforms," *San Francisco Examiner,* May 28, 1992, p. A18.

14. Joan Scott has argued that the right-wing attack on multiculturalism is primarily about the attempt to "neutralize the space of ideological and cultural nonconformity by discrediting it." (Joan W. Scott, "Multiculturalism and the Politics of Identity," *October,* 61 [Summer 1992]:13.) While this is certainly true, it is not the whole story. The conservative attack in not new, it is deeply rooted in a long tradition of anti-Catholic, antiethnic, and antiimmigration rhetoric that saw the "multicultural" problem as largely a racial issue. It is precisely this historical context that exposes the racist character of recent arguments against multiculturalism made by Arthur Schlesinger, Jr., Gary Sykes, Richard Brookshiser, and others. For an attempt to insert the history of racism back into the multicultural debate, see Stanley Fish, "Bad Company," *Transitions,* 56 (1992): 60–67.

15. Stuart Hall and David Held, "Citizens and Citizenship," in Stuart Hall and Martin Jacques (eds.), *New Times: Changing Face of Politics in the 1990's* (London: Verso, 1990), p. 178.

16. Jonathan Kozol, "If We Want to Change Our Schools," unpublished speech given to the Commonwealth Club in San Francisco, 1992, pp. 1–2.

17. Robert Bellah et al., "Breaking the Tyranny of the Market," *Tikkun,* 6(4) (1991): 90.

18. Steve Whitman, "The Crime of Black Imprisonment," *Z Magazine*, May 1992, pp. 69, 71.

19. Peter Dreier, "Bush to Cities: Drop Dead," *The Progressive*, (July 1992), p. 22.

20. Chester E. Finn, Jr., "Does Public Mean Good?" *Education Week*, 11(21) (February 12, 1992): 30.

21. On the relationship between democracy and cultural difference, see Henry A. Giroux: *Border Crossings: Cultural Workers and the Politics of Education* (New York: Routledge, 1992), and *Living Dangerously: Multiculturalism and the Politics of Difference* (New York: Peter Lang, 1993).

22. James Clifford, "Museums in the Border Lands," in Becker, et al., *Different Voices*, p. 119.

23. E. D. Hirsch, Jr., *Cultural Literacy: What Every American Needs to Know* (Boston: Houghton Mifflin, 1987).

24. Such pronouncements have become commonplace among traditionalists such as Lynn V. Cheney, John Silber, William J. Bennett, Chester E. Finn, and Allan Bloom. See, for example, Carolyn J. Mooney, "Scholars Decry Campus Hostility to Western Culture at a Time When More Nations Embrace Its Values," *The Chronicle of Higher Education*, January 30, 1991, pp. A15–A16.

25. James Davison Hunter, *Culture Wars: The Struggle to Define America* (New York: Basic Books, 1991), p. 44.

26. I have paraphrased this insight from Gregory Jay, "The End of American Literature: Toward a Multicultural Practice," *College English*, March 1991, p. 266.

27. Bhikhu Parekh, "Identities on Parade: A Conversation," *Marxism Today*, June 1989, p. 3.

28. Renato Rosaldo, *Culture and Truth* (Boston: Beacon Press, 1989).

29. For an analysis of the history and varied meanings of multicultural education, see Christine E. Sleeter (ed.), *Empowerment Through Multicultural Education* (Albany: State University of New York Press, 1991); Cameron McCarthy, *Race and Curriculum* (Philadelphia: Falmer Press, 1990). Also see Peter Erickson, "What Multiculturalism Means," *Transition* No. 55 (1992): 105–114.

30. Parekh, "Identities on Parade," p. 4.

31. Manning Marable, *Black America: Multicultural Democracy in the Age of Clarence Thomas and David Duke* (Westfield, NJ: Open Media, 1992), p. 13.

32. On this issue, see ibid.

33. Bob Suzuki, "Unity with Diversity: Easier Said than Done," *Liberal Education*, February 1991, p. 34.

34. Roger Simon, *Teaching Against the Grain* (Westport, CT: Bergin & Garvey, 1994), p. 47.

35. Iain Chambers, *Border Dialogues* (New York: Routledge, 1990), p. 114.

36. Jeffrey Weeks, "The Value of Difference," in Jonathan Rutherford (ed.), *Identity, Community, Culture, Difference* (London: Lawrence and Wishart, 1990), p. 98.

37. The issue of border pedagogy and border crossings is taken up in Giroux, *Border Crossings*.

6

Pedagogies of Dissent and Transformation: A Dialogue about Postmodernity, Social Context, and the Politics of Literacy

Kris D. Gutierrez and Peter McLaren

Kris Gutierrez: Your work on schooling, identity, and critical pedagogy is noted for its attempt to locate itself in a discussion of larger social contexts of consumer capitalism and identity formation. You are noted for discussing social and cultural issues related to power that exist outside of the classroom as much as you are for dealing with these issues as they inscribe social relations inside the classroom. This is one of the reasons that I find your work interesting and important. The language that you use is often quite literary and is situated in transdisciplinary theoretical terminology where poststructuralism and theories of postcolonialism, among other theoretical perspectives, play a significant role.

I think, however, that this mixture of the theoretical and, if you will, poetical, has both advantages and disadvantages. While it gives you new angles and perspectives on the production of subjectivity within capitalist social formations, don't you think it tends to restrict your audience to specialists in the critical social sciences and is less likely to find its way in teacher education courses, where I would think that you would want your work to be taken up? Your view of contemporary culture is sometimes considered to be quite pessimistic—although far from nihilistic—and I wonder if your criticisms of everyday life in the United States are perhaps deliberate attempts at overstatement for the sake of shocking your readers into an awareness of the very serious social problems that face us. For instance, I read some comments by you recently in which you talked about the "structural unconscious" of the United States resembling the minds of serial killers such as Ted Bundy. You write in *Thirteen Questions* (1992): "Serial killer Ted

Bundy has donated his multiple texts of identity to our structural unconscious and *we are living them.*" Is this a motivated exaggeration, a form of
theoretical hyperbole for the sake of making a point about the violence that
pervades everyday life?

Peter McLaren: Yes and no, Kris. I consider my writing to be simultaneously cynical and utopian. I think it was Theodor Adorno who once said
something to the effect that in every exaggeration there exists some truth.
And, of course, as somebody who lives in Los Angeles, you don't need to
be reminded about violence. Perhaps I focus on the more violent effects of
capitalism on social formations because I really do believe that violence exists
at the very heart of postindustrial capitalism as a structural precondition for
it; that capitalism, in fact, is steadfastly predatory on violence; and that it
fundamentally constitutes what could be called a "necessary contingency"
within what has come to be called "the cultural logic of late capitalism."
This is perhaps part of what Arthur Kroker (1992) refers to as "the contemporary human situation of living at the violent edge of primitivism and sim-
ulation, of an infinite reversibility in the order of things wherein only the
excessive cancellation of difference through violence reenergizes the process."

Kris: What about Los Angeles? In his book *City of Quartz*, Mike Davis
(1990) has described Los Angeles as existing "on the bad edge of postmodernity." Can you give us a cultural autopsy report?

Peter: Los Angeles is hemorrhaging from its social wounds. The steel fist
of despotic capitalism has pulverized the soul of this city. The cowardly
federal retreat from the big cities is certainly not going to help stop the
bleeding of Los Angeles, a city now referred to by some as the new capital
of the Third World. In fact, Los Angeles is now facing the worst economic
crisis since 1938. People seem to forget that after the Watts rebellion in
1965 there were 164 major riots that spread through urban ghettos across
the United States—a period sometimes referred to as the "Second Civil
War." This provoked Lyndon Johnson's administration to push its Model
Cities Bill through Congress. Yet this historical fact and the spring 1992
Los Angeles rebellion have not provoked any serious action on the part of
the federal government.

You mentioned Mike Davis, whose work I admire very much. Davis has
chronicled the crisis of Los Angeles very thoroughly and my comments simply rehearse what he has said on a number of occasions. The current crisis
of Los Angeles has to be seen in the context of the combination of international finance capital and low-wage immigrant labor and what some have
called the "Third Worlding" of the city (although I have problems with the
way this term is frequently used).

There is little cause for optimism about the future of Los Angeles when
the czar of the 1984 Olympics, Peter Ueberroth, is given the task of rebuilding Los Angeles through corporate coalition building and voluntarism.

Current government responses that center around the creation of microenterprise zones and "infrastructure" are not a great improvement on the former Bush administration's efforts to repackage existing programs under a new banner while at the same time preventing small business loans and food stamps from reaching needy neighborhoods. Not to mention Dan Quayle's advice to sell the Los Angeles Airport to help rebuild the city after the uprising.

Kris: Federal disinvestment policies have had a devastating effect on the city. But the problem is more widespread than California. Key industrial states are reducing welfare and educational entitlements. It's shameful that this could happen in a country that poured so much money into the Gulf War and the savings and loan bailout.

Peter: Mike Davis describes current government initiatives directed at rebuilding Los Angeles as "shoe string local efforts and corporate charity." He refers to government aid after the rapid deployment of federal combat troops to South Central as little more than an "urban fire sale." I agree with Davis' criticism of the Republican war on big cities. During the Reagan-Bush era, big cities became what Davis describes as "the domestic equivalent of an insolvent, criminalized Third World whose only road to redemption is a combination of militarization and privatization." So now we're faced with what Davis sees as white flight to "edge cities" along beltways and intercity corridors, the Latinization of manual labor, deficits in the jobs-to-housing ratios among blacks, and the new segregation in cities which Davis refers to as "spacial apartheid."

Kris: So how does this affect the average youth? I am the mother of a biracial twelve-year old. Despite the fact that he has had access to and participation in academic, cultural, social, and political activities and experiences that privilege him in so many ways, his "blackness/Latinoness," accentuated by his large frame and his ability and willingness to articulate elaborated sociopolitical analyses of his own life and the world around him, position him at the very margins, the borderlands, of most of his classroom communities. His strong literacy skills are not valued when they are used to write poems about the L.A. uprising or to critique or challenge the content of the classroom curriculum. For example, his Honors History class was recently studying about Mecca. In an attempt to provide the students with a visual portrait of Mecca, the teacher brought in the videotape of the movie "X." The teacher played a segment of the movie, the scene which shows Malcolm arriving in Mecca. After viewing this particular scene, the teacher asked the children to identify what was important. My son's hand shot up as he offered his response, "Well, I think that the fact that Malcolm is being followed by two white CIA agents as he goes to worship in Mecca is very interesting." He was publicly chastised for being off-topic, for not being focused, "we're studying Mecca not Malcolm" quipped his teacher. "But can't we study history when we're study geography?" asked my son. The teacher simply did not get it. His is not so much the "spacial apartheid" about which Davis writes. Instead, his is an "intellectual apartheid" that silences and marginalizes young adults in schools, particularly black/Latino males, who take up various forms of resistance and contestation to demand the affirmation of their particular existences.

But as Cornel West (1993) has asked, "How does one affirm oneself without reenacting negative black stereotypes or overreacting to white supremacist ideals?" How does this discourse of contestation not become what Michel Foucault calls "reverse discourse"? As Henry Louis Gates, Jr. (1989) has written, this discourse "remains entrapped within the presuppositions of the discourse it means to oppose, enacts a conflict internal to that 'master discourse'; but when the terms of argument have already been defined, it may look like the only form of contestation possible." How are these factors lived out in the everyday existence of today's urban students?

Peter. That's the key issue for me, Kris. I think we need to look beyond the transgressive desire of graffiti artists and taggers, P.T.A. groups, and anticrime community activists to find the seedbeds of a new cultural politics. We need to begin the fight against racism and social injustice in the schools. In doing so, educators need to ask themselves how students' identities are organized macrospatially and geopolitically as well as within the micropolitics of the classroom. How are students specifically positioned (in terms of race, class, gender, sexuality) within the grid of late capitalist economic containment and sociopolitical control? How are their structures of affect (what Larry Grossberg [1992] calls "mattering maps") organized? How are students situated in both libidinal economies as well as conceptual ones? These are pressing issues, many of which have been addressed by people such as Henry Giroux, Chandra Mohanty, Larry Grossberg, bell hooks, Michele Wallace, and others.

It's hard today to draw clear boundaries around the affective and cognitive modes of existence or even to identify ontological categories. This is partly due to the allegorical effects of technology, to what some writers refer to as hyperreality or the imploded regions of cyberspace created by the new rhetoricity of our media-saturated lives. Identity has become fluid, reduced to an abstract code not simply of difference but also indifference. Today it is difficult to have an identity, let alone pursue one. We are all, in a very grave sense, always traveling incognito in hyperreality. Students in classrooms are attempting to construct their identities through transgressive acts, through resisting those normalizing laws that render subversive, obscene, and unthinkable contestatory possibilities and a pragmatics of hope.

Kris. Fear has taken on a new meaning, it seems. It has become intensified in new ways.

Peter. Kris, I believe that we are witnessing the hyperreal formation of an entirely new species of fear. I live not far from the UCLA campus in Westwood and nearly every night I hear the wailing cries of drunken students, cries that at once evoke the empty humor of "Hee-Haw" and the more serious, reflective pain of youthful bodies responding to the slow commodification of their will under late capitalism. Their wails remind me of a desperate attempt to fill in the empty spaces of their souls with a presence-effect of pure intensity.

I think that as teachers we need to ask ourselves: What does it mean to live in this fear in an arena of shifting forms of global capitalism? How does such fear direct urban policy and school policy? How is everyday life saturated by such fear and what role does this fear play in student learning? What kinds of learning need to take place in order to resist or overcome the fear of participating in the construction of terminal identities? What politics of liberation must be engaged in as part of a struggle for a better future for our schools and our youth who attend them?

Brian Massumi (1993) has done a brilliant job in discussing the breaking down of the "humanistic" integrative strategy of Keynesian economics and the advent of "unapologetically ruthless strategies of displacement, fluidification, and intensification."[2] We're talking here about the utilitarian and socially unrepentant dismantling of the welfare state and the restructuring and dissolution of identities and entire lives that follow such a dismantling. Briefly put, Kris, displacement refers to exporting industrial production to the Third World, where the growing middle class there can provide an important market outlet for consumer durables.

In the United States, central economic forces mean producing more information and communication services in new and mostly nonunionized domains, leaving youth to their "McJobs" (to coin a term by Canadian novelist Douglas Coupland in his book, *Generation X* [1990]. Massumi uses the term "fluidification" to mean the increasing fluidity of capital and the workforce as well as creating rapid product turnovers. Use value in this case is increasingly replaced by image-value. Massumi uses the term "intensification" to refer to basically the merging of production and consumption, which is accompanied by the disappearance of leisure and a focus on self-improvement in the service of gaining a competitive edge in the marketplace. Massumi notes that the very contours of postmodern existence have become a form of surplus value as the wage relation virtually collapses into the commodity relation.

Capitalism has colonized all geographical and social space and schools have not been immune. In fact, they are perhaps one of the most vulnerable social sites for this kind of colonization as we can see in the example of Whittle's Channel One enterprise and the powerful forces that are being put in place by corporate logic to ensure the privatization of education. Massumi argues that capitalism is coextensive with its own inside, such that it has now become a field of both immanence and exteriority. There is no escape. There is only fear. Fear, reports Massumi, is now the objective condition of subjectivity in the era of late capitalism. In this sense it means

something more than a fear of downward mobility but rather the constitution of the self within a market culture and market morality. When non-
market values—such as love and compassion—disappear from everyday life
nihilism sets in. Cornel West speaks eloquently about this dilemma especially
in urban settings.

I agree with Anthony Appiah (1991) when he says that Max Weber mis-
took the Enlightenment universalization of the secular for the triumph of
instrumental reason. I believe, as does Appiah, that the Enlightenment has
more to do with the transformation of the real into sign value than it does
with the incursion of instrumental rationality into the multiple spheres of
the social. What Weber missed was the incorporation of all areas of public
and private life into the money economy. There exists no autochthonous
and monolithic space of pure culture or uncontaminated identity—everything has been commodified. Use value is now supported by what Massumi
calls "fulfillment-effect" or "image value."

We are, all of us, subjects of capital—the *point d'appui* between wage
relations and commodity relations, with commodification representing the
hinge between the future and the past. According to Massumi, consum-
mation and consumption are continually conflated under late capitalism, as
we increasingly come to live in the time form of the future perfect or future
anterior, which can be expressed in the existential equation "will have
bought = will have been." Surplus value has become, in effect, a metonym
for everyday existence. Of course, all of this points to the urgency of understanding how students invest in their lives and bring meaning to everyday
life. It suggests students need to understand more about the structural and
more fluid contexts that produce their everyday lives and how their identities
are constructed out of the vectors and circuits of capital, social relations,
cultural forms, and relations of power. It means understanding more than
simply how the media and dominant school curricula control the representation of the racialized Other and influence our attitudes and desires.

I will be the first to emphasize the importance of understanding the politics of representation and the ways in which our subjectivities are constructed through the economies of signs in our media-saturated world. But
as Giroux and others have emphasized, we need to go further than this. We
need to understand how identities are produced through structural relations
and constraints and the systems of intelligibility we have historically inherited and invented and that produce us on a daily basis. It means understanding the causes of oppression and exploitation and the material effects of
economic practices and capitalist logics.

Something that has struck me for quite some time has recently been articulated in a brilliant book by Rey Chow (1993), *Writing Diaspora*. Global
capitalism and its technological apparatuses of domination have ushered in
what Chow refers to as "a universal speed culture." Here she is referring,
after Paul Virilio, to the mediatization of information. Such mediatization

and human life, while incompatible, are now interchangeable. Electronic communication makes this possible. Chow notes that human labor is "finally exchangeable in digitalized form, without going though the stage of the concrete commodity whose mysteriousness Marx so memorably describes" (p. 180). We now live in a world of what Chow calls "electronic immigrants" who work in countries such as India and the Soviet Union, where well-trained but jobless technical professionals sell their labor for low wages to U.S. computer companies. They work through the phone lines (where there are no import duties) as cheap data processors. This digitalized form of labor has implications for the potential of developing critical forms of literacy in school.

Moving now to the question of schooling, you have been developing a politics of literacy that I think is extremely important in helping educators to understand how knowledge is constructed within a variety of social contexts. Can you talk about the role social context plays in your own work with immigrant Latino children?

Kris: As you know, Peter, the focus of my work involves communities and schools here in Los Angeles and concerns itself primarily with how contexts of learning in schools influence the nature of the teaching and learning of literacy for linguistically and culturally diverse student populations. This means doing intensive ethnographic fieldwork in both the schools and the communities. In the course of doing this ethnographic work, we[1] have examined how certain contexts provide or deny access to particular forms of learning and literacy learning in particular. I believe this kind of work helps make visible the ways in which literacy instruction continues to function as a way of socializing historically marginalized students into particular forms of knowing and being that make access to critical forms and practices of literacy in either their first or second language difficult. What becomes evident in this work is how this socialization process cannot be understood apart from the sociohistorical context in which it occurs and implicates how teachers' beliefs influence who gets to learn and how.

Peter: It seems to me, Kris, that teachers have a mandate to understand their own process of identity formation as well as those of their students. And in order to do this they need to at least have a rudimentary understanding of how their subjectivities are produced. They need to break free from the time-encrusted conceptions of identity, which, throughout the history of liberal humanism, have given credibility to the idea of the transparent ego, the autonomous will or the metaphysical illusion of self-identity. They need to escape from the hallucinatory idea of the boundaried, self-sufficient agent of history and see how anonymous political and economic structures colonize their life-worlds, instrumentalize forms of human agency, and sediment forms of desire. And then they need to engage such practices of colonization with some normative and regulative idea of justice and human freedom. Which is not to suggest that teachers develop some metaphysical or transcendental platform of ethicopolitical judgment.

Kris: That's true. However, this country has found itself completely unprepared and, in some cases, unwilling to address the educational and social needs of its multicultural student population. As a result of the shortage of multicultural, multilingual teachers, teachers are given emergency credentials to teach. These teachers have little opportunity to develop an understanding of what it means to teach in a multilingual and multicultural society. Moreover, teacher preparation programs continue to focus on the teaching and learning of monocultural and acontextual "models" of instruction such as the seven-step lesson plan. Who needs to be critical and reflective if the continued use of decontextualized "teacher proofed" methods, materials, and curricula is the normative practice in schools?

Peter: How do your students help teachers in this task?

Kris: I would argue that these long-term, classroom-based studies help us understand how teachers themselves, through their own experiences as students and through their preservice and inservice experience, have been socialized to particular understandings of "knowing" and "doing." Further constrained by deplorable working conditions and inadequate preparation, these teachers have little opportunity for reflective, critical practice. Understanding how these cycles of socialization influence classroom culture helps explain how the structures—that is, the social and discursive practices of many classrooms—reflect the relations of power and systems of knowledge distribution in the larger society. Critical theorists such as yourself, Michael Apple, and Henry Giroux provide the needed meta-analysis of the function of schools in corporate capitalistic societies and the effects of its pedagogies on multicultural student populations. However, to truly transform the nature of teaching and learning requires work at multiple levels and requires the development of situated understandings of what counts as teaching and learning in classrooms and the larger social context.

Peter: I agree with you. Your attentiveness to multiple levels of analysis is what I admire so much about your work. Of course, social life would be impossible without some form of discursive and nondiscursive domestication. All forms of nomination—of naming—are in some ways violent in that the world is reduced to objects of knowledge. I'm not opposed to naming social life but I am opposed to certain values that are embodied in the formation of the social at the level of micropolitics as well as macropolitics, whose persistent and motivated unnaming further reproduces existing relations of power and privilege.

Kris: I know that some theorists are critical of microanalytic educational research and I certainly agree with much of the criticism, of the failure to locate the dynamics of classrooms and school life in larger sociopolitical contexts. I also believe that much of educational research does not discuss the ways in which hegemonic classroom practices are both the coconstruction of particular sets of individuals, as well as the reinstantiation of larger sociohistorical processes and practices; however, I think that some critics of classroom-based, action-oriented research have not spent enough time in schools and, thus, do not understand that unless we can also unpackage the construction of these hegemonic practices at the microlevel, we will not be able to assist teachers in their attempts to transform the contexts for learning and their roles in that process.

Peter: Yes Kris, I agree. But we need to be wary of researchers who supply us with specific contextual data in ways that enable such data to become unwittingly recoded and reconverted so that practices professing to be liberatory actually become complicitous with the dominant ideology of colonialism.

Kris: That's always an important issue. An Antonio Gramsci reminded us, intellectuals are experts in legitimation and in defining what counts as knowledge. I'm reminded of linguistic anthropologist Charles Goodwin's (1993) analysis of the first Rodney King case. In his paper, he demonstrated how the prosecution recodified the data frame by frame, created new schemas, and provided an institutionalized scientific language to redefine Rodney King as the violent, crazed aggressor and the police behavior as the appropriate and measured response to imminent danger. The data were recodified and, thus, recoded to redefine the obvious brutality. A good lesson here. The fact that a researcher is engaged in an antiimperialist ethnographic study is no guarantee that a transformative politics and pedagogy will always emerge; it does not prevent at some level the recuperation of some of the very colonialist discourses one is contesting. That's what makes our work so difficult. I'm sure you noticed the reaction to Paul Willis's *Learning to Labor* (1990) by feminist researchers and to your early ethnographic work. I believe some of the engagements you had in your formative years as an ethnographic researcher with your critics has helped deepen and extend your own methods of analysis.

Peter: I try to be ruthlessly self-critical about my own work. When you are engaged in a collective struggle, the stakes are always higher.

Kris: The task for transforming instruction is an urgent one and, as you know, action-oriented, ethnographic research is one way of advancing this struggle. I believe that many teachers recognize the need for radical change. But teachers also need assistance in reimagining instructional contexts in which a problem-posing curriculum, an organic curriculum, emerges from the sociocultural and linguistic experiences of the participants—contexts in which the teaching and learning of literacy lead to critical, reflective practice.

Peter: Kris, elaborate if you would on the kind of ethnographic work that you feel is central to the emancipatory agenda of criticalists in the field.

Kris: I'm interested in ethnographic research that is informed by transdisciplinary work—cross-cultural, sociocultural, sociopolitical, and sociohistorical perspectives concerning the relationships among language, development, culture, and power. The works of Jean Lave (1991), Barbara Rogoff (1990), Elinor Ochs (1988), and Marjorie Goodwin (1990) come to mind. It is these kinds of studies that I believe are extremely useful in helping us understand the sociohistorical and sociocultural nature of development and in producing contextualized and situated understandings of the effects of current schooling practices on particular groups of students. But such work also has to have social and political agendas to be transformative.

Peter: When you talk about effects on "particular groups of students," I take it that you mean the contextual specificity of schooling practices in relation to the construction of gendered, classed, and racialized subjects.

Kris: Precisely. Classroom-based research that identifies what counts as knowledge in classrooms, and that describes how that knowledge is constructed, as well as whose knowledge gets constructed, is essential to transforming schools from the bottom up and for developing situated understandings of the social construction of classroom culture, of how gendered, classed, and racialized subjects are constructed. The hegemonic practices that structure the teacher-centered pedagogy of so many of the classrooms of bicultural students must be unpacked at the micro level— that is, in the moment-to-moment interactions of teacher and students as they participate in everyday classroom routines. I have found that this kind of research provides teachers both the theoretical and analytical tools and a language for transforming their own pedagogies. This process of becoming a critical teacher/researcher, however, requires a redefinition of the hierarchical social relationships between researcher and classroom teacher; it requires movement away from the traditional objectification of those studied to action-oriented research in which both teacher-researcher and researcher are brought together to define the research agenda, as well as their own positions in those processes. In short, these research agendas have social and political consequences.

Peter: What concerns me about the hegemonic articulations of dominant schooling practices is the way in which teachers participate in institutionalized structures, practices, and discourses that set up forms of racial differentiation and differential exclusion. It is the "whiteness" of the dominant ideology that metonymizes the standard curricula and constructs the legitimating norms for our pedagogies. I'm talking here about what David Theo Goldberg (1993) refers to as "the constitution of alterity." Goldberg is referring to the hold of racialized discourses and racist exclusions over subject formation and expression. I don't think that, as educators, we have carefully thought through this issue in our day-to-day teaching practices, especially the way in which racist discourses become conjoined with the discourses of class, gender, nation, and capitalism. As Goldberg notes, all racisms have to do with exclusions on the basis of belonging to particular racial groups, even though there is not a single transhistorical meaning of the word "race." I think we need to do more ethnographic work on how racial groups are constituted discursively and how race is inscribed by the interests of different groups and institutions and how racial preferences are assigned.

Some of my recent visits to Brazil have been very illuminating in terms of understanding the discursive constitution of racialized subjects. For instance, racialized descriptions of individuals based on morphology and skin color are much more nuanced there. Some of the descriptive categories include the *mulatto escuro* (dark skin) and the *mulatto claro* (light skin), which refer to persons of mixed racial groups (Caucasian and Afro-Brazilian). The *sarara* has light skin with blonde or red kinky hair and varied facial features, while the *moreno* has dark curly hair but light skin that is not white. The *cabo verde* has dark skin but lighter than, say, a *preto retinto*. The *cabo verde* has thin lips and a narrow straight nose, whereas the *preto retinto* has black skin and a broad nose and kinky hair. The *cabra* and *cabrocha* are lighter than the *preto* but darker than the *cabo verde*. Whites are also sub-classified according to skin color, hair, and facial attributes.

Here in the United States our system of classification is primarily in terms of binary oppositions—black versus white—whereas in Brazil there is a complex system of differences based more on distinctions. But these distinctions are still made on the basis of privileging whiteness. Whiteness is still a marker of special distinction and one has to see this historically and link it to the capitalist elites who have the power to suture ideological discourses to material relations of political, social, and economic advantage. How will global capitalism continue to reinforce such distinctions? That, to me, is an important issue. We need more qualitative work in this area.

Kris: But these distinctions are also made here in the United States. Chicano sociologists Eddie Telles and Ed Murguia have identified how phenotype influences which Chicanos have access to particular academic and economic opportunities. Still, I agree that we need more qualitative work that allows us to see how privileging on the basis of whiteness, language, and class is instantiated in the classroom. I also believe that qualitative work that is informed by a very different epistemology allows us to see the effects of unidirectional socialization processes of schools. For example, the socializing nature of institutional contexts is made evident in the institutional nature of the classroom discourse and interaction among participants and in the instantiation of teacher beliefs in the contexts for learning.

We have observed how the uniform turn-taking pattern of speech in the many classrooms we have studied exhibits overwhelming adherence to institutionally appropriate procedures—procedures that are both historically and socially situated. In particular, a differential and restricted system of knowledge distribution and access to meaningful conversation and participation characterize the normative teaching and learning practices of many classrooms of linguistically and culturally diverse children. Moreover, we found that the rules and rights of participation were set by the teacher—

that is, the teacher determined who was allowed to speak, how often, for how long, when, to whom, and for what purpose. Thus, the social hierarchy and the asymmetrical social relationships among participants and their roles in the learning process privileged the teacher's knowledge in the knowledge exchange system. Consequently, the linguistic and sociocultural experiences of these Latino children rarely became incorporated into the classroom narratives, as they were routinely denied access to meaningful and legitimate participation—that is, access to practice as a means of learning.

Moreover, access to the means and forms of learning for Latino children is restricted at several levels of instruction. For example, these students are provided limited opportunities to develop comprehensive literacy skills (i.e., reading, writing, talking, critical thinking, as well as the sociocultural knowledge needed for successful participation in this discourse community) in both their native and second language—that is, few opportunities to become biliterate.

Further, the classroom discourse that serves as the medium of instruction is itself restrictive and, thus, limits opportunities for students to engage in and produce the very discourse they are expected to learn. Even when they are encouraged to produce written and oral text, they are not encouraged to use literacy in ways that allow them to narrate their own experiences, much less to critique the sociopolitical and economic realities of their everyday lives. In this way, both the language of instruction and the form of discourse reconstruct and preserve the traditional forms of language use, interaction, and the traditional knowledge exchange system constitutive of teacher-centered instruction—instruction that is centered around a decontextualized and uncritical curriculum. Thus, the relationships between discourse, power, and forms of knowledge are made evident in everyday practices of literacy instruction (see Gutierrez and Larson, 1994, for more discussion).

Current language practices in schools, despite attempts to incorporate bilingual instruction, provide the most effective means of denying access to both knowledge and practice. Richard Ruiz's (1992) research on language policies and practices points out that particular language policies are, in fact, responses to the presence of particular language communities rather than a need or desire to improve or expand language practices. Current language policies aimed at quickly moving children from native language usage to English are no different.

Such language programs are historically rooted in the policies and practices of a monocultural and monolingual society in which assimilation is highly valued and necessary. Multiculturalism and multilingualism are seen as threats to the social, political, and cultural stability of this country. In these times of economic crisis, as support for the wave of antiimmigrant legislation increases, it becomes even more critical to understand how these sentiments manifest themselves in school policies and practices, in classroom instruction.

In our literacy studies, we find that the linguistic, economic, educational, and sociocultural needs of immigrant Latino children, particularly the Mexican immigrants, are still defined by the same Eurocentric lens used to define earlier immigrant experiences. However, these children are not monocultural, monolingual; they, and their families, transmigrate from Los Angeles to Mexico, for example, at least several times each year. The sociocultural, political, and linguistic realities of their everyday lives require them to draw on their bicultural experiences and their various languages and discourses. If we continue to define these students' experiences as being similar to the immigrant experiences of European-American and even of other linguistically and culturally diverse immigrants, we simply will not be able to understand the educational and larger social needs of this immigrant student population. In defining them as traditional immigrants, we fail to understand how transmigration better explains their existence, and to understand how these students are not monocultural but bicultural children in a multicultural society. From this perspective, the linguistic and cultural characteristics of this student population are not the same as those of children who have previously immigrated to this country. Thus, a more appropriate response to the linguistic needs of these students would be to create language policies that move beyond monolingualism and bilingualism to policies that promote biliteracy; that is, language practices that focus on the acquisition of a more comprehensive set of literacy skills, including writing, in both the native and the second language.

Such policies and practices acknowledge the complex linguistic and social needs of a multicultural society. Further, this recognition is an important first step in redefining bicultural children as a tremendously valuable national resource. This redefinition, however, will necessarily challenge the folk knowledge that currently informs so much of school practice and will also challenge current attitudes that underlie the growing antiimmigrant sentiment in our country.

Peter: One of the crucial issues for criticalists working in the field of literacy is to rethink the conditions of possibility for the subaltern to speak, to escape the labyrinth of subjugation, to make critical counterstatements against the logic of domination that informs the dominant white supremacist ideology of patriarchal capitalism, and to transform the ideological precepts that make up the "imponderability" of everyday life where social relations of power and privilege are naturalized throughout the curriculum.

As Brackette Williams (1993) has pointed out, if you use the term "American" without a hyphen you are taken to be white and if you do hyphenate the term, then you are not only categorized as nonwhite but also as "ethnic." Nonwhite groups are often defined in our schools as "problems," a status that Vine Deloria (1987) argues "relegates minority existence into an adjectival status within the homogeneity of American life." The conservative multiculturalists writing under the sign of whiteness are trying to protect the unitary cohesiveness of cultural life, making culture isomorphic with the logic of assimilation and homogenization and a unified racionational configuration. Even the difference-in-unity of the liberals and Left liberals attempts a cultural balancing act in which harmony and consensus is sought while minorities continue to be excluded and oppressed.

Interestingly, David Theo Goldberg (1993) suggests that capitalism's new demands for flexible accumulation loosens the sociocultural and spacial boundaries that help to promote racialized antagonisms. There is a greater opportunity for transgressing "the established racialized limits of spatial confines and political imagination." At the same time Goldberg notes that diversity in the public domain is challenged and delimited by the privatization of "univocality, exclusion, and exclusivity." In other words, diversity itself has become commodified in the interests of corporate capitalism. Multiculturalism is one of the hottest commodities at present circulating in the global marketplace. I want to know more about the direction of your work in relation to multiculturalism.

Kris: In our work, we attempt to redirect the discourse on multiculturalism from an exclusively sociopolitical discussion to one that is also informed by theories and research that help us better understand the relationship between language, culture, development, and power. To make the shift to include sociocultural frames, however, requires a brief discussion of how socioeconomic and sociopolitical forces gave rise to the emergence of multiculturalism. Although multiculturalism is most often identified with educational reform movements, the roots of multiculturalism are grounded in economic and sociopolitical processes. Specifically, multiculturalism is the ideological reflection of two medium-term processes that have unfolded in the core area of the world system (e.g., Europe, the United States, and the other rich countries of the advanced capitalist societies).

The first process is a structural response produced by the workings of global capital in the post–World War II era. These world processes are eroding and recreating national boundaries and are diffusing the notion and practice of nation stateness. Thus, global production and simultaneous widespread global migration are challenging the notion of monoculturalism—a concept inextricably linked to that of nation-building. From this perspective, multiculturalism has emerged as a consequence of global capitalism and its accompanying great migration has thrown monoculturalism into a crisis; multiculturalism has emerged as a consequence of these worldwide socioeconomic processes.

Peter: But we need to be reminded of the specificity of these processes, especially in light of growing nationalism in places like the former Soviet Union and Yugoslavia.

Kris: Of course. It's also important to understand that the need for multiculturalism has also been created by sociopolitical forces. From a world systems perspective, for example, multiculturalism is the sociopolitical challenge of the subordinated peoples both in the peripheral areas of the global world system and in the racialized areas of the core countries—the people participating in national liberation struggles in the Third World and those struggling for human and civil rights in the First World.

Multiculturalism is a new paradigm of race relations, a new concept of the proper relations between ethnic groups and races and is a reflection of the post–World War II challenge by people who have been marginalized and colonized. The ethnic and discriminated races have challenged the assumption of the inherent superiority of European cultures and have demanded the elevation of their cultures to equal those of Europe or white America. This particular sociological analysis attributes the emergence of multiculturalist movements to the inability of the monocultural systems to control the processes of globalizing capital and to enforce the sustained subordination of a racialized strata of its working people. However, until an overarching concept of nationhood is created—a concept that accommodates the globalizing tendencies of postindustrial capitalism and the inherent instability it creates—multiculturalism itself cannot serve to resolve the crisis, as you point out in the examples of the former Soviet Union and Yugoslavia.

Thus, despite its limited impact, multiculturalism has already begun to challenge monocultural beliefs and practices and has begun to destabilize Eurocultural strongholds. Yet we need to recognize that we are in a period of transition for which the social order has yet to be established. We need to understand that monoculturalism requires a hierarchy of cultures and particular power relations. Multiculturalism requires a transformation of these hierarchies and the accompanying social relationships among diverse populations.

In an educational context, however, few who are doing work in multicultural education address the necessity of transforming traditional hierarchical relationships and redefining the purposes of education. Some forms of multicultural education have emerged as a means for celebrating difference. But these are additive models that do not challenge existing paradigms and frames of reference. Educators, then, have come to terms in limited ways with addressing some issues of ethnicity but still have difficulty understanding how to deal with culturally and linguistically diverse communities. The discourse around the education of bicultural children still defines the educational and social needs of these black, Latino, Native American, and Asian children as problems that need to be addressed. Cornel West (1993) underscores this point: "we confine discussions about race in America to the 'problems' black people pose for whites rather than consider what this way of viewing black people reveals about us as a nation." That's why you and others are using the term "critical multiculturalism" to distinguish the criticalist multiculturalist agenda from those of conservatives and liberals.

To fully understand the difficulty in reforming practices that promote inequity, we must recognize that such practices, as Goldberg suggests, are deeply and historically rooted in beliefs about racial hierarchies and capacities; beliefs that are an inherent part of monocultural/monolingual societies. So part of the resistance to the implementation of radical pedagogies that call for transformative practice, such as language programs that promote biliteracy, for example, is a resistance to multiculturalism and multilingualism and other changes that disrupt the maintenance of racialized ways of life.

Peter: I'm wondering if we can discuss some of the possibilities that are emerging from criticalist work such as yours.

Kris: While I recognize that only limited change can occur without major reform on a wider scale, critical educators, in collaboration with classroom teachers, must begin the process of rethinking teaching and learning in a multicultural society. I'm very hopeful about the possibility of transforming classrooms into very different kinds of communities in which dialogic rather than monologic forms of instruction are evident—heteroglossic communities in which the social relationships and discourses are dramatically transformed. In our studies of the social contexts of literacy, so many of the classrooms we studied reinstantiated traditional social relationships of teacher as information giver and student as receiver of knowledge and, thus, created very restricted forms of learning and limited opportunity for the linguistic, social, and cultural experiences of the children to become organically constitutive of classroom life. However, we did identify some classrooms in which very different contexts for literacy learning existed.

In these classrooms, the coconstruction of discourse, activity, and knowledge were the normative practices for both teacher and students. Instruction was not driven by what Stanley Aronowitz (1993) calls methodologically oriented practice; instead, in these more interactive contexts for learning, or what we call "responsive/collaborative" classrooms, the nature of participation for both students and teachers was transformed and created new, as well as more, opportunity spaces for students to function as apprentices and as experts in the literacy learning process. In these communities of practice, the socialization process was bidirectional and students with varying levels of experience and expertise were full participants in legitimate and meaningful praxis. They were not relegated to skill-drill-and-kill work; instead meaningful discourse and practice were both the means and the ends to critical literacy. (See Gutierrez, 1993, for a comparison of the effects of various contexts for learning on bicultural children.)

In these more democratic classrooms, there were zones of possibility for both teachers and students to dialogue, to pose critical questions, to coconstruct both process and product. Both teachers and students were critical ethnographers in both their classrooms and surrounding communities. In this way, the curriculum of the classroom relied on "funds of knowledge" that existed in children's families, social networks, and communities. (See Moll, 1990, for more discussion of the notion of "funds of knowledge" in Chicano communities.) Literacy learning, then, necessarily addressed the lived experiences of children. While it is true that these classrooms had not resolved issues of power relations, racism, and sexism, these were themes that informed many of the classroom narratives. In this way, I believe that responsive/collaborative classrooms set up the conditions for problem-posing pedagogy and increase the potential for radical pedagogy, for different representations of and stances toward knowledge and different ways of "doing and being student and teacher." It's an encouraging beginning. (See Marc Pruyn, 1994, for a discussion of the social construction of critical pedagogy in elementary school classrooms.)

As we develop new pedagogies for teaching the new student population, there is much to be learned from the struggles in ethnic, women's, and cultural studies. For example, cultural studies programs have brought together transdisciplinary perspectives and methods of inquiry to more comprehensively examine the social, economic, political, cultural, and historical dimensions that shape the lives of America's ethnic and racial groups. Thus, cultural studies reflect the intersection of issues of race, ethnicity, class, gender, culture, and power.

One of the central aims of ethnic studies has been to make visible the essential philosophies, cultures, and histories of ethnic peoples and, thus, to produce a complete scholarship that necessarily challenges prevailing Eurocentric thought and methods. From this perspective, then, ethnic studies is not the inclusion or integration of new themes or experiences into the existing curriculum; that would simply require studying new subjects through the same Eurocentric lens, rather than a process by which students, teachers, and researchers develop new forms of agency. Instead, ethnic studies seeks to locate itself in a much broader sociocultural terrain in which groups of color and women of color are integral to the understanding of everyday life in an American context.

Because ethnic studies was not conceptualized as an addition or an appendage of existing curricula, the development of ethnic studies provided the occasion not only to create a new epistemology but necessarily to become an occasion to substantively transform both pedagogy and curricula, to develop a very stance toward the production of knowledge. Curricular transformation, then, was not an inadvertent by-product of ethnic studies. Rather, the epistemological roots of ethnic studies were reflected in the interdisciplinary and cross-disciplinary nature of its methodology, in the content of the curriculum and its pedagogy. In this way, ethnic studies was constitutive of a coherent content, methodology, and pedagogy that allowed the development of curricula that focused on an examination of the interactions among particular groups of people and others and on the explication of these experiences within and across the total population. Transforming the general curricula for a multicultural student population requires the same processes. I would argue, however, for a pedagogy that does not promote an essentialist agenda.

I spend a great deal of time working with teachers and in the teacher education programs. There's so much to be done. This transformation is not about using the right materials, reform-oriented pedagogies, or celebrating ethnic life in the form of food, fun, and fiestas, or simply "retraining" teachers so that they become tolerant or sympathetic to difference. It's about developing a very different space for teachers, students, and parents in the educational process.

Peter: I think one of the biggest problems in establishing a criticalist movement in pedagogy on a wider scale than exists at present has been the pervasiveness of the way experience is understood and employed by bourgeois educators. There has been a strong tendency to essentialize experience, to view experience as self-evident. Some groups argue that there is an essential Chicano/Chicana experience, or Anglo experience, or African American experience, or gay experience. Personal history is spoken about as if it somehow affords transparent access to the real, as though it were removed from the effects of larger structures of mediation. This is to hold to the mistaken belief that experiences constitute some ordinary or foundational event. Identity is therefore conceived as an original authorship, as possessing the means to foreclose contingency and stabilize or impose a unity on the process of signification. It's my contention that in such cases the employment of experience as a referent for a transformative pedagogy needs to be rethought, because too often it leads to the reproduction of those strategies of containment, regulation, and normalization that one is trying to contest.

I've been in classes where students demand to speak from their own experiences and where the voice of experience for them is a license to render as the ultimate authority whatever they happen to "feel" about an event. Classes based on the privileging of personal experience and a fear of theory tend to degenerate into a forum for telling personal anecdotes or stories. Now I believe stories are extremely important, since they "narrativize" our cultural world in important ways. And life experiences are absolutely crucial to identity formation and historical agency.

However, as I have argued elsewhere (1992) (along with Henry Giroux (1992), Joan Scott (1992), and others), experience is fundamentally discursive. That is, we cannot separate experience from language and the conflict among and contradictions within systems of signification. Experience permits us to establish a system of similarities and differences. But we can never "have" an experience and then simply attach a word or concept to that experience. Because experience is always a form of languaging—it is always an event. A material event in the sense that language always reflects and dialectically reinitiates social relations, structural relationships to Otherness, and the world of objects and events. But it is always an aftereffect, too, since it is always housed within particular conceptual frameworks and can never exist in a pure state unsullied by ideology or interest. Experience, in other words, never occurs outside of its specific forms of intelligibility or signification. It always occurs in relationship to the normativizing power of social life and the exclusionary logics of dominant subject positions. All experiences occur within more or less established regimes of signification or meanings.

We need a theoretical language if we want to be able to interrogate the manner in which we enable our experiences to be understood and acted upon. Joan Scott (1992) notes that since experience is discursive it "is at once always already an interpretation *and* is in need of interpretation." She adds something very insightful when she says: "Experience is a subject's history. Language is the site of history's enactment." We cannot separate experience from language. After all, experience is produced by systems of intelligibility that help to recognize it as experience. When we acquire a new language of analysis we reinvent experience retroactively.

When my students discover feminist theory, some of them are motivated to return to their prior experiences and relive them through the conceptual frameworks of this new language and their experiences become transformed as a result. Confronting the often-suffocating and periphrastic values of the controlling patriarchal and white supremacist hegemonic formations often leads these students to new ways of understanding, of acting *in and on* the world. Students acquire a new form of agency. While experience is a linguistic event, Scott emphasizes that it is not confined to a fixed order of meaning. We read texts but are also read by them. But because texts read us—that is, install us as readers within particular discursive communities—this doesn't mean we are simply the dupes of our language use. Experiences don't determine our agency in the world but certainly help constitute it. Of course, to a certain extent our experiences are overdetermined by larger social, cultural, and economic structures. They are installed and constituted by signifying a chain of prior meanings and usages. Yet they don't determine our identities but often create the conditions of possibility for our ability to understand them and recreate them.

In order to make the experiences of the oppressed more visible and more central to our way of understanding the world, we need to be able to understand the discursive processes and practices that constitute our experiences and subjectivities. We need to be careful that our denaturalizing strategies (making the familiar strange and the strange familiar) do not recuperate whiteness as a foundational referent against which alterity and abjectness are constructed.

Kris, I'm growing weary of the banner flown by the liberals that announces that we must be merely tolerant of difference. This suggests to me that the Other to whom they hope to show tolerance is considered to be quite repugnant. Of course, liberal multiculturalism sees racism as some personal lifestyle problem and not a serious social and historical problem in which teachers must be called upon to interrogate the linkage of epistemological and social history as well as education and political culture.

We don't need a pedagogy of lifestyle tolerance. Nor do we need a pedagogy of attitude adjustments—the police carry that out successfully with batons and tear gas. We need to understand racialized discourse as complexly linked to the totality of discourses that make up our "empire of signs." We also need to understand how this linkage is reproductive of social relations of domination and oppression. In other words, our experiences are always constrained by conditions of possibility—systems of power that give significance to particular experiences. We need to transform these systems of power when they unwittingly give legitimacy to racist and homophobic social and pedagogical practices.

Critical pedagogy tries to contest the imperial and soverign discourses of the controlling hegemonic formations. It is a disintegrative stance, refusing to allow the marginalized, the immiserated, and the powerless to be absorbed into the cultural dominant. It works against the incrementalist position of slowing "adding on" minorities to the mainstream by creating spaces for the construction of minority voices *here* and *now*. It renegotiates sociopolitical space. It moves toward the direction of Goldberg's (1993) "transformative incorporation" by following an "antiracist insistence upon incorporative politics over some exclusionary social standard." Critical pedagogy strikes at the practices of oppression in their many guises, limiting and, where possible, eliminating the conditions of possibility for their ongoing production.

Kris: Peter, I agree with your analysis of how experience has been essentialized by liberal educators. What we're arguing for is not a liberal "I'm Okay. You're Okay" pedagogy. Instead, like Lisa Delpit (1988), we also expose the effects of liberal pedagogy on bicultural students. In our research, for example, we have identified the consequences that some forms of liberal reform pedagogies, such as the teaching of "the writing process" to second language learners, have on the development of literacy and biliteracy.

As I previously stated, in many of the classrooms we studied, there is almost no opportunity, neither in the curriculum nor in the participation structures of the classroom, for students' voices and experiences, in either written or oral form, to be affirmed and to become constitutive of classroom knowledge. There is little opportunity to build on prior knowledge and experience and, thus, to expand, revise, or challenge prior understandings of both the local and larger societies. Such practices are fundamental to development.

In our work, we also insist that teachers be theoretically grounded so that they can examine the local and folk knowledge that informs their assumptions about how children learn and who can learn. Simultaneously, we, along with other educators and classroom teachers, are helping to create a theoretical language to help us describe and critique the processes we observe in schools that affect both teachers and students. In a qualitative study with nineteen novice teachers last year, I gathered empirical data that substantiated what I already knew from my experience as a classroom teacher and my continued experience with teachers. When teachers are treated as intellectuals, are provided occasions for reflective and informed practice, and are assisted in developing ways of knowing and doing that are informed by theory, research, critical practice, and systematic observation of children in a variety of contexts, they begin to understand the political, social, and cognitive consequences of schooling, to understand how classroom culture is constructed, how certain contexts for learning deny or increase access to particular forms of literacy, and to understand the importance of developing agency and new frames of reference for both students and teachers. These teachers are not intimidated by research and theory; instead, they coconstruct the discourse of theory and practice. In this way, we are attempting to conduct research that has multiple agendas—that is, research that has academic, social, and political consequences.

NOTES

This interview session will appear in slightly different form in *International Journal of Educational Reform*, 3(3) (1994): 327–337; and in Peter McLaren, *Critical Pedagogy and Predatory Culture* (London: Routledge, in press).

1. I will use "we" to talk about this research because research assistants have always been an important part of the ongoing study. Assistants such as Joanne Larson, Marc Pruyn, William Saunders, Terese Karnafel, Cindy Tuttle, Tracy Rone, and Claudia Ramirez should be acknowledged for their contributions.

REFERENCES

Appiah, K. A. (1991). "Is the Post- in Postmodernism the Post- in Postcolonial?" *Critical Inquiry,* 17 (Winter): 336–357.

Aronowitz, Stanley (1993) "Paulo Freire's Radical Democratic Humanism." In P. McLaren and P. Leonard, (eds.), *Paulo Freire: A Critical Encounter.* London: Routledge.

Chow, Rey (1993). *Writing Diaspora.* Bloomington: Indiana University Press.

Coupland, Douglas (1991). *Generation X: Tales for an Accelerated Culture.* New York: St. Martin's Press.

Davis, Mike (1990). *City of Quartz.* New York: Verso.

———. (1993). "Who Killed LA? A Political Autopsy." *New Left Review,* 197: 3–28.

Deloria, Vine, Jr. (1987). "Identity and Culture." In R. Takaki, (ed.), *From Different*

Shores: Perspectives on Race and Ethnicity in America (pp. 94–103). New York: Oxford University Press.

Delpit, Lisa (1988). "The Silenced Dialogue: Power and Pedagogy in Educating Other People's Children." *Harvard Educational Review*, 58(3): 280–298.

Gates, Henry Louis, Jr. (1989). "Transforming of the American Mind." Paper presented at the Annual Meeting of the Modern Language Association, San Francisco.

Giroux, Henry (1992). *Border Crossings: Cultural Workers and the Politics of Education*. New York: Routledge, Chapurca & Hall.

Goldberg, David Theo (1993). *Racist Culture: Philosophy and the Politics of Meaning*. London: Blackwell.

Goodwin, Charles (1993). "The Discursive Constitution of Rodney King." Paper presented at the annual meeting of the American Anthropological Association, Washington, DC.

Goodwin, Marjorie Harness (1990). *He-Said-She-Said: Talk as Social Organization among Black Children*. Bloomington: Indiana University Press.

Grossberg, Larry (1992). *We Gotta Get Out of This Place: Popular Conservatism and Postmodern Culture*. London: Routledge.

Gutierrez, Kris (1993). "How Talk, Context, and Script Shape Contexts for Learning." *Linguistics and Education*, 5:335–365.

Gutierrez, Kris and Larson, Joanne (1994). "Language Borders: Recitation as Hegemonic Discourse." *International Journal of Educational Reform*, 3(1): 22–36.

Kroker, Arthur (1992). *The Possessed Individual: Technology and the French Postmodern*. Montreal: New World Perspectives.

Lave, Jean and Wenger, Etienne (1991). *Situated Learning: Legitimate Peripheral Participation*. Cambridge: Cambridge University Press.

Lefebvre, Henri (1990). *Everyday Life in the Modern World*. New Brunswick, NJ: Transaction.

Massumi, Brian (1993). "Everywhere You Want to Be: Introduction to Fear." In Brian Massumi (ed.), *The Politics of Everyday Fear* (pp. 3–37). Minneapolis: University of Minnesota Press.

McLaren, Peter (1992). "What Is the Political Role of Education?" In Joe Kincheloe and Shirley Steinberg (eds.), *Thirteen Questions: Reframing Education's Conversation* (pp. 249–262). New York: Peter Lang.

Moll, L. (1990). "Introduction." In L. C. Moll (ed.), *Vygotsky and Education: Instructional Implications and Application of Sociohistorical Psychology*. Cambridge: Cambridge University Press, pp. 1–27.

Ochs, Elinor (1988). *Culture and Language Development*. Cambridge: Cambridge University Press.

Pruyn, Marc (1994). "Becoming Subjects through Critical Practice: How Students in One Elementary Classroom Critically Read and Wrote Their World." *International Journal of Educational Reform*, 13(1): 37–50.

Rogoff, Barbara (1990). *Apprenticeship in Thinking: Cognitive Development in Social Context*. New York: Oxford University Press.

Ruiz, Richard (1992). "Language and Public Policy in the United States." In W. A. Van Horne (ed.), *Ethnicity and Public Policy Revisited: Selected Essays*. Milwaukee: Institute on Race and Ethnicity.

Scott, Joan (1992). "Experience." In Judith Butler and Joan Scott, (eds.), *Feminists Theorize the Political* (pp. 22–40). New York: Routledge.

Telles, Edward and Marguia, Edward (1990). "Phenotypic Discrimination and Income Differences among Mexican-Americans." *Social Science Quarterly,* 71(4): 682–696.

West, Cornel (1993). *Race Matters.* Boston: Beacon Press.

Williams, Brackette (1993). "The Impact of the Precepts of Nationalism on the Concept of Culture: Making Grasshoppers of Naked Apes." *Cultural Critique,* 24: 143–191.

Willis, Paul (1990). *Common Culture.* Boulder, CO: Westview Press.

7

Adult Education and the Politics of the Theoretical Text

Daniele D. Flannery

INTRODUCTION

Adult education has multiple purposes: literary education, community-based education, cooperative extension, continuing higher education for pursuit of degrees, continuing education for the professions for the update or change of career-related needs, worker education, and popular education that seeks to transform society, among others. Therefore, demands for life-long learning opportunities[1] and increasingly diverse populations of learners[2] present a major challenge for adult educators today. As a field, adult education can engage in an emancipatory pedagogy. This includes understanding the communicating, valuing, and knowledge-making differences of multiple cultures and enforcing a struggle against educational, cultural, and political efforts to reduce groups of persons to a single uniform cultural identity. Achieving this can work toward a radical democratic notion of liberty, justice, and equality. The question is, "Can adult education really engage in an emancipatory pedagogy that is empowering to different individuals?"

One of the values that adult education espouses is the empowerment of persons as fundamental to adult learning (Stanage, 1986). I argue that adult education can also be viewed as emancipatory. With that in mind, adult learning can "free people from personal, institutional and environmental forces that prevent them from seeing new directions, from gaining control over their lives, their society and the world" (Apps, 1985, p. 151). These notions of empowerment and emancipatory learning have been historically situated in the philosophy of liberal humanism (Elias and Merriam, 1980). Two major assumptions at the center of the teaching/learning exchange in liberal humanism are an emphasis on the individual as the controller, definer, and selector of personal empowerment; and an emphasis on behavior change as the sole domain of the individual. This focus on the individual demands consideration of whether adult education can continue to rely on liberal humanism as the basis for empowerment. Rather, it is suggested that an alternative paradigm, such as a critical postmodern humanism, is necessary for the empowerment and emancipation of multiple and diverse cultures in the twenty-first century.

The emphasis of postmodernism consists of border crossing (Giroux, 1992), voice (Orner, 1992; McLaren, 1989), narrative (Weiler, 1988), and similarities within differences (Kanpol, 1992),[3] which offer an alternative philosophical base for adult education. Yet postmodernism has failed to be seriously considered in adult education. The purpose of this chapter, then, is to connect tenets of postmodernism to adult education through the critique of present adult learning theory. I suggest changes in adult education learning theory based on postmodern theory that would enhance both the empowerment and emancipatory potential of adult education in general. In conclusion, I discuss the benefits such postmodern changes could have for multiple settings of adult learning in an increasingly multicultural society.

ADULT EDUCATION LEARNING THEORY

Three learning theories have dominated adult education: andragogy, self-directed learning, and perspective transformation. The theory of andragogy, the art and science of helping people learn, is based on the following assumptions:

People have a deep psychological need to be generally self-directing as they mature, although they may be dependent in certain situations.

Peoples' experiences are an increasingly rich resource for learning.

People are ready to learn something when they experience a need to learn it in order to cope more satisfyingly with real-life tasks or problems.

Learners see education as a process of developing increased competence to achieve their full potential in life. (Knowles, 1980, pp. 43–44)

The literature on self-directed learning grew out of the assumption in andragogy that people have a need to be self-directing. The development of "self-directed individuals—that is, people who exhibit the qualities of moral, emotional, and intellectual autonomy—is the long-term goal of most, if not all, educational endeavors" (Candy, 1991, p. 19). Further, Brookfield (1986, p. 25) proposes that the "exercise of autonomous self-direction in learning is the distinguishing characteristic of adult learning."

The research on self-directed learning emphasizes two domains of self-direction: "the process in which a learner assumes primary responsibility for planning, implementing, and evaluating the learning process, and the learner's desire or preference for assuming responsibility for learning" (Brockett and Hiemstra, 1991, p. 24).

The literature of perspective transformation as the goal of adult learning continues the philosophy of increasing personal growth (Beder, 1989), enhancing the learner's ability for self-direction in learning (Mezirow, 1981, p. 21), and adds a liberal progressive aspect of critical reflectivity (Brookfield, 1986) to it. Mezirow (1990), who builds on the works of Paulo Freire and Jürgen Habermas, introduces the concept of perspective transformation to adult education:

Perspective transformation is the process of becoming critically aware of how and why our presuppositions have come to constrain the way we perceive, understand and feel about our world; of reformulating these as to permit a more inclusive discriminating, permeable and integrative perspective; and making decisions or otherwise acting on these new understandings. (p. 14)

INTRODUCTION TO THE TENETS OF POSTMODERNISM UTILIZED TO CRITIQUE ADULT LEARNING THEORY

A postmodern lens focuses on the relationship of the self to the society. A more critical postmodernism deconstructs race, class, sex, and gender differences, and other power relationships. Critical postmodernism posits that individuals are more than the product of historical and social forces that are controlled by the dominant class (group) and that are further reproduced through major socializing forces such as family, school, church, and state. All persons, be they African American, Latino American, European American, Gay, or Lesbian, are viewed as being in "constant creation and negotiation within structures of ideology and material constraints" (Weiler, 1988, p. 467). Peoples' voices, shaped by their culture, their history, and their relationships to power (McLaren, 1989), are heard through their personal narratives. Specifically, critical postmodernism rejects absolutes of rationality, morality, totalizing theoretical frameworks, and practice. There are no "metanarratives" that are not themselves the partial expressions of a particular point of view (Lyotard, 1984). Society, inherently unequal because of the dominance of favored groups over the less favored, must be transformed. Therefore, critical postmodernism celebrates differences (Burbules and Rice, 1991) and constructions of social and historical conditions (Giroux, 1988). Furthermore, critical postmodernism offers hope to a democratic ideal, a process that accepts and empathizes with differences, continues to deconstruct existing meanings, and seeks also to understand common elements in peoples' lives and struggles against oppression and exclusion (Kanpol, 1992). Thus, "difference and sameness are in constant interaction with one another" (Burbules and Rice, 1991, p. 403). With this in mind, conditions are created under which persons are valued as diverse, where power is transformed from the domination of a few into collective action, where there is a concerted effort to live in respect, and where there exists acceptance and tension with sameness and difference.

An important goal that postmodernism has called critical pedagogy is emancipation and transformation through the teaching/learning exchange. However subtly, the true essence of any teaching/learning exchange emanates from the paradigm established by the prevailing learning theory text. I submit in the section that follows that the prevailing learning theory text in adult education must be radically transformed if the goal of critical pedagogy can be realized.

A POSTMODERN CRITIQUE OF ADULT LEARNING THEORY

Postmodernism views the forces of the individual and social, historical, political, and economic forces as intertwined (Giroux, 1992). Yet adult learning theory is not built on the premise of relationships of the person to society. Adult education scholarship and practice in North America have paid only lip service to social aspects of learning (Candy, 1991; Rubenson, 1989; Brookfield, 1986). Clearly, the focus of discussion, research, and writing has been on the individual learner and individual education (Merriam and Caffarella, 1991). *Andragogy* concentrates on the individual, views the group as unimportant (Tennant, 1986), and assumes that all people can or want to accept individual freedom in learning (Brockett and Hiemstra, 1991). Andragogy views learning as separate from the preparation of the activity. While creating circumstances for some cognitive and/or factual learning (Rubenson, 1989), andragogy doesn't really distinguish between individual purposes and the social consequences of learning (Griffin, 1983). With the above in mind, the *self-directed learning* literature also omits critical analysis of taken-for-granted assumptions about cultural, sociopolitical, and institutional constraints (Brookfield, 1986). Finally, because of the lack of critical postmodern critique in adult education, adult educators do not recognize that their efforts, while well-intentioned, accommodate institutional and societal needs (Collins, 1991). For example, instead of providing opportunty for optimum learning, the imposing of self-directed learning projects on the teaching/learning exchange is one way to accommodate a large number of students admitted to classrooms by institutional needs for increased financial advancement.

The emphasis of *perspective transformation* learning theory is on the individual, but departs from theories of andragogy and self-direction. Perspective transformation moves from a philosophy of consciousness to one of more communicative interaction with social beings. Unlike the other two theories, within perspective transformation, individuals are not fully aware of their own needs and best interests. Therefore, they are not self-directed. According to perspective transformation theory, self-directed learning occurs only when individuals are free to understand the context of their needs and wants from historical, cultural, and biographical influences, and are able to make choices from among alternatives (Mezirow, 1985).

Finally, what perspective transformation, andragogy, and self-directed learning continue to omit is that learning itself is not a purely psychological phenomenon. Rather, the epistemological structure of learning and knowing must be radically changed. Learning and knowledge must be acknowledged as a cultural phenomenon, intricately interwoven in the setting in which they occur. In reality, all cognition is dialectically structured by activity and setting (Lave, 1988), and hence the social cannot be separated from the personal.

In critical postmodernism, "all culture is worthy of investigation. . . . Furthermore, European tradition (White, patriarchal, middle class) as the exclusive referent for judging what constitutes historical, cultural or political truth must be rejected" (Giroux, 1988, p. 168). Prevailing adult learning theory is "elitist by nature" (Cunningham, 1988, p. 133), transmitting the dominant culture of Western, middle-class white male values that glorify autonomy (Mezirow, Darkenwald, and Knox, 1975; Rubenson, 1989, Clark and Wilson, 1991; Brockett and Heimstra, 1991). "In the process it reproduces the cultural system which, in itself is a force for the retention of the status quo rather than for societal change" (Jarvis, 1985, p. 139). As such, learning theories and learning activities that accompany them are value-laden political activities (Jarvis, 1986; Rubenson, 1989; Cunningham, 1988). Specifically, the three adult learning theories previously discussed promote this elitism in two ways. First, each of these theories is put forth as universal— that is, as representative of how all people learn (Flannery, 1994). But these theories are by no means universal. "The notion of individuality as a desirable personality goal is not universal, but is culturally specific and tends to be found in those cultures (such as ours) where high status is obtained by competitve individual achievement" (Keddie, 1980, p. 54).

Contrary to adult learning emphases, individualism is not equally valued by all groups within our own society. Learning for many women is interactive and collaborative (Haring-Hidore et al., 1990), or "connected learning" (Belenky et al., 1986). Persons of non-Western cultural backgrounds, such as Mexican Americans, African Americans, Native Americans, and Canadian Indians, tend to have learning processes based on communal values rather than on individualistic values (Pratt, 1988). Also, "working class culture places emphasis on collective values" (Keddie, 1980, pp. 54–55). Communal values include which knowledge is valued, how learning occurs, communication patterns, and patterns of working together for the good of the community. For among adults there is a need for explicit teacher direction paralleling reliance on authority and leadership rather than on individual autonomy or communal leadership (Hvitfeld, 1986).

Second, the proponents of these three learning theories have neglected to address the fact that diverse voices can, and do, express their learning habits and preferences. Among the missing voices in the adult education learning literature are women, who learn to keep silent as their meanings differ from those of men (Belenky et al., 1986); people of color (Ross-Gordon, 1990; Cassara, 1991); and people of varying classes (Lutrell, 1989). These voices are missing in research on learning theories, in the construction of knowledge about learning, and regarding what knowledge is considered valuable (Thompson, 1983).

In critical postmodernism, while persons must speak from their own histories, collective memories, and voices, they must also simultaneously challenge the grounds on which their knowledge and power are constructed and legitimated (Giroux, 1988, p. 175). Furthermore, forms of subordination that create inequities among different groups as they live out their lives must be called into question (Giroux, 1988). The three adult learning theories discussed here are political. They have governed adult learning and the teaching/learning exchange from a philosophical perspective of universal individualism. Yet neither the theory of andragogy nor the theory of self-directed learning has acknowledged that they are political, and that forms of political and cultural subordination occur through the use of prevailing learning theories. Although perspective transformation theory (Mezirow, 1990) does not acknowledge its political base, it encourages critical reflection on all social and cultural aspects that influence peoples' beliefs. However, perspective transformation ignores the deconstruction of history and culture (Hart, 1990). Hence, perspective transformation does not challenge forms of subordination that create inequities. People therefore do not have an understanding of the reality of the power that defines their lives. Additionally, perspective transformation does not directly criticize current economic, social, and political arrangements that are inherently tied to these distortions (Hart, 1990; Collard and Law, 1989). Clearly, even though perspective transformation describes true communication, it does not take place, because there is no mutuality and reciprocity where the powerful and powerless exist.

Finally, the goal of critical postmodernism is toward democratization, which is a process that accepts and empathizes with difference, seeks to emancipate and transform society through shared struggle (Kanpol, 1992; Giroux, 1992), and works to promote a creative tension of similarities. The adult education learning theories based on individualism and self-direction stress the importance of citizens who are informed, think for themselves, and participate actively toward a democratic process. The problem is that andragogy and self-direction do not allow for differences in learning, nor consider that the very theory and processes of learning may be oppressive, and hence are antidemocratic. Only perspective transformation promotes the rudiments of an emancipatory education that is based on praxis following critical consideration of historical and social factors that influence persons. However, even this is not enough. Acceptable action, according to perspective transformation, may be individual change of thought or behavior, which does not necessarily foster social change through collective efforts (Collard and Law, 1989). Hence, the liberal democratic character of Mezirow's ideas suppresses the concept of a critical postmodernism. Finally, in these theoretical adult learning texts, which ignore a democratic imaginary of difference and struggle for power, there can be no working toward understanding similarities.

SUGGESTED CHANGES IN ADULT LEARNING THEORY BASED ON POSTMODERNISM FOR AN EMANCIPATORY AGENDA

How must adult learning theory change to move from liberal humanism, with its myopic focus on the individual, to the critical humanism of the postmodern, which is a continual working tension between the similarities and differences of individuals, of cultures, and of learners? First, people must be understood as social beings. Any construction of learning theory must include both considerations of the socialization of individuals within their various societies, including the learning societies, as well as the historical and economic conditions that have influenced those societies. Learning theory must include an understanding of the institutions and organizations in which learning often takes place and their relationships to individuals and cultures (Courtney, 1992). Any attempt to put forth an adult learning theory or explanation of behaviors in the teaching/learning setting that focuses on the individual as a psychological entity alone must be critiqued as incomplete. For example, adult learning theories assume that if adults really wanted to learn (i.e., were psychologically motivated), they would. Yet many adults who participate in adult basic education endeavors do not succeed. Research has shown that students from minority groups are the least successful in the public school system, not because of psychological reasons, but because of the social stereotyping that exists in the classroom (Frey, 1993). If adult learning theories promote a classroom that presents the same monocultural environment of language, teaching/learning styles, and communication patterns, and ignore the influence of the social context from which the learners come, failure to learn may well be perpetuated.

Second, differences must be accepted without promoting competition among different persons, cultures, or learning patterns. Rather than the universal promotion of the theories of andragogy, self-directed learning, or a linear process of engaging in perspective transformation, adult learning theories must acknowledge that people and cultures vary in how they learn (Flannery, 1991). Universality must be avoided. Adult learning theory must include, along with self-directed learning, the place of other-directed learning, of collaboratively directed learning (Flannery, 1991), of community-directed learning, of global processes of engaging in perspective transformation, and other ways of learning that people and cultures use (Flannery, 1992a). For example, Latino culture promotes community through the reality of the extended family. Learning for Latino persons is likely to occur using community-directed learning (Ramirez, 1982; Ramirez and Casteneda, 1974). In Latino community-directed learning the problem arises in the community, is worked at collaboratively by members of the community, and uses methods, language, and communication patterns that are valued in the community. Obviously, to impose self-directed learning theory on a community-directed group would be inappropriate.

Third, in order for learning theory to "stretch the borders of the narrow circle of the self" (Bordo, 1990), it must become inclusive and give voice to all people and groups, allowing missing voices (women, working-class persons, persons of color) to narrate their diverse stories of how and where they learn, and about their values of learning. To give voice to multiple individuals and cultures, learning theory must also understand the social, cultural, political, economic, and historical constructs that silence and influence them (Weis and Fine, 1993).

Fourth, learning theory must be critical. Critical implies that all human interactions, including the theoretical text of learning that supports the teaching/learning exchange, must be viewed as political. This means not contributing to or sustaining the alienation and oppression of people or groups. The underlying philosophical assumptions of the learning theories discussed earlier are exclusive and limiting. Future critical postmodern learning theorists must agree on a mechanism to continually confront issues of power, control, and conflict. For critical learning theory to flourish, we must address the inequities that are revealed in the learning theories themselves in the production of meaning, and in actual learning encounters (Merriam and Caffarella, 1991, p. 281).

An example of both voice and the political is found in the following. Little is known about the multiple meanings that women attach to learning in their lives and its relationship to the concrete conditions of their lives. A study of women's learning within the context of leisure (Flannery and Freysinger, 1993) showed that women used leisure to engage in emancipatory learning. In leisure, women resisted definitions of themselves that society, their spouses, families, and learning settings gave them. Instead, the women used leisure to learn to understand who they were as women—separate from their roles, to be self-determined in their choices of self-expression, and to be free from the roles of spouse and/or mother.

Women's choices of self-expression included going to college week for women; learning how to weave, how to use a computer, how to be a landscape architect. Their choices emphasized seeking assistance from others. These were usually women who were friends or who became friends through the teaching/learning exchange. Their processes of learning were global and simultaneous rather than linear. Finally, the women's learning in leisure was described as freely chosen to develop the self and as "fun" by all of the women. This learning was juxtaposed with formal learning that was "not freely chosen" and described as a power situation in which the women had to learn what someone else decided and in the way in which someone else prescribed. Clearly, this study's results, as have many others, challenges adult education learning theory's universal adherence to autonomy in the sense of "rugged" individualism, the power relations of persons deciding what is good for others, and the power of gender politics as experienced by the women in previous learning settings. Learning theory must engage in "genuinely democratic communicative action" (Collins, 1991, p. 89). The following questions, adapted from Lather (1991, p. 84) are offered to adult education learning theorists and pedagogues in the deconstruction of their efforts and in the promotion of a truly emancipatory text and pedagogy:

- Did I create a text that was multiple without being pluralistic, double without being paralyzed? Have I questioned the textual staging of knowledge in a way that keeps my own authority from being reified?

- Did I focus on the limits of my own conceptualizations?

- Did I make resistant discourses and subject positions more widely available? Did my work multiply political spaces and prevent the concentration of power in any one point? Perhaps more importantly, did it go beyond critique to help in producing pluralized and diverse spaces for the emergence of subjugated knowledge and for the organization of resistance?

- Did I encourage ambivalence, ambiguity, and multiplicity, or did I impose order and structure? What elements of legislation and prescription underlay my efforts? How have I policed the boundaries of what can be imagined?

- What is most densely invested? What has been muted, repressed, unheard? How has what I've done shaped, subverted, complicated? Have I confronted my own evasions and raised doubts about any illusions of closure?

Changing the basic tenets of adult learning theory to a critical postmodern worldview will contribute not only to the democratization of the theoretical text, but because the theoretical text is the philosophical basis for the practical text of the teaching/learning exchange in adult education, the practice of adult education will also be changed. These changes will immensely benefit diverse learners participating in adult education.

BENEFITS OF CHANGES FOR MULTIPLE SETTINGS OF ADULT LEARNING IN AN INCREASINGLY MULTICULTURAL SOCIETY

Adult learning theories must engage in a serious paradigm shift. For an empowering and emancipatory agenda, the superficially objective liberal humanist perspective must evolve to one that focuses on critical humanism. In this way the construction of knowledge is everyone's task and is the product of many individual and collective social and contextual perspectives.

These potential changes in the theoretical and practical text can influence how adult educators think and feel, and thereby influence the teaching/learning exchange. Under a critical postmodern learning theory rubric, personal and cultural narratives of multiple groups can be included. A curriculum to this effect will reflect the multicultural society through academic thinking and language, reading requirements, teaching/learning exchanges, and research design. These more democratic learning approaches can include the imperative to "listen"; to become aware of one's biases, prejudices, and ignorance; to be multiculturally informed; to attend to the "multiple cultural crosscurrents that persons are likely to have experienced" (Adams, 1992); and to engage in an interdependence of theory testing and creation.

The role of the critical postmodern teacher will be multiple—a combination of critical pedagogue, and andragogue, and mediator. A critical pedagogue challenges, models, and confronts the social, political, economic, historical, and organizational forces that influence dominant and oppressive beliefs in and out of the classroom. The critical pedagogue offers an emancipatory "language of possibility" (Aronowitz and Giroux, 1985). As andragogue, the teacher facilitates a setting where teacher and students co-learn, believing that if truth is the product of multiple perspectives, it is the job of everyone. As mediator, the teacher works to establish respect, understanding, and empathy to encompass differences of all points of view and to establish true dialogue across differences. Finally, as critical pedagogue, andragogue, and mediator, the teacher is responsible for crossing borders in order to ignite "the nurturance of a new morality of non-oppressive, caring relationships among all the participants in an educational situation" (Hart, 1990, p. 126).

In conclusion, for adult education to be empowering and emancipatory in the twenty-first century, there must be changes in the adult learning

theory text. The changes must be border crossings of the making of knowledge by multiple knowledge makers, of differences, of ethics, of politics, and
of power. Also, these borders of difference must exist in an "unoppressive
city where there is understanding of social relationships without domination,
in which persons live together in relations of mediation among strangers
with whom they are not in community" (Young, 1990, p. 303).

NOTES

1. Continuing education for the professions has grown so that universities and
professional schools may serve from a few hundred persons to 40,000 persons a year
per school, while at least 3,000 national professional agencies provide educational
offerings for their clientele each year (Cervero, 1989). Forty-two percent of all students in colleges and universities were registered in the fall of 1987 were twenty-five
years of age or older (National Center for Statistics, 1987). By the year 2000 "75
percent of all workers currently employed will need retraining because of changes in
the nature of existing jobs or because of the creation of new jobs that will require
new and higher levels of skills" (Watkins, 1989, p. 429).

2. There is a growing and different ethnic diversity in the population. If current
trends persist, "the Hispanic population is projected to further increase 21%, the
Asian presence about 22%, African Americans almost 12% and Anglo Saxon Americans a little more than 2% when the 20th century ends" (Henry, 1990, p. 28). There
is diversity in the workforce. For the first time in U.S. history, demographic profiles
of the workforce indicate that white males are the minority—only 46 percent (Copeland, 1988). Racial and ethnic minorities are projected to constitute 29 percent of
labor force entrants between now and the year 2000, twice the current percentage
(Goddard, 1989). "There is diversity of educational levels based upon race with the
gap between the educational achievements of the majority populations and those of
most minorities widening at an alarming rate" (Briscoe and Ross, 1989, p. 584). In
1986, 64.4 percent of African Americans, 50.6 percent of Hispanics, and 76.8 percent of Anglo-Saxon Americans had completed high school (National Center for
Education Statistics, 1988). There is a growing age diversity. The average age of
European Americans, who have more education, is increasing. The average age of
the minority population, who are less well educated, is decreasing.

3. To me, there are two major processes in postmodernism. The first is border
crossing; the second is sustaining a communication between differences and similarities.

Border crossing is facing the boundaries we as individuals and groups have erected
over time with regard to other individuals and other groups. Border crossing involves
three primary activities: trying to get to know others as they want to be known;
deconstructing the historically and socially constructed meanings we have that exist
based on power of a group of people over any other group of people; and celebrating
human differences and diversity by encouraging narratives. Narratives are the life
stories of people set in the socioeconomic and historical meaning structures of their
lives. These life stories can be garnered by considering "text"—that is, those aspects
external to individuals that have impinged on their lives—and by listening to "voice,"

the personal stories individuals tell in their own language and with their own meanings.

Sustaining a communication between differences and similarities is the ongoing and fluid effort to respect plurality of meaning and to join in a transformative stance that seeks to work for common purposes of freedom from invisibility, alienation, and oppression.

REFERENCES

Adams, M. (1992). "Cultural Inclusion in the American College Classroom." In K. B. Border and N. Van Note Chism (eds.), *Teaching for Diversity* (New Directions for Teaching and Learning, No. 49) (pp. 5–18). San Francisco: Jossey-Bass.

Apps, J. W. (1985). *Improving Practice in Continuing Education.* San Francisco: Jossey-Bass.

Aronowitz, S. and Giroux, H. (1985). *Education under Siege.* South Hadley, MA: Bergin & Garvey.

Beder, H. (1989). "The Purposes and Philosophies of Adult Education." In S. B. Merriam and P. M. Cunningham (eds.), *Handbook of Adult and Continuing Education* (pp. 37–50). San Francisco: Jossey-Bass.

Belenky, M. F., Clinchy, B. M., Goldberger, N. R., and Tarule, J. (1986). *Women's Ways of Knowing: The Development of Self, Voice and Mind.* New York: Basic Books.

Bordo, S. (1990). "Feminism, Postmodernism and Gender-Skepticism." In L. J. Nicholson (ed.), *Feminism/Postmodernism* (pp. 133–156). New York: Routledge.

Briscoe, D. B. and Ross, J. M. (1989). "Racial and Ethnic Minorities and Adult Education." In S. B. Merriam and P. M. Cunningham (eds.), *Handbook of Adult and Continuing Education* (pp. 583–598). San Francisco: Jossey-Bass.

Brockett, R. G. and Hiemstra, R. (1991). *Self-direction in Adult Learning: Perspectives on Theory, Research, and Practice.* London: Routledge.

Brookfield, S. D. (1986). *Understanding and Facilitating Adult Learning.* San Francisco: Jossey-Bass.

Burbules, N. C. and Rice, S. (1991). "Dialogue across Differences: Continuing the Conversation." *Harvard Educational Review,* 61(4): 393–416.

Candy, P. C. (1991). *Self-direction for Lifelong Learning.* San Francisco: Jossey-Bass.

Cassara, B. B. (1991). *Adult Education in a Multicultural Society.* London: Routledge.

Cervero, R. M. (1989). "Continuing Education for the Professions." In S. B. Merriam and P. M. Cunningham (eds.), *Handbook of Adult and Continuing Education* (pp. 513–524). San Francisco: Jossey-Bass.

Clark, M. C. and Wilson, A. L. (1991). "Context and Rationality in Mezirow's Theory of Transformational Learning." *Adult Education Quarterly,* 41(2): 75–91.

Collard, S. and Law, M. (1989). "The Limits of Perspective Transformation: A Critique of Mezirow's Theory." *Adult Education Quarterly,* 39(2): 99–107.

Collins, M. (1991). *Adult Education as Vocation: A Critical Role for the Adult Educator.* London: Routledge.

Copeland, L. (1988). "Learning to Manage the Multicultural Work Force." *Training*, 25:49–56.

Courtney, S. (1992). *Why Adults Learn: Towards a Theory of Participation in Adult Education*. London: Routledge.

Cunningham, P. M. (1988). "The Adult Educator and Social Responsibility." In R. G. Brockett (ed.), *Ethical Issues in Adult Education*. New York: Teachers College Press.

Elias, J. L. and Merriam, S. B. (1980). *Philosophical Foundations of Adult Education*. Malabar, FL: Krieger.

Flannery, D. D. (1994). "Changing Dominant Understandings of Adults as Learners." In S. Colin III and E. Hayes (eds.), *Confronting Racism and Sexism in Adult and Continuing Education* (New Directions for Adult and Continuing Education, No. 61) (pp. 17–26). San Francisco: Jossey-Bass.

———. (1992a). "Towards an Understanding and Implementation of Culturally Diverse Learning Styles." *Community Education Journal*, 19(4): 10–12.

———. (1992b). Book Review: R. Brockett, and R. Hiemstra (1991). Self-direction in Adult Learning. *Adult Education Quarterly*, 43(2): 110–112.

———. (1991). "Adult Education: Little Boxes All the Same?" *Adult Learning* 3(3): 31.

Flannery, D. D. and Freysinger, V. J. (1993). "Learning in the Context of Leisure." Manuscript under review.

Frey, J. F. (1993). "A Legacy of Cultural, Social and Linguistic Hegemony in Education: Understanding the Adult Learner's Educational Past." *PAACE Journal of Lifelong Learning*, 2: 33–48.

Giroux, H. A. (1988). "Border Pedagogy in the Age of Postmodernism." *Journal of Education*, 170(3): 162–181.

———. (1992). *Border Crossings: Cultural Workers and the Politics of Education*. London: Routledge.

Goddard, R. W. (1989). "Work Force 2000. *Personnel Journal*, 68(2): 65–71.

Griffin, C. (1983). *Curriculum Theory in Adult and Lifelong Education*. London: Croom Helm.

Haring-Hidore, M., Freeman, S. C., Phelps, S., Spann, N. G., and Wooten, H. R. Jr. (1990). "Women Administrators' Ways of Knowing." *Education and Urban Society*, 22(2): 170–181.

Hart, M. (1990). "Critical Theory and Beyond: Further Perspectives on Emancipatory Education." *Adult Education Quarterly*, 40: 125–138.

Henry, W. A. (1990). "Beyond the Melting Pot." *Time*, April 9, 1990, pp. 28–31.

Hvitfeld, C. (1986). "Traditional Culture, Perceptual Style and Learning: The Classroom Behavior of Hmong Adults." *Adult Education Quarterly*, 36(2):65–77.

Jarvis, P. (1985). *The Sociology of Adult and Continuing Education*. London: Croom Helm.

———. (1986). *Adult Learning in the Social Context*. London: Croom Helm.

Kanpol, B. (1992). *Towards a Theory and Practice of Teacher Cultural Politics: Continuing the Postmodern Debate*. Norwood, NJ: Ablex.

Keddie, N. (1980). "Adult Education: An Ideology of Individualism." In J. L. Thompson (ed.), *Adult Education for a Change*. London: Hutchinson.

Knowles, M. (1980). *The Modern Practice of Adult Education: Andragogy versus Pedagogy*. New York: Association Press.

Lather, P. (1991). *Getting Smart: Feminist Research and Pedagogy with/in the Postmodern*. New York: Routledge.

Lave, J. (1988). *Cognition in Practice: Mind, Mathematics and Culture in Everyday Life*. Cambridge: Cambridge University Press.

Lutrell, W. (1989). "Working-class Women's Ways of Knowing: Effects of Gender, Race and Class." *Sociology of Education*, 62:33–46.

Lyotard, J. F. (1984). *The Postmodern Condition: A Report on Knowledge*. Minneapolis: University of Minnesota Press.

McLaren, P. (1989). *Life in Schools*. New York: Longman.

Merriam, S. B. and Caffarella, R. S. (1991). *Learning in Adulthood*. San Francisco: Jossey-Bass.

Mezirow, J. (1981). "A Critical Theory of Adult Learning and Education." *Adult Education*, 32(1): 3–27.

———. (1985). "A Critical Theory of Self-directed Learning." In S. Brookfield, (ed.), *Self-Directed Learning: From Theory to Practice* (New Directions for Continuing Education, No. 25) (pp. 17–30). San Francisco: Jossey-Bass.

———. (1990). "How Critical Reflection Triggers Transformative Learning." In J. Mezirow & Associates, *Fostering Critical Reflection in Adulthood: A Guide to Transformative and Emancipatory Learning* (pp. 1–20). San Francisco: Jossey-Bass.

Mezirow, J., Darkenwald, G. and Knox, A. (1975). *Last Gamble on Education*. Washington, DC: Adult Education Association.

National Center for Education Statistics. *1988 Digest of Education Statistics*. Office of Educational Research and Improvement and the National Center for Education Statistics. Washington, DC: U.S. Government Printing Office, 1988.

Orner, M. (1992). "Interrupting the Calls for Student Voice in "Liberatory" Education: A Feminist Poststructuralist Perspective." In C. Luke and J. Gore (eds.), *Feminism and Critical Pedagogy* (pp. 74–89). London: Routledge.

Pratt, P. (1988). "Cross-cultural Relevance of Selected Psychological Perspectives on Learning." In M. Zukas (ed.), *Proceedings of Transatlantic Dialogue: A Research Exchange*. Leeds: University of Leeds.

Ramirez, M. (1982). "Cognitive Styles and Cultural Diversity." Paper presented at the Annual Meeting of the American Educational Research Association (ERIC document ED 218 380).

Ramirez, M. and Casteneda, A. (1974). *Cultural Democracy, Bicognitive Development, and Education*. New York: Academic Press.

Ross-Gordon, J. M. (1990). "Serving Culturally Diverse Populations: A Social Imperative for Adult and Continuing Education." In J. M. Ross-Gordon, L. G. Martin, and D. B. Briscoe (eds.), *Serving Culturally Diverse Populations* (New Directions for Adult and Continuing Education, No. 48) (pp. 5–15). San Francisco: Jossey-Bass.

Rubenson, K. (1989). "The Sociology of Adult Education." In S. B. Merriam and R. S. Caffarella (eds.), *Handbook of Adult and Continuing Education* (pp. 51–69). San Francisco: Jossey-Bass.

Stanage, S. M. (1986). "Unrestraining Liberty: Adult Education and the Empowerment of Persons." *Adult Education Quarterly* 36(3): 123–129.

Tennant, M. (1986). "An Evaluation of Knowles' Theory of Adult Learning." *International Journal of Lifelong Education*, 5: 113–122.

Thompson, J. L. (ed.) (1983). *Learning Liberation: Women's Response to Men's Education*. London: Croom Helm.

Young, I. M. (1990). "The Ideal of Community and the Politics of Difference." In L. J. Nicholson (ed.), *Feminism/Postmodernism* (pp. 300–323). New York: Routledge.

Watkins, K. E. (1989). "Business and Industry." In S. B. Merriam and P. Cunningham (eds.), *Handbook of Adult and Continuing Education* (pp. 422–435). San Francisco: Jossey-Bass.

Weiler, K. (1988). *Women Teaching for Change: Gender, Class and Power*. South Hadley, MA: Bergin & Garvey.

Weis, L. and Fine, M. (1993). *Beyond Silenced Voices: Class, Race and Gender in United States Schools*. Albany: State University of New York Press.

8

Learning the Hard Way: Maria's Story

Bonny Norton Peirce

Everybody is aware of how people look at Thompson. It doesn't bother
some people. Me, on the other hand, it really bugs me. I don't like to
be judged because my parents are from Italy. I deserve the same respect
as anybody else. I'm not saying I'm better. I want to be considered an
equal.

Maria Sabatini

In June 1990, a board of education in a predominantly Anglo-Saxon town
in the province of Ontario, Canada, closed down a secondary school in a
neighborhood populated mainly by people of Italian and Portuguese heritage. For two years prior to the closing of this school, the students at the
school took a range of actions in their struggle to keep the school open.
Primarily through the voice of one of the senior students in the school,
Maria Sabatini (a pseudonym), this chapter documents the actions by the
local school board to secure powerful Anglo-Saxon interests in the town at
the expense of the less powerful Italian community. This chapter explores
Maria's ambivalent responses to her Italian culture and history, particularly
as they relate to her experience of schooling in multicultural Canada. In
giving voice to Maria's experiences, the chapter addresses the social and
historical context in which Maria's narrative unfolds, the particular circumstances that led to the marginalization of Maria's school in the local community, and the extent to which Maria's school paradoxically represented a
place of refuge and possibility for her. Data for this chapter were collected

from interviews with the students and parents in the town from March to May 1989.

INTRODUCTION

It is difficult to do justice to Maria Sabatini's story. It is a narrative that links identity formation, schooling, work, language, culture, and community into a complex web that defies neat analysis. But it is a story that must be told if educators wish to understand how schools and communities impact on the social identities of students and the daily conduct of their lives. If educators believe that pedagogy should promote the enhancement of human possibility (Simon, 1992), it is important to understand why John Thompson Secondary School in Richmond, Ontario, Canada, which was closed down in June 1990, officially due to dwindling enrollment, was a contradictory place for Maria Sabatini. For Maria Sabatini, Thompson was denigrated by the wider Richmond community as a "wop" school, while at the same time offering refuge to Maria, a place where she could be whatever she wanted to be. In giving voice to Maria's story, this chapter addresses three different but related questions: First, what historical circumstances might serve to explain why a predominantly Italian school in multicultural Canada was marginalized in the Richmond community? Second, how did John Thompson Secondary School come to represent a place of possibility for Maria Sabatini? Third, how can the closing of Thompson inform our understanding of the ways in which relations of power structure and are structured by dominant and subordinate group relations in Canadian society? The three sections of this chapter address each of these questions in turn.

THE HISTORY OF JOHN THOMPSON SECONDARY SCHOOL, 1962–90

In order to understand the marginalization of John Thompson Secondary School within the wider community, it is necessary to examine the time/space location of the school in the town of Richmond. The years 1956 and 1961 are particularly significant. In 1956 a multinational company opened a large manufacturing plant on the outskirts of the sleepy town of Richmond, Ontario. The opening of the plant had a major impact on the economy of the town, accelerating its growth and providing employment for hundreds of European immigrants entering Canada after the ravages of World War II. The character of the predominantly Anglo-Saxon town changed as immigrants arrived from different European countries, particularly Italy and Portugal. While most of the original town of Richmond was settled on the south side of town, the new immigrants settled primarily on the north side of town.

As the population of the town increased, so did the need for new schools.

The majority of the elementary schools in Richmond were built between 1955 and 1962, and by 1956 there was a growing need for more secondary school accommodation. The only secondary school in Richmond was Richmond High, to the south of the town. In 1957 Northern High was opened by the Winchester School Board, which had jurisdiction over all the non-Catholic schools in the Richmond area. Northern High, however, was at some distance from the area densely populated by the Italian and Portuguese communities. By 1959 there was talk of another secondary school being built, named for a well-known local educator, John Thompson.

While members of the Winchester School Board were debating where this new school should be located, events on the other side of the Iron Curtain had overtaken them. In 1961 the Soviets sent the satellite *Sputnik* into space, and set the course of Thompson's history. According to a teacher who had taught at Thompson for twenty-five years, the launching of *Sputnik* threw federal and provincial governments into a panic over Canada's technical education capabilities. The Federal-Provincial Technical and Vocational Training agreement was struck and federal grants were suddenly available to school boards across Canada to cover 75 percent of the construction and equipment costs for composite schools. Thompson was to be Richmond's first school of this kind, embracing a complete program of academic, commercial, and technical education, and it was to be located in the heart of the town's immigrant Italian and Portuguese communities.

According to a student leader who vigorously opposed the closure of Thompson, the historical foundations of the school led to its marginalization within the Richmond community. He noted that the particular ethnic composition of the school and its technical orientation doomed it from the start. One parent indicated that a school with a technical orientation would never be highly regarded in the wider Richmond community. Another parent indicated that Thompson was a vulnerable school in Richmond because it served a community of first-generation Canadians who did not play a large role in the politics of the town. New Canadians, he said, would not tell the chairman of the board to "jump in the lake." The thinly veiled disdain for Thompson had not escaped Maria Sabatini.

Everyone I talk to, I tell them I go to Thompson High School. It's like "Oh, the wop school." It's just so annoying—"the wop school." They refer to us as "the wops"—immigrants without papers—that's what they call Italian people around here. You would not believe the remarks I get around here.

According to Maria, the marginalization of Thompson Secondary School was perpetuated by the subtle practices of people who worked in the interests of the dominant Anglo-Saxon community. She provided two examples, given below, to support her position. The first example documents how teachers in other schools in Richmond denigrated Thompson Secondary

School. For teachers in predominantly Anglo-Saxon schools in Richmond, the equation was clear: Italian = immigrant = "a bad name." The second example portrays how people with whom Maria came into contact during her part-time work at a local store in Richmond labeled and marginalized her as soon as they were aware of her background and the school she attended.

Example 1

OK. I know a family member that supplied [substituted] at Richmond High School. All the teachers were saying, "Oh, Thompson is such an immigrant school." She went to Thompson High School—she was Italian. She couldn't say anything because she was a supply teacher. She didn't want to get herself in—in a bad name—how can you say? But she couldn't believe it that another—even teachers, not kids—but teachers themselves were saying it. And of course students are going to think that way if teachers think that way.

Example 2

A lot of people have said it in front of my face. For example, I worked with a lady— I don't think she knew I was Italian yet—and she asked me: "So what grade are you in?" "13." I think she asked me what my background was. I said, "Italian." She said, "Oh. So what school do you go to?" I said, "Thompson High School." She said, "Ooooh." Just the way she said it. "So I guess you're not going to university, right?" She said that. She's a WASP, from Middleton. I thought that was mighty rude.

Over time, the school was framed as academically inferior to other Richmond schools. As Maria said:

They think it's easier if you can get an 80 average at Thompson. I used to work with some people [who would say] like "Our classes are harder than your classes. So, if you get higher marks, that doesn't mean anything." If we all have the same course, how can our courses be easier if the Winchester Board tells us what to teach? That's what I don't understand.

Thompson was established by the Winchester Board of Education in 1962 because the dominant Anglo-Saxon community feared that it would not be able to compete technologically on the world market. Immigrant populations in Richmond worked hard to provide Canada with professionals, skilled tradespeople, and artisans. But the dominant Anglo-Saxon community chose to close the school in the interests of securing Ontario Ministry funding for schools in other parts of Richmond. As the needs of the dominant Anglo-Saxon community changed, the "wop" school became dispensable.

JOHN THOMPSON SECONDARY SCHOOL: HOME FROM HOME

In this section I will argue that Thompson paradoxically represented a place of refuge from the fragmented discourses that faced Maria in the daily course of her life by replicating the conditions that existed within the supportive environment of her family and her Italian neighborhood. Furthermore, I will examine how the Richmond discourse on Thompson was implicated in the construction of Maria's social identity. By Maria's "social identity" I reference how Maria understood her relationship to the social world; how that relationship was socially and historically constructed across time and space; and how Maria understood what possibilities were available for her future. Drawing on Cornel West (1992), I also take the position that Maria's social identity references desire—the desire for recognition, the desire for affiliation, the desire for security and safety. As West argues, such desire cannot be separated from the distribution of material resources in a particular society: A person who has access to a wide range of resources in a society will have access to power and privilege, which will in turn influence how the person understands his or her relationship to the social world.

Maria describes her home as one that is loving and supportive and her parents as having "a good marriage." Her mother in particular "tries really hard; she tries to be friends with the neighbors, she really tries hard, and if she can do anything for them, she'll do it." Her father had worked at the manufacturing plant before undergoing eye surgery five years previously. His limited literacy skills in English had prevented him from reaching the level of foreman at the factory. Maria describes her father as a man who had many experiences in Canada of "being made fun of" because he was Italian. "He resents a lot of people. And British people he resents very much because when he came to Canada, those were the people that really hurt him."

The family has been back to Italy many times and her parents have never thought of themselves as Canadian. They might have returned to Italy, but believed it was in Maria's best interests to remain in Canada. Her father's English is good, but her mother's English is limited. She has never worked outside the home. The Sabatinis participate in many activities in the Italian community: they go to the local Italian church, attend weddings and festas, and watch the multicultural channels on television. Maria has aunts, uncles, and cousins in the community. However, she tries to get involved in the wider community through a variety of volunteer organizations. In her home environment, she can be whatever she wants to be.

I'm the only child, believe it or not—in an Italian family. It's kind of hard being an only child because I'm like their one-shot deal. "If she doesn't do it no-one will." They would like me to go to postsecondary education—preferably university, but they have never pressured me. "Whatever you can handle, whatever you can do, you can do." They give me some advice. They don't know very much about the programs here. So I've decided things mainly on my own and with the counselor at school. He was a great help too, my counselor. We have other Italian people around me, where I live, at school. When we go to church, we communicate with Italian people that go there. There are others: British, German, too, Croatian. But we really speak to Italian people more because I go to school with their sons and daughters at Thompson High School.

As I questioned Maria closely about her experiences at Thompson, I had expected to hear that the staff were unsupportive, the headmaster ambivalent, and the students divided and alienated. Such was not the case. Maria's experience at Thompson was a positive one; in fact, it seemed to replicate the lived culture of her own Italian community. It is for this reason that I believe the school represented a place of possibility for Maria. Consider the parallel imagery that Maria evokes when she describes cultural practices in the Italian community and in her school, respectively:

My dad loves Italy. He adores it. He loves it because it's so—everyone is like a family—since everyone speaks the same language and since he doesn't feel out of place, right? He thinks it's great. Like I mean, you see people in the street, "Hi, how are you?"
I think the people in Thompson get along. We're like a family. Since we're such a small school everybody knows each other. And when you see each other, it's like "Hi, how are you?"

In both her community and at Thompson, Maria's heritage and culture were validated: in both places, she felt at "home." Maria could comfortably take up a number of subject positions within the school: Italian, Canadian, student, female, friend. The cosmopolitan nature of the school, the supportive faculty, and the limited number of students served to affirm a sense of community among both faculty and students. One student told me that Thompson had not been "ghettoized" into different groups; students of all backgrounds were made to feel at home in the school, and there was a good relationship between staff and students. Yet another noted that it didn't matter whether a student in the school was Italian, black, or green. "At Thompson you are accepted for what you are. And that's what Canada is all about." One parent explained how this school culture developed by saying, "When you have a mixed community, everybody is a stranger." He indicated that there was no one dominant group that made other students feel uncomfortable; it was what he called a "humane kind of environment."

Many critical accounts of the experiences of students from minority communities tend to focus on the way schooling is implicated in the marginalization and alienation of these students. Witness Peter McLaren's account of the experiences of Italian and Portuguese students in an inner-city Catholic school in Toronto (1986, p. 220):

The feelings which frequently surfaced from the students' engrossment in the instructional rituals were those of hostility and indifference. After all, a major purpose of the instructional rituals was social control. Rituals shored up a wall of densely packed symbols covered with barbed wire behind which instructional alternatives were kept in check.

Maria's depiction of her experiences at John Thompson Secondary School, which was echoed by other students and parents I interviewed, presents a very different picture from that described in McLaren's study. Such an account has an important place in the literature on cultural studies because it demonstrates that progressive educators need to exercise caution when making generalizations about schooling, culture, and identity formation. This case study suggests that schools in minority communities can become important sites of possibility for students, even as they struggle against their marginalization within the wider community.

However, even though Thompson was a "home from home" for Maria, both the school and the home as sites of identity formation could not help Maria resolve her fundamental ambivalence toward her Italian culture and heritage. She could not escape the struggle for ownership of the "Italian" label in the Richmond community. Within Thompson Secondary School, Maria was subject of the discourse on Italian: she could comfortably claim to be Italian, to have Italian friends, to live in an Italian neighborhood. In other sites, she became subject to the discourse on Italians. To claim ownership of the Italian label was to invite assaults to her identity, her relationship to the social world, and her desires for the future. The very source of Maria's sense of self-worth became the object of disdain. She could not find a subject position for herself as "Italian" within the dominant culture:

People don't judge you until they know what your background is, or what school you go to—my school especially. The ladies I work with are such a good example: I work at the Prestige. In my department it's all mainly ladies, and they're all either from Middleton or Richmond. And just when they ask me about my background and stuff, and just the way they look at me—I don't know—it might be in my head.

In her attempt to deal with her identity as a site of struggle, Maria frequently attempted to reframe references to her Italian culture and heritage. The kinds of contradictions that emerged in Maria's discussion of her background, school, and culture are evidence by such comments as:

My culture has a great influence on me—a very great influence on me—the way my parents brought me up. Because of my morals and values, I find that people that don't have a cultural—well not a cultural—not a European background—they think different than me. I find that people here, it's like they tend to pull back. Being raised in an European family I find that I like to hug someone and to kiss someone. People just think that's awkward.

Maria's frequent references to her culture as "European" in character was indicative of her ambivalence toward her Italian identity. Although she resisted being equated with Portuguese people ("people find that offensive"), she nonetheless wished to promote a notion of herself as "European." At other times, Maria saw herself as Canadian, sometimes as Canadian Italian, sometimes as Italian. Consider the following extracts taken from the data:

- I consider myself Canadian. I'm very proud of it too.
- I'm very proud to be Italian.
- The melting pot would be a good idea. But for some reason I want to be considered Italian—I don't know why. I think it's a good idea to have a melting pot. But my culture has had such an effect on me, I can't be considered just Canadian, I have to be considered Canadian Italian.

A fragmented and multiple sense of self was symptomatic of Maria's ambivalent social identity in the Richmond community. Within her home and within her school Maria could happily live with a multiple sense of self: the multiple discourses of Italian, Canadian, child, student, and friend were complementary. As Maria entered the wider Richmond community, she moved from the center to the margins of power and privilege. The multiple sense of self became fragmented and the contradictions frightening. And few would buy into the discourse of the European.

THE CLOSING OF THOMPSON: A BLOW FOR MULTICULTURALISM

In this section I will examine how the closing of Thompson can help to inform our understanding of the way power relations between dominant and subordinate groups operate in Canadian society in general and in Richmond in particular. This has important implications for schooling because the Thompson community lacked the political clout to keep it open. The three overlapping themes that need examination are linguistic, political, and economic.

Command of the English language seems to be necessary (but not sufficient) requirement for entry into mainstream Canadian society. Maria was very aware that her parents' lack of proficiency in the English language had marginalized them within the wider Richmond community. As she said, "Thompson is going to close down, right? I think people took advantage of our school because our parents were immigrants. The majority of people who go to our school have parents who are immigrants—who can't speak English very well. And I think that if it was a WASP school I don't think they would have even tried to do anything like that."

One of the parents in the school commented that the parents who had taken up the fight for Thompson had been the parents who lived beyond the borders of the Italian and Portuguese communities in the Thompson area. He said that the lack of proficiency in English among Italian and Portuguese parents had restricted their involvement in the struggle to keep Thompson open. Maria herself commented on the relationship between political activism and language proficiency: "When it comes to politics, they [my parents] haven't had that much experience with it. On the other hand, people here have always been involved. People who speak the language better have always been involved—have learned how the system goes. But my parents don't know anything about it—my father knows a bit."

John Mallea (1987, p. 48) has convincingly expressed the political role of language in the relationships between dominant and subordinate groups, particularly within the context of schooling:

The language of the dominant group is accorded the highest value and therefore it is its linguistic capital that is reproduced and legitimated in the schools. Correspondingly the linguistic capital of the minority language groups is considerably undervalued, downplayed and marginalized. Hence the language of instruction reinforces the more general role of language—one of the most effective mediators of relationships between groups—in helping reproduce dominance and subordination among Canada's racial and ethno-cultural groups.

The lack of involvement in political activity also has a sociocultural base in the Italian community, although this too can be explained in terms of historical relations of power and dominance. As Maria said, "I think my parents—European people—were brought up to believe not to fight against what the law says—you know what I mean. Just whatever they say, goes. My parents will fight for other things; for what they believe in, like family, cultural things."

E. Auerbach's (1989) research on family literacy in the United States also suggests that language-minority parents are alienated from educational structures of power in the wider society. As she argues, "The need to take on an advocacy role presents a particular challenge for low-income language-minority parents. They may, for cultural reasons, defer to the authority of the school, assume that the school is always right, or feel unable to intervene between themselves and school authorities" (p. 175).

When Maria told her parents that there were plans to close Thompson, her parents, although dismayed, had put up little resistance:

"Oh, that's too bad, dear. Is there anything anybody can do?" I said, "I think it's just political." Well, I'm very offensive when it comes to cultural things. I told my parents, "I think they're just closing us down because people won't stick up for their rights, the parents won't help, and because there's just not enough support from the public."

Maria's final comment requires further analysis. First, Maria clearly thought people would be within their "rights" to oppose the closing of the school, but believed the Thompson community would not exercise these rights. Presumably, Maria had faith that if people exercised their rights, they would have had greater success in their efforts to keep the school open. Second, she had also learned that parents can have a powerful influence on school politics, and that their absence from school politics will make the community vulnerable to subordination and exploitation. ("I think people took advantage of our school because our parents were immigrants.") Third, she understood that the wider community must share the interests of the Thompson community if the latter is to have any success on exercising its rights. However, Maria was aware that not only was the wider community not supporting them—it was actively working against them.

The lack of public support for Thompson can partially be explained by the competition for resources among different schools within one board of education in Canada. A characteristic of school politics and school funding is that a number of school communities within a region are always in competition with one another for funding, staffing, and facilities. The people who represent the interests of the various school communities are those who "know the system," who speak the dominant language, and who do not accept that "what the laws says, goes."

The attitudes of the dominant Anglo-Saxon community in Richmond, and the practices it supports to maintain its dominant position, fly in the face of the federal government's expressed commitment to multiculturalism, as expressed by Gerry Weiner, minister of Multiculturalism and Citizenship Canada in the Canadian Multiculturalism Act: A Guide for Canadians:

When the Canadian Multiculturalism Act was passed into law in 1988, it established that our multicultural diversity is a fundamental characteristic of our society. Gone are the days when multiculturalism was a side show for new Canadians and those labelled as "ethnics." Today's multiculturalism is about removing the barriers of discrimination and ignorance which stand in the way of acceptance and respect.

Maria was aware that the discourse on multiculturalism negates the lived experience of minority-language communities in Canada: "But a lot of the commercials you see are about ethnic people. They show commercials about Canada and different ethnic people. And it's like they're trying to say, 'This is an ethnic country, be proud.' But then you get the people themselves in Canada who just don't look at Canada that way."

While the Italian community has made economic progress in Canada, this progress has not translated to political clout. Maria says that her father believes the following:

Now he tells me: "The Italian people have made their stand." I think he means economically—like there are a lot of rich people here—but I don't think he means politically. There are Italian lawyers, and doctors and stuff, but there aren't as many British and—you know what I mean.

According to Maria, most Italians who have been economically successful have made their money in real estate and the construction business, "not really something you need an education to do." The only Italian people who get involved in the wider community are the wealthy ones—"maybe people respect them because they're rich Italians, they're not middle class or poor."

As suggested earlier in the chapter, the distribution of material resources in a society cannot be understood apart from the social identity of individuals. The people who have access to socially valued linguistic/ political/economic resources have access to power and privilege—which intersects with their relationship to the wider society and their desires for the future. The students at John Thompson Secondary School passionately desired recognition and validation in multicultural Canada. But they lacked the linguistic, political, and economic resources to insist that what they say, goes.

CONCLUSION

The struggle for Thompson was characterized by sets of opposition that are constituted in and by Canadian society: wop/WASP, ethnic/mainstream, subordinate/dominant. In many ways, Maria was caught in the crossfire between these oppositions. She simultaneously embraced and resisted the Italian label; she took pride on her culture but yearned for acceptance in the wider community; she saw her school as a place of refuge and familial support, but recognized its marginal position in the Richmond community. The lessons that Maria learned at John Thompson Secondary School were not part of the formal school curriculum, but they were lessons that Maria learned the hard way. Despite almost two years of resistance by students, parents, and teachers, Thompson was closed by the Winchester Board of Education. The Winchester Board did not choose any unlucky target, but a school that was indeed different from others in Richmond. It had a vision of Canada in which people from different ethnocultural backgrounds, with different income levels, and with different language backgrounds could nevertheless share in a project of possibility for all students. The lessons that Maria learned are captured in the words of Shehla Burney (1988:1), who argues convincingly that "official multiculturalism boils culture to curry, perogies and Caravans—excluding 'others' from the mainstream of discourse where actual power resides."

NOTE

I wish to express my gratitude to the participants in this study for their generous cooperation. In particular, I am indebted to Maria Sabatini, who spent many hours in conversation with me and offered valuable comments on an earlier draft of this chapter. I would also like to express my thanks to the Social Sciences and Humanities Research Council of Canada for its financial support.

REFERENCES

Auerbach, E. (1989). "Towards a Social-contextual Approach to Family Literacy." *Harvard Educational Review*, 59(2): 165–181.

Burney, S. (1988). "The Exotic and the Restless: Representation of the "Other" in Colonialist Discourse." Paper presented at ISSISSS '88, University of British Columbia.

Mallea, J. (1987). "Culture, Schooling and Resistance in Plural Canada." In J. Young (ed.), *Breaking the Mosaic: Ethnic Identities in Canadian Schooling*. Toronto: Garamond Press.

McLaren, P. (1986). *Schooling as a Ritual Performance*. London: Routledge & Kegan Paul.

Peirce, B. N. (1993). "Language Learning, Social Identity, and Immigrant Women." Unpublished PhD thesis, Ontario Institute for Studies in Education/University of Toronto.

Simon, R. (1992). *Teaching Against the Grain: Texts for a Pedagogy of Possibility*. Westport, CT: Bergin & Garvey.

West, C. (1992). "A Matter of Life and Death." *October*, 61 (Summer): 20–23.

Multiculturalism and Citizenship Canada (1990). *The Canadian Multiculturalism Act. A Guide for Canadians*.

9

Multiculturalism and Empathy: A Border Pedagogy of Solidarity

Barry Kanpol

INTRODUCTION

Over the last five years or so, an emerging body of literature on postmodernism and education has heavily impacted the theoretical constructs within which educational and social theory are associated (Cherryholmes, 1988; Wexler, 1987; Giroux, 1988a&b, 1990a&b, 1992; McLaren, 1988, 1991a&b; McLaren and Hammer, 1989; Lather, 1989, 1991a; Shapiro, 1989, 1991; Kanpol, 1992a,b&c, among others). Through the multiple uses of the concept of difference, these critical educational theorists have viewed how the constructions of race, class, and gender disparities exhibit signs of oppression and hope: oppression when these incongruities exacerbate forms of subordination and alienation, and hope when new constructions and cultural resistances possibly create new social relations which are not subordinating or alienating.[1]

I have argued elsewhere (Kanpol, 1992a,b&c) that if radical intellectuals cannot find similarities within their arguments, tension, conflict, and cacophony will subsume one of the dominant tasks of critical theorists—the liberation from dogmatic forms of reasoning. To focus on difference and thereby allowing it to divide and conquer as is so often the case with academics (Ellsworth, 1989; Lather, 1991a&b; Bowers, 1991) becomes a hegemonic trap—a form of facile relativism with little or no direction for solidarity so as to enable us (critical social theorists) to address the multiple forms of oppression inside as well as outside the academy.

With the above in mind, and as we move to the public school arena,

Henry Giroux (1992) convincingly argues that at least one way to create some form of unity, despite difference, is for teachers and students to operate within what he terms a border pedagogy, where both educators and students can rethink the relations between the centers and the margins of power structures in their individual and collective lives. Giroux argues that to create a border pedagogy would allow teachers and students to accept and understand differences that often include cultural symbolic codes, particularly situated histories, alternative languages, and multiple and varied experiences. This would provide the impetus for teachers and students to explore the multitudinous race, class, and gender configurations. Concurrently, a border pedagogy also requires educators and students to join in unity in a mutual pedagogy that crosses the boundaries of differences into a terrain of similarities and solidarity. Put simply, I speak of similarity in terms of common effects as they relate to aspects of subordination, oppression, and alienation that exist contradictorily within a *seemingly* democratic, yet capitalistic, society (Shapiro, 1990).

I have also argued (Kanpol, 1992a,b&c) that without understanding "similarities within our differences," public school educators, as well as radical academics, have little to cling to in terms of alleviating the frustrations of intersecting race, class, and gender relations. One aspect of postmodernism is clearly meant to redraw the boundaries of various cultures and their race, class, and gender relations. One just has to observe world events to understand that if, for instance, despite their historical, cultural, social, and religious differences, Israel and its Arab neighbors cannot both cognitively and affectively[2] empathize with each others' similarities of oppression, pain, and guilt, there will be little or no chance for creating peaceful relations. During the on-going unstable Middle East peace process, I keep asking myself: How does one develop *empathy* that allows for a unification of minds, a form of intersubjectivity, despite the multiple and clearly confusing differences between these particular peoples? Put succinctly, a border pedagogy would speak to a unification between centers and margins of power that include an empathetic incorporation of the Other's voice in an effort to seek similarities *without ever* losing sight of multiple differences that precede.[3] With all of this in mind, multicultural education becomes a central concern for me.

Over the last ten years or so, and within a particularly modernistic framework,[4] public schools have been influenced by the now standard notion that multicultural education is a necessary ingredient to enhance equity for minority groups. In academe, in general, the diversity issue has also become central to most institutions. Yet I sense a flare of ignorance in the on-going discussions about diversity.[5] At present on my campus, the diversity issue has become a question of course numbers, not the empathetic incorporation and understanding of others as the dominant multicultural theme. In the Harrisburg, Pennsylvania, inner-city schools, we see minority students subjected to what I consider a better depiction of multiculturalism than in the suburban schools. There is within the inner-city schools a movement to incorporate other cultures through activities involving understanding different dress and food and on-going experimental research activities about cultures among students. In the suburbs of Harrisburg, in predominantly white middle-class Anglo schools, multiculturalism is, quite simply, a myth. The assistant superintendent of an affluent school district commented that "we have an all white population so we aren't exposed to many cultures." This is sadly so due to a nondiverse student population. Clearly, the inner-city schools' population consists of black and Hispanic people, yet they still explore difference. Viewed in a different light, how can one understand differences or seek similarities as a border pedagogy, especially if these differences are not central to one's life (personal or, as the cause may be, in a particular district)? I would agree with Giroux (1990a, p. 10).

Multiculturalism is generally about Otherness, but is written in ways in which the dominating aspects of white culture are not called into question and the oppositional potential of difference as a site of struggle is muted . . . by refusing to identify culture as a problem of politics, power *and* pedagogy.

If educators are to continue to develop a critical pedagogy (McLaren, 1988, 1989; Giroux and Simon, 1989; Simon, 1988; Kanpol, 1992a,b&c), with what I shall later depict as a postmodern theory and practice of multiculturalism, both the theory and practice of multiculturalism must begin to include a notion of border pedagogy as a form of cultural politics that includes identifying and empathizing with differences as well as unifying similarities between race, class, and gender intersections. The concept of similarity within difference becomes central to such an agenda. First I will expand on these concepts, then connect them to a postmodern notion of multiculturalism. I will portray through my own particular research experiences (Kanpol, 1992a&b) how one may conceive of similarities within differences through a border pedagogy of multiculturalism. I will conclude with a discussion on how the above issue may effect a multicultural agenda.

SIMILARITY WITHIN DIFFERENCE AND EMPATHY

A border pedagogy of multiculturalism considers the concept of similarity within difference as connected to a view of what can be loosely defined as empathy. Traditionally, within a multicultural context, "differences are politicized into borders that define different kinds of people as antagonists in various realms of everyday life" (McDermott and Gospondinoff, 1981, p. 216). However, I have recently argued (Kanpol, 1992a,b&c) that at the base of individual differences lie the commonalities or similarities of oppression, pain, and feelings, albeit in different forms. For example, while all immigrants may share *similar* feelings of frustration with forms of acculturation (which may include personal insecurities, low self-esteem, certain paranoias, and, quite possibly, a low socioeconomic status), many immigrants, within their personal histories and various experiences, would *differ*. This could be evidenced by various immigrants being hegemonized by a patriarchal father and subservient mother, a matriarchal mother, or having differing illiteracy problems.[6]

Some immigrants may assimilate into a new culture better than others. A similarities within difference theme can clearly represent all groups, not only immigrant groups. For instance, some inner-city and even suburban schools that are racially divided possess their particular cultural forms, histories, and experiences. For instance, as a teacher, I bring my cultural capital to the classroom. This cultural capital will be different in many ways from the multiple cultural representations in any single classroom. Within a border pedagogy, teachers will simultaneously seek similarities within differences to empathetically incorporate the Other into social relations, as well as identify with those who have felt alienation and certain forms of suffering and oppression, even though our respective particular circumstances may have differed. In part, I am calling for the educator to recover her or his history and experiences that allow meeting points with the Other's history and experiences.

As a teacher, then, it becomes a moral responsibility to understand my actions as both oppressed and oppressor, teacher and learner, deconstructionist and reconstructionist, passive bearer of dominant ideologies (Eagleton, 1990) as well as active appropriator of counterhegemonic possibilities. While I can never physically, mentally, or socially be black, Puerto Rican, Hispanic, or Asian, the challenge within a multicultural society and a border pedagogy is for me, as a white middle-class male, to locate those intersections of race, class, and gender where individual and group identities are understood through similarities, despite the celebration of multiple differences. Similarities within differences would then allow for what M. Bakhtin (1984) calls a politics of representation or a multivoiced community. Under this rubric, individual differences can be celebrated as representations of particular individuals. It is precisely within community relations (be it a single school or classroom as examples) that an individual's voice can be represented in communion with others' despite individual differences. This opens up the possibility for a border pedagogy of multiculturalism.

Therefore, a border pedagogy that considers multiculturalism as essential for an emancipatory agenda will take seriously the concept of *empathy* in its cognitive and affective domain.[7] Empathy, then, can and must for this educative agenda be viewed within the subjectivity and intersubjectivity dialectic. Western thought depicts the subject or individual as

carrying overtones of segregation and willful arrogance. . . . Through their implication in the mastery of nature, individual reason and the thinking subject were part
and parcel of anthropocentrism, constructed as the quest for general human supremacy or species liberation. . . . As a result of these and related trends, the possessive
and manipulative traits of traditional individualism gained preeminence. (Dallmayer,
1981, pp. 1 & 2)

A border pedagogy that includes intersubjective traits presupposes that
interaction among individuals can be conceived of as a system within a natural world. An intersubjective border pedagogy calls for the binding of the
mental life of different others. That is, community consciousness, as a form
of multiculturalism, calls for a plurality of centers of consciousness enjoying
mutual intercourse, a "we-synthesis—the intentional interpenetration of ego
subjects and their transcendental life" (Dallmayr, 1981, p. 43). A border
pedagogy that begins to recount personal and community experiences has
the possibility of creating an intersubjective consciousness that transcends
dividing, cutting, and competing differences into an arena of mutual tolerance, celebration over difference and joy over unity, solidarity, and similarity.

Empathy, then, is reached through one's different subjective experiences
of racism, alienation, and various other forms of domination, combined with
an understanding of the dialectical meeting points of the similarities of these
oppressive experiences. Empathy becomes the border crossing (Giroux,
1992) where educators within their multicultural contexts recount and/or
recover lost moments in personal memories and histories so as to reconstruct
them within a similarity within difference framework of mutuality, cooperation, connectedness, and care,[8] despite the clear celebration of my whiteness, your blackness, and/or her femaleness, whatever color, gender, or age.
A border pedagogy considering the above begins to outline directions that
we may see for a deeper multicultural society.

POSTMODERN MULTICULTURALISM

In the broadest sense, postmodern multiculturalism is about an Otherness
that questions the potential of difference as a site of cultural transmissions,
where dominant forms of ethnicity, race, and power relations make both visible and questionable the varying struggles of different groups. Specifically,
postmodern multiculturalism does not only directly involve nonwhiteness,
but includes introspective negotiation by both Anglos (in their multiplicities
and fragmentations) and non-Anglo groups (in their various ethnic make-
ups) who will critique their "selves" and ideological configurations. In large
part, a border pedagogy of postmodern multiculturalism moves away from
the individual as the central figure (without losing sight of unique individual
talents and creativities) and, rather, steers us to a direction of a connected

individual within community relations that, in his or her construction, seriously considers the similarities within differences and empathy between individuals and groups, irrespective of color, race, or gender.

At this point, a number of political points should be made. First, teachers and/or students in a similarity within difference environment will displace what Giroux (1992) depicts as ideological expressions of a hegemonic theory of multicultural education. Technically, different learning styles and celebrating different, yet important, cultural events will still remain central to any multicultural education. However, these facets of an education will no longer displace the knowledge and power (Foucault, 1980) dialectic that smother race, class, and gender relations. It seems to me that a border pedagogy of multiculturalism incorporating a similarities within differences theme lends itself to a political expression of variance within and between individuals and groups that no longer view schools as innocent places, free from social and racial intrigue. A postmodern multicultural border pedagogy calls for educators to consider the multiple and always varying and displaced differences of peoples (both extrinsic, such as color, gender, etc., and intrinsic, such as the values, norms, rules, and beliefs that make up religious and moral platforms) within a context of reconceptualizing similarities of power, domination, oppressive, joyful, and spiritual forces that frame the dominant and nondominant cultures. It is here that the politics of pedagogy and voice become paramount to a multicultural society. Voice becomes a part of the "multilayered, complex, and often contradictory discourses" (Aronowitz and Giroux, 1991, p. 100). In a similarity within difference theme, the concept of voice is more fully explored, providing students with Other histories, experiences, cultural artifacts, and narratives of personal and Other cultures. Clearly, *Otherness* becomes central to a postmodern border pedagogy of multiculturalism. It is to this theme that I now turn.

MULTICULTURALISM AND OTHERNESS

Otherness involves the understanding, acceptance, and celebration of multiple differences. Giroux (1990b, p. 15) is insightful here:

Postmodernism has provided the conditions necessary for exploring and recuperating traditions of various forms of otherness as a fundamental dimension of both the cultural and the sociopolitical sphere. In other words, postmodernism's stress on the problematic of otherness has included: a focus on the importance of history as a form of countermemory; an emphasis on the value of the everyday as a source of agency and empowerment; a renewed understanding of gender as an irreducible historical and social practice constituted in a plurality of self and social representations; and an insertion of the contingent, the discontinuous, and the unrepresentable as coordinates for remapping and rethinking borders that define one's existence and place in the world.

Within the context of the above use of Otherness, much is made of the value of representation and difference, agency and voice, and history and social practice. Little representation, however, is made of the commonalities of voice,[9] representation, agency, and social practice. Clearly, it seems to me, a postmodern border pedagogy of multiculturalism must begin to re-shape thinking over fundamental extrinsic and intrinsic differences and social practices (especially those that are economically determined). Multicultur-alism must also begin to focus on a form of Otherness that intimates com-mon pluralities of struggles that within their collective identity consider a notion of democratic impulse or democratic imaginary (Shapiro, 1988; Kan-pol, 1992a&b; Laclau and Mouffe, 1985) as part of citizenship education.[10] Clearly, this form of postmodern multicultural education argues for the par-tial, the particular, and the specific viewed within a common framework of struggle for a just and more equitable society. It is here that the similarity within difference theme is *not* meant to be a claim of ultimate truth, higher authority, or master narrative. Within the context of a border pedagogical postmodern multicultural analysis, similarities within differences would allow for moments of representation of Others and a place for situating collective, intersubjective identities. Here, Otherness within multicultural education becomes part of a political project of multidifferences intersected with the empathetic incorporation of a deep sense of understanding similarities. While traditional multicultural approaches suggest helping to clarify, reflect, and evaluate separate ethnic identities (Banks, 1988, pp. 193–202), a more radically oriented multicultural approach argues for voice representation of similarities of identity without losing sight of multiple differences. The "pol-itics of representation" that T. O'Conner (1989, p. 62) speaks about would then include an intersecting border pedagogy of differences entwined with similarities. It is precisely this kind of theoretical fuzziness that makes post-modern multicultural border pedagogy such a difficult concept to grasp.

In order to continue and refine a postmodern multicultural border pe-dagogy's development, I turn to particular ethnographic-oriented accounts of its possible construction. In the following examples, the reader must keep in mind that I will relate two particular snippets of data within two different contexts: each instance can be viewed separately for what I have termed as border pedagogy multiculturalism; and the different instances in their to-tality share common border pedagogy postmodern multicultural traits.

Sarah: History and Empathy Connected

In a recent naturalistic study of mine (Kanpol, 1992a), in an inner-city high school with an 82 percent Hispanic population, five English as a Sec-ond Language (ESL) teachers were studied. Sarah, a tenth-grade teacher, exemplifies a commitment to a border pedagogy multiculturalism.[11]

Sarah was born in Egypt and has been in the United States for twenty-three years. She is so committed to her students that the principal comments: "She is extremely enthusiastic about helping kids, that sometimes she forgets to look at things within the context of the entire school."

One outstanding quality in Sarah is that she both cognitively and affectively empathizes with her students. Once an immigrant herself, Sarah is well aware of a new immigrant's assimilation problems. Sarah links her history to her student's lives:

Let me share something with you now that you are just new immigrants. A home is never the same once you leave it. Finding a new home is like transplanting a plant. This is what happened when you left Mexico and I left Egypt. Everything would look different to me. It doesn't mean you are going to be less in the new place. It only means you are going to be different. Don't forget your good qualities. Choose the good things America has to offer you. Then you'll be unique. This is how I feel. Just because you are different doesn't make you worse. We are richer because of our differences.

Additionally, Sarah connects her own experiences as a female to her female students' experiences: "I do encourage females and I've had a lot of success with them going on to do their own thing."

As I enter Sarah's class, I am struck by the large colored poster on top of the blackboard: "We take pride in the differences that make us unique. As individuals we find joy in the sameness that makes us all sisters and brothers."

Empathy is built into Sarah's class and is related to *one's home, differences*, and *conflict and empathy*. On one's *home* and the poem "Alone":

Sarah: What does a home represent?

Student 1: A place.

Student 2: Mexico.

Student 3: A place where you can feel good at.

Student 4: Where you can be peaceful.

Student 5: Mexico, I belong. Love and warmth there.

Student 6: I feel alone!

Sarah: What does alone mean?

The concept of loneliness as related to the students has great personal dimensions to it. Sarah empathizes with her students, commenting to them on the connecting aspects of *difference*:

Just because you are different doesn't make you worse. Differences make us richer—we have so much more to offer others. We share our differences and can understand each other better. By understanding our differences we can see in what ways we are the same too.

Sarah believes that *conflict* must be related to students' personal lives. She connects conflict with empathy for her students:

I give them a conflict situation before we read on conflict such as if we had a small house or my two ways of solving conflict are presented—fight or flight. So I say it's better to work things out and fight out conflict. They have many of the same conflicts when I came from Egypt. I am a role model for them. I also suffered . . . just like these kids. I was in a similar situation—had to make a choice—fight or flight. I know what they go through. I interrelate personal conflict with the general conflict they face every day. As immigrants they will always have conflict.

To exemplify her desire to deal with conflict, much of the literature curriculum that Sarah chooses has to do with conflict situations. In one of the stories ("The Lady or the Tiger") Sarah asks this question:

Sarah: What is the meaning of conflict?

Student 1: A problem.

Sarah: A problem that arises from what?

Student 2: A difficult situation.

Sarah: Very good, a conflict comes from difficult decisions.

After elaborating on the conflicts of the story, in which the students learn about plot, theme, characterization, and place, Sarah continues the intense interaction with her students on conflict:

Sarah: There's one thing very important about this story. What is it?

Student 3: She's an individual.

Student 4: She's independent.

Sarah: Oh, wonderful, yes, she did what she wanted. She was disobedient to her father.

Student 3: The king didn't approve of the relationship . . . his daughter and the slave.

Sarah: So what conflict do we have here?

Student 5: Inner conflict.

Students begin to understand the nature of inner conflict. Only a week later, Sarah connects this conflict to what a theory is:

Sarah: What is a theory?

Student 1: An idea.

Sarah: Is the idea always correct?

Student 6: No!

Sarah: Yes, someone has to prove it's right or wrong. Let's see, Christopher Columbus had a theory.

Student 7: Yes, the world goes around.

Sarah: Did people believe him?

Student 8: Not everyone.

Sarah: Then we have a conflict between what's right and wrong.

Through personal experience and her past history, Sarah is able to understand her students from their intersecting race, class, and gender formulations. This has important ramifications for a postmodern border pedagogy of multiculturalism, which I will elaborate in further detail in the final section.

Betty: Where There Is Difference There Is Hope

In another naturalistic study of mine (Kanpol, 1990), Betty, a fourth-grade teacher, was chosen for observation primarily because of her involvement and interest in global education as an important pedagogical theme. Betty is a very committed teacher. Her students are her life. A high percentage of Betty's students are Hispanic. Betty, who is also Hispanic, speaks fluent English and Spanish.[12]

As one enters Betty's class, what strikes the eye is the message decorating the front portion of the class wall: "The limits we have are those we set for ourselves." Rules are also noticeable: "Respect your neighbor, listen to others, talk and share with others."

Betty builds self-esteem in her students. She accomplishes this, in part, through a continual appraisal of a student's worth. At approximately 8:15 every morning, students shout "My Creed" at the top of their lungs:

Today is a new day. Today I believe in myself. I respect others and I care about my friends. Today I will work hard to learn all I can learn. I am intelligent. I am wonderful. I know I am very special. I'm glad I'm here and I'm going to make today a great day.

Additionally, Betty's class underwent an energy circle ritual. After the creed was repeated, Betty called the class to the front of the room. Betty comments to her students: "First we must have everyone supporting each other. Let's hold hands and give each other energy. Close your eyes. Now, pass the energy around, feel the energy go through you. We are now connected, we now have energy." Through these exercises, an atmosphere of building self-esteem and respect for one's peers became the dominant themes around which lay other themes.

Building of Self and Community

Within her curriculum, Betty decided to create a three-week unit group project, where each group was to be a different country. Asked why she used this form of curriculum (which strayed from official ITV, or Instructional Television program), Betty commented: "Some prejudice that I experienced made me want to know what others were like and why there's discrimination and so on. Our regular curriculum doesn't go into that stuff." While not discounting the ITV as a form of curriculum, Betty commented about her use of alternative curriculum:

The ITV is just the tip of the iceberg. The real teaching comes when I connect peoples of the world with the ecology movement, for example. I will do more simulations that could also be political. For instance, we will learn about some countries' hunger problems, and why we must do away with that. At the same time, while we work on these ideas, we do them in groups, for the purpose of working together and sharing ideas, accepting and understanding different points of view, just being a community.

Within the three-week unit, the concepts of difference, empathy, community, and competition were paramount.

Different Points of View: The Building of Empathy

Betty extracted student feelings about their viewpoints concerning other people in class and different countries. In one exercise, for instance, Betty placed different items on a round table at the side of the class. Students listed everything they saw from where they were seated. After five minutes the class met on the floor:

Betty: What did you discover?

Student 1: I can't see from a distance.

Student 2: That nobody's perfect.

Betty: Would you like to have a perfect list? How would you feel about not seeing everything: good about it; upset?

Student 1: Upset. Cheated because some people saw different things and we were all sitting at different places.

Betty: What would you wished you'd have done?

Student 3: I felt mistreated.

Betty: How could you get all the information?

Student 4: Look differently.

Student 5: Look for different points of view.

Betty: How many points of view are there?

Student 2: Many, at least two. You can see different things if you stand in different places.

Betty: Can you see everything when you are really close?

Students: Yeah.

Betty: What can you tell me about your point of view? What can change your point of view?

Student 1: When you look different.

Betty: If I put more makeup on or dress differently, does that change my point of view? What can you do to change your point of view?

Student 7: Use your imagination.

Betty: Can you learn to like someone and accept their point of view?

Student 8: Yes, by sharing with them your ideas, to take them as your partners.

Student 1: Yes, by working with them.

Betty: How do you feel about different points of view?

Students: (All together) Good!

Betty places a white sheet on the board and immediately asks her students for similarities and differences between people. After this exercise is completed, and numerous similarities and differences are mentioned, the conversation continues:

Betty: Are we the same?

Student 9: We all work.

Student 10: Poor people don't.

Student 5: We all have some money.

Betty: Do all people have some money? I want to know similar things. Not that all people have money.

In all, Betty teaches that members of the group will have different points of view and different countries will have different customs and habits. In closing, she comments:

You need to pay yourselves on the back, support and encourage everyone, and say "you're doing a good job." Remember, in this exercise we learn about different points of view, different countries. We don't just memorize the different facts about the countries. We must be on task and check our feelings, that everyone is feeling good about themselves. You all have important jobs to do. Let's go to work and do our research on the different countries.

Community and Competition

The sometimes contradictory traits of community and competition are emphasized in Betty's class. Betty comments:

I always break the class into groups in order to learn that we can work together. Many times, though, groups don't work well together and often I have to sit down with individuals and talk with them about why they aren't working well together. It becomes difficult for students to "stick together" as a unit. Many times, differences of opinion arise. Joshua is continually upset that he cannot do things his own way. He often looks disgruntled:

Joshua: Ms———. I want to do this my way and he says I can't.
Betty: Can't you work this out together?

When the situation gets out of hand, Betty motions to Joshua on more than one occasion. They perform a role-reversal ritual. Joshua assumes the role of the *Other* student and is asked to feel for that person. Over the following two days and more role-reversal situations, Joshua becomes a cooperative working member of the group.

Groups begin to compete with each other. Many times a group member from Kenya or Sri Lanka will wander to another "country" and check who has "the better project." Betty's main concern at the beginning of the unit, however, is expressed in her journal. "The groups are not yet bonded. These groups compete with each other and with themselves as well. To get bonded will be a challenge that will help us all."

By the end of the first week of student research, Betty comments: "I am a nervous wreck. I want this to work out so much. I can see groups beginning to settle down and bond nicely. I want so much for each child to feel successful and to do their part for their group."

By the end of the student research project, Betty comments: "I feel really good today. All the groups are really making progress and supporting each other. Of course, some groups are ahead of others and some children need to be directed daily."

As I move to my concluding remarks, readers should keep in mind: (1) The above data reflect different research avenues that share similarities within differences. (2) Similarities within differences (incorporating empathy) as connected to a postmodern notion of multiculturalism through ongoing (and never-ending) meaning construction is an indispensable (and ideological) postmodern trait and *never* final in its formation. (3) A practical platform is only as good as flexibility allows. In short, there is no final practical solution to incorporating a postmodern multiculturalism. I turn to these three concluding themes.

CONCLUSION: BORDER PEDAGOGY AS A CRISIS IN MEANING

Similarities within differences has guided how I view public school sites as places of struggle, hope, and possibility. The accounts of Sarah and Betty depict how differences are commonly both taught and negotiated, albeit in various ways. That is, the different research venues I visited can be viewed for both multicultural similarities and differences within a framework of a postmodern border pedagogy.

The two accounts exhibit how the female teachers share similar ideological orientations (women, minority teachers, teaching minorities). Both teachers use a "multicultural" pedagogy of difference to create empathy and care for the "Other" in their respective students. Additionally, both teachers allow room for student interpretation (and meaning-making) of a scenario (either the exercise of placing items in the room as in Betty's case, or an interpretation of a story with a conflict situation as in Sarah's case). Meaning is an open-ended construction related to students' feeling structures ("so what conflict do we have here" [Sarah] or "how do you feel about not seeing everything" [Betty]). By creating the grounds for empathy, both teachers *similarly* open the possibilities for tolerance of others, respect and celebration over differences, and hearing the Other (role-reversal games [Betty] or Sarah putting herself in the students' shoes as a former immigrant).

Put simply, what binds these two teachers (despite their different teaching assignments) is that their border pedagogy of multiculturalism depicts a crisis in curriculum meaning. Similarity within difference as both a practical and theoretical construct has created for these teachers and their respective students the widening boundaries of possibility and hope out of an older predetermined and closed view of a standardized curriculum or a prepackaged student stereotype.

It seems to me that a border pedagogy of multiculturalism that incorporates this negotiated meaning is always in flux, never predetermined, fixed, or in total control of the teacher or student. If both educational theorists and teaching practitioners (in academe and at public school sites) can similarly agree that differences (in their multiple race, class, and gender configurations) are *so* different yet can concurrently be part of a binding form of opposition to ideologically oppressive forms (sex, race, and class stereotypes, for instance), then teacher and student group solidarity over these differences may similarly take place as a catalyst to change at either school or higher education sites.[13] I would emphatically agree with McLaren (1994), who calls attention to meaning systems that are imposed on "Others." McLaren's call is to interrogate the culture of whiteness itself, in order not to naturalize whiteness as a cultural marker against which Otherness is defined.

I would also further add that a border pedagogy of multiculturalism would mean the interrogation of "dominant" (and, quite possibly, oppressive, subordinative, and alienating) values of any culture. This could mean, for example, an interrogation of matriarchy. Additionally, a border pedagogy of multiculturalism calls for introspection of blacks, Hispanics, women, and so on, and other cultures as markers and/or signifiers to negotiate similarity within difference. Perhaps Richard Kearney (1991, p. 180) sums this point up well. The task of postmodernism, what he calls a postmodern imagination, is "to interpret the images of the other and to transfigure one's own image of the world in response to this interpretation." McLaren (1994) poignantly comments that this involves transcending beyond Martin Buber's liberal "I-thou" ethic—that is, beyond the realm of face-to-face encounters and into the terrain of engaging a border pedagogy of multiculturalism that begins to engage "Others' " worlds in both a "language of social criticism and a language of social dreaming" (pp. 18–19). Here, perhaps, a "dialectics of difference" (Salvidar, 1990, p. 175) is a catalyst for engaging students to resist the absolutizing of their own culture (and personal subjectivity) as a closed and fixed entity (in its multiple race, class, and gender forms).

This is not the place to lay out a practical "how to" multicultural border pedagogy platform. I have attempted this sporadically elsewhere.[14] Clearly, however, no practical platform is final in its configurations, especially given the shifting identity that a border pedagogy of multiculturalism argues for. Given the dominating themes of this chapter, any practical platform must conform to changing differences (and identities) and similarities across these differences. For example, teaching English as a Second Language would do well to incorporate "different" stories in English that are represented by many cultural differences. Dialogue over cultural similarities could also take place, thus unifying modern and postmodern tendencies. Teaching Social Studies would include various historical perspectives, and multiple race, class, and gender positions on issues all similarly considering the notion of multiple differences as a guiding motif. History classes, for example would similarly point out how conflict has been *the* highlight of international, national, and local differences, and depict how these differences have been co-opted into mainstream culture. The list of what a practical border pedagogy of multiculturalism could continue.

Teachers and professors who undertake such an agenda as I have suggested become what Giroux (1992) has described as "cultural workers"— people who interrogate the dialectical Self and Other in their intersecting similar and different forms. Cultural workers explore multiple subjective intentions of Self and Other as well interrogate those intentions as a starting point for social transformation. Moreover, a "cultural worker" is a political agent who acts to resist forms of oppression, subordination, and alienation. Teacher introspection that dialectically views the Self and Other and Other as Self is the beginning process within which a postmodern border pedagogy of multiculturalism raises its shoulders. To avoid the essentializing of Self and Other becomes the politics and language of hope and possibility within a multicultural community. The two teachers depicted are exemplars of how this process might begin.

Clearly, there is a lot of legwork to be done. Postmodern ethnographers like myself must continue to regularly enter public school sites to search for continuing avenues that depict these multicultural similarities within differences. This is not a call for all postmodern educational researchers to agree how or when to conduct their research. This *is* a call, however, for these researchers to explore the notion of a border pedagogy of solidarity within a multicultural setting whose starting emphasis is a dialectical and ongoing hermeneutic inquiry of similarities within differences inside the context of Self and Other.

NOTES

1. For more on cultural resistance as distinguished from institutional resistance, see Kanpol (1992b).

2. The distinction between cognitive and affective empathy is blurry. Cognitive presupposes a mental understanding of the *need* to accept differences, while affective presupposes that at some time one can literally *feel* difference precisely because one has been in similar situations.

3. For more on this see McLaren (1989) and his discussion of the relevance of the concept of "voice" for educational theory and practice.

4. The distinction between modernism and postmodernism has been made elsewhere. In the sense I use it here, modernism refers to the positive enlightenment traits of equity, community, and respect for others.

5. McLaren distinguishes between diversity and difference: diversity is the mainstream liberal notion of pluralism—the accepting of others in general under common universal principles of equality and justice in which lies the illusion of the acceptance of difference. Difference, on the other hand, speaks to specific historical and cultural race, class, and gender multiplicities that avoid essentializing of Otherness into one pluralistic society. In this sense, difference is never essentialized, totalized, but, rather, new, emerging, arbitrary, and contingent. See McLaren (1994) for more in his second edition of *Life in Schools.*

6. For more on these statistics, see McLaren (1989).

7. In its cognitive domain I refer to the modernistic trait of understanding the *need* to accept a border pedagogy. In the affective domain, I refer to the postmodern notion of *feeling*, accepting, and celebrating difference through one's own subjective experience.

8. I refer here to a construction of the feminist argument that considers a *morality* of care and connectedness as vital to social transformation. See Gilligan (1982) and Lyons (1983) for more.

9. For more on the concept of "voice" and how it is portrayed in the inner city, see McLaren (1989) and Yeo (1992).

10. This democratic impulse or imaginary, argue Mouffe and Laclau, arises when there are struggles in different times and places that share the same, common effort to end various forms of oppression, alienation and subordination. For even further discussion on this see Laclau (1990) and Mouffe (1988).

11. For the sake of anonymity I am naming this research subject Sarah.

12. For the sake of anonymity I am naming this research subject Betty.

13. For more on teacher group solidarity and its construction, see Kanpol (1991).

14. For a more practical use of critical pedagogy using the similarity within difference theme, see Kanpol (1992a,b&c).

REFERENCES

Aronowitz, S. and Giroux, H. (1991). *Postmodernism and Education: Politics, Culture and Social Criticism.* Minneapolis: University of Minnesota Press.

Bakhtin, M. (1984). *Problems of Dostoevsky's Poetics,* C. Emerson (ed. and trans.). Minneapolis: University of Minnesota Press.

Banks, J. (1988). *Multiethnic Education: Theory and Practice,* 2nd ed. Boston: Allyn and Bacon.

Bowers, C. (1991). "Critical Pedagogy and the 'Arch of Social Dreaming': A Response to the Criticisms of Peter McLaren." *Curriculum Inquiry,* 21 (4): 479–487.

Cherryholmes, C. (1988). *Power and Criticism: Poststructuralist Investigations in Education.* New York: Teachers College Press.

Dallmayr, F. (1981). *Twilight of Subjectivity.* Amherst: University of Massachusetts Press.

Eagleton, T. (1990). *Ideology: An Introduction.* New York: Verso.

Ellsworth, E. (1989). "Why Doesn't This Feel Empowering? Working through the Repressive Myths of Critical Pedagogy." *Harvard Educational Review,* 59 (3): 297–324.

Foucault, M. (1980). *Power and Knowledge: Selected Interviews and Other Writings,* C. Gordon (ed.). New York: Pantheon.

Gilligan, C. (1982). *In a Different Voice.* Cambridge, MA: University Press.

Giroux, H. (1988a). "Border Pedagogy in the Age of Postmodernism." *Journal of Education,* 170 (3): 162–181.

———. (1988b). "Postmodernism and the Discourse of Educational Criticism." *Journal of Education,* 170 (3): 5–30.

———. (1990a). "The Politics of Postmodernism: Rethinking the Boundaries of Race and Ethnicity." *Journal of Urban and Cultural Studies,* 1 (1): 5–38.

———. (1990b). "Rethinking the Boundaries of Postmodern Discourse: Modernism, Postmodernism, and Feminism." *College Literature,* 17 (2–3): 1–50.

———. (1992). *Border Crossings: Cultural Workers and the Politics of Education.* New York: Routledge, Chapman & Hall.

Giroux, H., and Simon, R. (eds.) (1989). *Popular Culture: Schooling and Everyday Life.* South Hadley, MA: Bergin & Garvey.

Kanpol, B. (1990). "Self and Community in a Fourth Grade Global Education Class." *Urban Review* 23 (4): 163–179.

Kanpol, B. (1992a). "The Politics of Similarity with Difference: A Pedagogy for the Other." *Urban Review,* 24 (22): 105–131.

———. (1992b). "Postmodernism in Education Revisited: Similarities within Differences and the Democratic Imaginary." *Educational Theory,* 42 (2): 217–229.

———. (1992c). *Towards a Theory and Practice of Teacher Cultural Politics: Continuing the Postmodern Debate.* Norwood, NJ: Ablex.

Kearney, R. (1991). *Poetics of Inquiry.* London: HarperCollins.

Laclau, E. (1990). *New Reflections on the Revolutions of Our Time*. New York: Verso.

Laclau, E. and Mouffe, Chantal. (1985). *Hegemony and Socialist Strategy*. London: Verso.

Lather, P. (1989). "Postmodernism and the Politics of Enlightenment." *Educational Foundations*, 3 (3): 7–28.

———. (1991a). *Getting Smart: Feminist Research and Pedagogy with/in the Postmodern*. New York: Routledge.

———. (1991b). "Post-critical Pedagogies: A Feminist Reading." *Education and Society*, 9 (2): 125–143.

Lyons, N. (1983). "Two Perspectives: On Self, Relationships and Morality." *Harvard Educational Review*, 53 (2): 125–143.

McDermott, R. and Gospondinoiff, K. (1981). "Social Contexts for Ethnic Borders and School Failure." In H. T. Trueba et al. (eds.), *Culture and the Bilingual Classroom*. Rowley, MA: Newbury House.

McLaren, P. (1986). "Postmodernity and the Death of Politics: A Brazilian Reprieve." *Educational Theory*, 36 (4): 389–401.

———. (1988). "Schooling and the Postmodern Body: Critical Pedagogy and the Politics of Enfleshment." *Journal of Education*, 170 (3): 53–83.

———. (1989). *Life in Schools*. New York: Longman.

———. (1991a). "Postmodernism, Post-colonialism and Pedagogy." *Education and Society*, 9 (1): 3–22.

———. (1991b). "Post-colonial Pedagogy, Desire and Decolonialized Community." *Education and Society*, 9 (2): 135–158.

———. (1994). *Life in Schools*, 2nd ed. New York: Longman.

McLaren, P. and Hammer, R. (1989). "Critical Pedagogy and the Postmodern Challenge: Towards a Critical Postmodernist Pedagogy of Liberation." *Educational Foundations*, 3 (3): 29–62.

Mouffe, C. (1988). "Hegemony and New Political Subjects: Towards New Concepts of Democracy." In Cary Nelson and Lawrence Grossberg (eds.), *Marxism and the Interpretation of Culture* (pp. 89–101). Urbana: University of Illinois Press.

O'Conner, T. (1989). "Cultural Voice and Strategies for Multicultural Education." *Journal of Education*, 172 (2): 57–74.

Salvidar, R. (1990). *Chicano Narrative: The Dialectic of Difference*. Madison: University of Wisconsin Press.

Shapiro, S. (1988). "Education and Democracy: Constituting a Counter-Hegemonic Discourse of Educational Change." *Journal of Curriculum Theorizing*, 8 (3): 89–122.

———. (1989). "Towards a Language of Educational Politics: The Struggle for a Public Discourse in Education." *Educational Foundations*, 3 (3): 79–100.

———. (1990). *Between Capitalism and Democracy: Educational Policy in the Welfare State*. South Hadley, MA: Bergin & Garvey.

———. (1991). "Postmodernism and the Challenge to Critical Pedagogy." *Education and Society*, 9 (2): 112–122.

Simon, R. (1988). "For a Pedagogy of Possibility." *Critical Pedagogy Networker*, 1 (1): 1–4.

Wexler, P. (1987). *Social Analysis of Education: After the New Sociology of Education.*
    London: Routledge & Kegan Paul.
Yeo, F. (1992). "The Inner-city School: A Conflict of Rhetoric." *Critical Pedagogy
    Networker*, 5 (3): 1–5.

10

The Conflicts of Difference in an Inner-City School: Experiencing Border Crossings in the Ghetto

Fred Yeo

INTRODUCTION

Within the discourses of postmodernist educational literature, there has been an increasingly strident dialectic framed by the issue of difference(s). In particular, one major issue has been whether it is possible to bridge the gaps constructed of difference between various Others to effect educational political projects. These projects are often contexted within the university of generalized (hypothetical) classrooms and positioned to represent the impossibility or the potentiality of crossing differential borders to construct emancipatory connections within education.

The postmodern debate coincides with an American educational system that finds itself increasingly befuddled by questions of diversity and difference; where the population of other-than-white is proliferating and concerns over race, ethnicity, gender and class are no longer muted. It is a system that "finds itself increasingly in a crisis of difference and we can no longer sanctimoniously count on a harmonious society that simply embraces a dominant status quo and its values and norms" (Kanpol, 1992a, p. 217).

In the liberal touting of certain educational schemes (excellence, multiculturalism, effective teaching) and the postmodern concern for an often-hypothetical marginalized Other, there is a certain irony. Ignored and/or denied, the diversity issues of the liberal educator and the postmodern contentions of difference and the margins all come together in the miasma that is the inner city school. Here the Other sits, struggles, succeeds, and drops out, living within multiple realities of nightmares where narratives of oppression, alienation, and subordination rule supreme.

The issue of difference and marginalization is far from being esoteric in an urban school classroom; it is the stuff of life. It is constructed of fear, frustration, oppressive conditions, and educational paradigms that frame daily conflict and failures to find connections between people and systems.

My intent is to configure the postmodern debate over difference and commensurability, position and representation, within the context of urban education to argue that dialogue and empathetic connections can occur between Others. In order to posit the possibilities for such a dialogue, I will first describe the postmodern debate as it portends to the issue of differences and dialogue (or not) across same. Second, I will briefly attempt to convey an understanding for the environment of an inner-city school and classroom as experienced by its clientele and this writer, a white male teacher in a predominantly African American school. Last, I will relate what I believe are potentials for dialogue bridging gaps between our differences, allowing for empathetic connections to elicit emancipatory conditions within classrooms and the school site; and will suggest potentialities for implementation of critical dialogic pedagogy in similar cultural boundary situations.

In order to place the argument for such dialogue, we must place it within the postmodern debate over difference, the Other and marginality, and the question of whether it is possible to cross borders of difference. Additionally, since so much of urban education is structured by liberal educational theories of learning and responses to diversity, it needs some brief discussion in theoretical contrast to postmodern arguments, which I will do in the following section.

POSTMODERNISM, DIFFERENCE, AND DIALOGUE

In general, the postmodern approach is an acknowledgment of the multiplicity of voices, positions, and representations without seeking combination into a unified account; a state of heteroglossia (Burbules and Rice, 1991). It is the denial of modernism's universal logics and totalizing ethnocentricity in favor of individuals and communities constituted out of and by multitudinous and shifting frames of difference.

Perhaps its major impact in the sphere of difference and multiethnicity is the attack on the modernist construct of universality that construes the Western (American) dominant ideologies and culture:

The achievements and contributions of all other cultures are considered . . . only in terms of appendage (filtered through the lens of Eurocentric interpretation), adornment (to prove the superiority of the Euro-derived tradition) and esoteric specialization (to prove that other traditions, unlike those derived from Europe) are narrow and provincial. (Rose, 1992, p. 407)

Postmodernism itself is configured by a multiplicity of theorems, particularly as to difference. Burbules and Rice (1991) differentiate postmodernism into two camps on this issue. One is the antimodernists, who contend that all differences are constructed as expressions of a subjective tension of identities that are totally incommensurable. This means that virtually no commonality between groups and/or individuals is possible across the spaces of difference. This posits what has been termed as the "dilemma of difference"—that is, "a denial of the possibility of intersubjective understanding, and an exaggerated critique that any attempt to establish consensual discourse across difference inevitably involves the imposition of dominant groups' values, beliefs and modes of discourse on others" (Burbules and Rice, 1991, p. 401).

The problem for the antimodernist is the immutability of difference, the perception that the spaces can not be bridged, reducing them to political impotence by virtue of their inability to theorize connectivities or community: "a pluralism which regards different perspectives as incommensurable; and the decentered anarchistic pluralism which celebrates uncertainty or lapse into a brooding and nihilistic retreat from life" (McLaren, 1988, p. 71).

The second approach is a postmodernism that desires to extend modernism's political project of possibility (Giroux, 1992). This construct is equally concerned with notions of difference and fracturing modernism's "universalism" and oppressive ideological and cultural regimes, but does so by "a broadening of positive modernist tenets (such as dialogue, cooperation, pluralism, democracy, community or intersubjectivity) that incorporate a myriad of differences, realities and truths as ingredients of a democratic society" (Kanpol, 1992b, p. 219). Here the postmodernist perceives that the multiphonic, multitextured subject gives rise to individual and social differences.

The problem for the postmodernists is how to construct connectivities across differences in order to frame political projects for a more emancipatory society and education. Primarily the effort to theorize such bridges derives of construing experience to ground solidarities in resistance to modernism's marginalization, oppressions, alienation, and subordinations. The intent is to interpret lived experiences such that one can "understand how acts of meaning and interpretation, politicizing identity and ending subordination can share similar features" (Kanpol, 1992b, p. 222) in order to concretize commonalities of experience between Others to effect solidarity of struggle, reducing inequalities and subordinations in society. This would mean

to find ways by which dissimilar people with distinct, sometimes divergent interests can come together and find common ground. It means to seek a language—an agenda—for education which reflects the particular struggle and aspirations of social groups and can reconcile their differences without denying or subordinating any of them. (Shapiro, 1993, p. 20)

Chantal Mouffe (1988) inscribes the concept of struggles and societal frictions that can lead to a "democratic imaginary" based on commonalities of resistant struggle. Henry Giroux (1988, p. 176) argues for what he terms a "border pedagogy" that "can generate an ethos of solidarity that speaks to what educators as critical agents . . . share in the common struggle against domination and for freedom while preserving the specificity of difference."

The postmodernist emphasis has become to locate syntheses of experience to derive a dialogue of difference to effect emancipating educational projects. The gist of the argument is to facilitate mutual understandings with and between "marginalized peoples, at the base of whose differences lie similarities of oppression, pain and feeling, albeit in miscellaneous forms" (Kanpol, 1992b, p. 221). Kanpol argues that a praxis of "similarity within differences" can be derived from interrogating one's own experience(s) so as to empathize with the "Other." He states: "Given my own life experiences, I can begin to identify with those who have felt alienation, suffering and oppression, even though our respective circumstances have differed" (Kanpol, 1992b, p. 221).

"To empathize with these forms of the 'other' is to transcend one's own ethnocentric view of what counts as correct culture and, instead, to understand, incorporate and change oneself in light of the other culture in order to shape a common emancipatory and democratic purpose" (Kanpol, 1992b, p. 221).

The problematic with constructing bridges over the troubled waters of difference with experiential empathy is the risk of equivalizing experiences. It presumes that alienating and/or marginalizing experiences are equivalent one to the other; that the alienation of a middle-class white male equates to that of a sexually abused, inner-city black female student; however "the issue here is not whether we may find equivalence in the forms of pain and oppression" (Shapiro, 1993, p. 14).

Yet, if we assume that difference is incommensurable, we are left in a state of nullity, forced to accept the status quo. Kanpol, Mouffe, McLaren, Giroux, and other educational postmodernists have, however, pointed to one potential bridge. Equivalent or not, we all share the fact of experience and the need for connectedness. What is needed to find "similarity within difference" is to move beyond our own isolated experience to effect experience with the Other.

In order to effect an understanding of another's difference and locate points of similarity, one must place the self where one becomes as an Other; to experience Otherness: "We can transcend the blinders of our own social location, not through becoming objective, but by recognizing the differences by which we ourselves are constituted, and . . . by actively seeking to be partially constructed by work with different groups" (Welch, 1990, p. 151).

Experience as Other is neither presumed nor proclaimed, but nodes of similarity can be gained with engagement:

we can never speak inclusively as the Other, though we may be the Other with respect to issues of race, class or gender; but we can certainly work *with* diverse others to deepen both our own and their understanding of the complexity of the tradition, histories, knowledge and politics that they bring. (Giroux, 1992, p. 35)

To experience connectivity to the Other assumes at least minimal communication—that is, a dialogue across differences that leads to understanding and cooperation without alienating differences or imposing one's views on others (Burbules and Rice, 1991). Burbules and Rice have argued that dialogue across differences has two aspects, both integral to and constituting a critical pedagogy in education. One is that such dialogue can result in an intersubjectivity formulating new common meanings, or, two, be nonconvergent aimed at tolerance and respect rather than agreement.

Such a dialogue across differences argues for "a language in which different voices and traditions exist to the degree that they listen to the voices of Others" (Giroux, 1992, p. 134), based on a notion of open cultural borders that are "a shifting sphere of multiple and heterogeneous borders where different histories, languages, experiences and voices intermingle amid diverse relations of power and privilege" (Giroux, 1992, p. 42).

In search for such a dialogue, and to locate and build solidarity and community of "similarity within differences" (Kanpol, 1992b), perhaps the framework for a bridge across differences could begin by acknowledging experiential similarities. However, such acknowledgment is insufficient in and of itself; the initiation of empathetic community must move beyond disconnected self-experience to "shared sensibilities which cross the boundaries of class, gender, race, etc. . . . ties that would promote recognition of common commitments and serve as a basis for solidarity and coalition" (hooks, 1990, p. 27).

This posits a move from the self-reflective to a proactive stance of seeking dialogue and being open to similarities of experience, which can be used in reformulating one's educational practices.

One arena in dire need of critical reformation of its framing educational paradigms and practices is that of the inner-city school. Contra to the arguments of those who negate the possibility of dialogue across differences, urban school sites can be the locus of both liberatory dialogue and commensurate experience, but they can also simultaneously frustrate bridging expectations, suggesting both of Burbules and Rice's (1991) aspects of dialogue. Both possibilities derive of the multiplicity of struggles within the school and its urban environment. Certainly, it would seem hard to argue that the barrios and ghettos of America's inner cities and their schools constitute anything less than marginalized, oppressed Others. However, it is possible to effect dialogue across differences and intersubjective similarities within its educational environs.

Before describing and examining this teacher's experience in both construction and frustration within an inner-city school, the scope of the marginality and difference of the inner city and its schools needs description, to which I now turn.

THE INNER-CITY SCHOOL AND COMMUNITY

Simply put, the schools of America's urban centers are appalling; bankrupt districts, burgeoning populations of minorities and immigrants, classrooms empty of materials but packed with children, pandemic drug and alcohol abuse, gang violence, and impoverished communities malignant with anger and frustration waiting for a spark (e.g., Los Angeles, April 30, 1992). Some 25 percent of America's children live in poverty and 80 percent of them are in our ghettos (Marable, 1992). The national dropout percentile for secondary schools is in the low 20s, but it is 65–75 percent in urban schools (Fine, 1991). In Chicago's ghetto schools, only 8 percent of a ninth-grade class will graduate reading at grade level, only 15 percent will even graduate (Fine, 1991). Many urban children come to school hungry, abused, and/or poorly clothed. They come to school from communities distinguished by empty buildings, boarded-up shops, proliferating liquor stores, random violence, pent-up anger and dehumanizing marginalization, poverty, and self-inflicted crime. "Youths who begin their lives at the greatest risks of class, racial or ethnic or gender exploitation attend the most traumatized schools and receive the most impoverished educations" (Fine, 1991, p. 23).

The school conditions ostensibly arise from those of the locating community and the forces that have relegated urban centers to poverty, unemployment, and the home of America's underclass:

The economic relations of the ghetto to white America closely parallel those between third-world nations and the industrially advanced countries. The ghetto has a low per-capita income and a high birth rate. Its residents are unskilled. Local markets are limited. Goods and services tend to be "imported." . . . The ghetto is dependent on one basic export—its unskilled labor power. (Tabb, 1970, p. 22)

"No fanciful detention centers 'secretly' being built to house niggers could be worse than the reality of the modern ghetto trap. . . . No one is spared the destructive consequences of ghetto living" (Glasgow, 1980, p. 10).

Within the geographical and political enclaves of these urban communities exist in inner-city schools. While no description of their dehumanizing conditions can be complete,[1] some specifics need relating as they frame the exigencies of staff and students in these schools.

The overwhelming pattern is demarked by educational failure; among black and Hispanic students in the five largest U.S. cities, the dropout rate exceeds 55 percent, and for black males it approximates 75 percent nationwide (Comer and Haynes, 1990). African American children are three times as likely as whites to be placed in classes for the mentally retarded and subsequently drop out; Latino students drop out of school at a rate higher than any other group—in some areas, 80 percent (Nieto, 1992).

Dominant cultural ideologies and motifs construct particular school-site reasons for these statistics: the irrelevance of the school's practices to students' lives and experience, the disconnection between the teachers and students, and the curricular approach administratively mandated and promulgated in the classroom.

Urban, public schools serving low-income students are organized in ways that offer sparse educational expenditures to children based on race/ethnicity, social class and community; lend academic and social legitimacy to prevailing ideologies . . . which often deny and betray the historic and current lived experiences of these youths. . . . Privileged are notions of individualism, competition, mobility, meritocracy, and silenced are discussions of social class, race, gender and sexual arrangements. (Fine, 1991, p. 199)

These paradigms are played out under the rubric of a mandated curricular approach termed "Basic Skills Programs," devised to ensure that urban students attain at least minimum literacy and computational skills, with the objective being to enter the workforce (Carlson, 1989). The question the schools never ask is: "what jobs?", thereby underscoring the disconnection between urban educational schema and students' existential realities. The major components of the "Basic Skills" agenda are performance-based guidelines that require *quantitative* data on student and school achievement; performance-based "skill" kits, workbooks, drillsheets, and texts; criterion-referenced pre- and posttests for use with specific curricular materials for specific subjects; and teacher evaluations measuring test effectiveness and appropriate "time on task."

The irony is that many inner-city districts are too poor to purchase the materials, and the "official" version becomes quickly distorted even where materials are available. The packages are used to facilitate teacher standardization necessitated by faculty turnover (80 percent in some districts), to sidetrack disruptive relations between teachers and students, and by principals who regularly promote "increases" in scores. Moreover, the program worsens relations with parents and students who view the schools as repressive, isolated, and racist (Carlson, 1989).

Parents, students, and community leaders perceive the school bureaucracy as insulated and not committed to the students—repressive in its overuse of rigid tracking schemes, inadequate counseling, and anxiousness to push "at-risk" kids out; isolated in the sense that school staffs are not involved in the community and are often arrogant to poor parents, especially where there is a racial or ethnic difference. Parents and students perceive an overuse of discipline and structured control coincident with schools' stated views that "ghetto kids" are unable to handle freedom or innovative classroom experiences. Typically, this is exacerbated by the feeling of being betrayed by black teachers who should have been allies, and whose structure and control emphasis is felt as a nonblack distancing and rejection (Glasgow, 1980). Many parents and students feel betrayed by the black-managed districts for hiring under various international education exchanges; districts see foreign teachers as "cheap" and the parents/kids see them as nonblack "Africans." Additionally there is the tension between middle-class teachers and administrators who do not live in the community and underclass parents and students; the first preferring disconnection from the latter.

Blacks see inferior education perpetuated through devices they suspect are white originated (e.g., biased tests, tracking, biased texts, biased counseling, etc.) and because they doubt that these schools understand Black children and their needs. Black mistrust and conflict with schools reduce the degree . . . of acceptance of the legitimacy of schools' goals, standards and instructional approaches. As a result, they do not perceive a need to cooperate . . . or follow rules and requirements." (Ogbu, 1990, p. 127)

An additional factor in the irrelevance and failure of the "Basic Skills" program is the students themselves and the experiences they bring to the classroom. The "failure" of the program and of the students must be understood as a complex dialectic of differences—between the students on the one hand with their survival strategies and "street knowledge" versus the teachers who value their middle-class, white cultural capital over that of the students:

In the streets, knowledge was "felt" classroom knowledge was objectified and often sullied by an inflated rationalism. . . . In the street, students made use of bodily engagement, organic symbols and intuition. Students struggle daily to reconcile the disjunction between the lived meaning of the streets and the subject-centered approach to learning in the classroom. (McLaren, 1989, p. 215)

Ultimately, students are prepared to pass tests and time, prepared for jobs that do not exist in the inner city, and are constantly battered with the dissonance of schooling ways (pedagogy) and values that contradict what they know. The emphasis in the "Basic Skills" program is on competition, individualism, and meritocracy and runs contra to the value system of the black community that emphasizes holism, group orientation, and self-effacement (Fordham, 1988; Solomon, 1988; Ogbu, 1988; McLaren, 1989).

The result is massive dropouts, illiteracy, and school rhetoric attempting to justify the failure of promulgating a white, Euro-Western education on Hispanics, Asians, and African Americans by blaming its clientele for those failures.

> The present failure of inner-city education is not in the genes or the attitudes of the poor, but in the failure of society to change the economic and social structures which regulate their lives. Rather than blaming the victims . . . we need to take into account our tolerance of the existence of grinding poverty, frightened and conde- scending teachers, self-serving politicians, irrelevant curricula . . . and the reluctance of educational officials to meet the needs of inner-city students. (McLaren, 1989, p. 153)

In like manner to the inner cities from which they derive, the urban schools are constructed by a matrix of synergistic forces and paradigms: economic, racist, the state's hegemonic inflections and the oppositional and diversity-based cultural understandings of the schools' clientele. Given all of the foregoing and multiplying the fracturing by the continuing influx of diverse populations, the maintenance of the current school schema would suggest that inner-city education will continue to spiral into a welter of irrelevance, diminished polities, and massive numbers of frustrated and dis- enchanted dropouts and their communities.

EXPERIENCING PEDAGOGY IN AN INNER-CITY SCHOOL

Ignorant of both the desmenses of inner-city schools and the potentialities of the praxis of critical pedagogy, armed with instrumental techniques of teacher education and the excitement of embarking on the experience of transmitting valuable knowledge (value, ideologic, and cultural constructs were taken for granted) to avid learners, I approached my teaching assign- ment at Washington Middle School[2] located in a south Los Angeles district. Although aware that the surrounding area was known as the site of the 1965 Watts Riot, somehow the ethnic and cultural connotations went unnoticed.

Escorted by the janitor, without a gradebook or class roll (or a welcome by the principal), openly gaping at the broken windows, the graffiti, and the ubiquitous trash, I clutched my carefully crafted lesson plans and entered the room. Filled with forty-four students, all yelling, arguing, and pushing, the cacophony exacerbated my shock—"They're *all* black, it's a room full of Them!" I was immediately and vividly conscious of my whiteness, and their blackness; the plans quickly became spurious and techniques of class- room management were drowned in the sheer volume of fights, obscene language, and everyone's anger. Later, meeting the other teachers, I found I was the only male teacher on campus and the ONLY white! Silence or snickers followed in my path as I walked the corridors, obscene and violent language assaulted my senses, and classes and instruction were an unmitigated disaster. Nothing in my experience, certainly not teacher education, had prepared me for the crushing humiliation and frustration as the "white boy," as the other.[3]

As time progressed, although I didn't know the term, I became inundated with the paperwork indigenous to the "Basic Skills" program. I struggled with pre- and posttests, futilely demanding attention, no cheating, and "please stop talking!" I wondered how the other teachers survived—was it a "black thang?" I found other classrooms were structured with rows of desks, worksheets, and a plethora of packaged tests. I listened while teachers routinely yelled at students to "shut up" and pushed them from the room for trivial excuses (anything, they would say, to lighten the load). I listened to the exhortations to work hard, follow directions, be on time, stay on task, so as to graduate and get a job. I learned from students that there weren't any jobs, except on the street. I heard staff rail against the gangs, and the students describe how joining meant survival in the "hood." I talked at first about oceans, geology, and space, and then began to listen about lives of abuse, hunger, and only knowing a few square blocks of squalid streets. I wondered why they refused to stop talking to each other during tests, until I realized they walked, talked, and lived in a group-cooperative world. I learned gang signs and how to speak AAL;[4] they learned about whites. I wondered how they could have so many brothers, sisters, and cousins, until understanding that "it refers to a kinship-like connection between and among persons, . . . a sense of peoplehood of collective social identity . . . [which is a] collective ethos of a fictive-kinship system challenged by the individual ethos of the dominant culture when the children enter school" (Fordham, 1988, p. 56).

A significant amount of administrator and teacher time is configured by a continuing conflict over what constitutes the school's dominant rhetoric. Superficially, the official language of the school (used almost entirely by teachers and staff) is framed by a white, middle-class language (both syntactically and in content) versus the often-obscene, oppositional "street" talk of the students. However, through dialogue and listening unassumptively, one comes to perceive that the contentiousness is polyphonic and multivoiced; what will be observed is that most of the issues surrounding school site rhetoric has little to do with pedagogy or instructional efficiency. Rather, most of the issues are political issues with serious social and cultural consequences (Williams, 1991).

This conflict in the content and educational practices of the school is closely related to a dimension of the relation of language and power; the distinction between *language* and *voice*.

Language is general, abstract, subject to an arbitrary normalization; voice is particular and concrete. Language has a life of its own—it exists even when suppressed; when voice is suppressed, it is not heard—it does not exist. To deny people their language, . . . is, to be sure, to deny them voice; but to allow them "their" language (as in bilingual education . . .) is not necessarily to allow them voice. To have a voice implies not that people can say things, but that they are heard (that is, that their words have status, influence). (Ruiz, 1991, p. 220)

At the school, although to some restricted (disciplinary) extent the students were allowed their language, their voice had little or no power or influence over the contested areas, educational content or practices, particularly within the classrooms: "schools do not allow students from subordinate groups to authenticate their problems and experiences through their own individual and collective voices" (Giroux, 1992, p. 135).

What has potential for critical reform in inner-city schools, perhaps, is that the staff was relatively unsuccessful in its efforts at cultural value imposition, excepting those students who were struggling to educationally and culturally conform in a form of "racelessness"[5] to the social cultural values implicit in the staff's rhetoric.

Three years later I was fully enmeshed in the school and the lives of students and families. Classes were swollen beyond *fifty* by the administration or by "floaters" ejected from other classrooms; I was cornered constantly for advice on school, studies, fights, sex, AIDS, race, and the myriad conundrums of my students' lives. Asked to break in new teachers of different ethnicities, including black, "cause you know how it is here," my own consciousness was caught up and changed by language, culture, dialogue, community, and empathetic connections.

The difference came about because of the intense realization that the educational practices and cultural capital promulgated by the school staff, texts, and official policies were inconsistent with the knowledge, culture, and experience of these children and their community. Struck by the irony of the distance between the language of the staff and that of the students, it became obvious that some new pedagogical dynamic was needed to contravene the former. The conflict for control over knowledge and voice between staff and students is illustrated by two vignettes, which, it should be understood, were not isolated events, but common occurrences, and exemplify the dichotomy of vision between the two groups.

Vignette 1

Overheard is an assembly where the principal spent the P. E. department's entire budget for a speaker to tell students to study hard, follow the rules, be quiet and obey teachers to get As and a "Cadillac job," students could be heard—"That man's fulla boosheet, dere ain't no fuckin jobs fo niggers, man!" "shit man, my homie's gettin me a Cad for heppin to move da blow [crack]!"; "My brother grageated from the 'Two' [a local high school] wid a four-o and he cain't get no job!". These comments (along with many others) expressed by A students!

Vignette 2

One afternoon after a day of fights, "misbehavior" and three teachers fleeing (quitting due to classroom "conditions"), the principal came on the P.A. and announced to the school that students should be good and obey the school codes: "If you want to be free, you have to obey our rules!"— never realizing the contradiction. The students responded with laughter and disdain: "Man, Mr. Yeo, that ole bitch, she be all fucked up—she don't know what she say, do she!". I could only agree and we spent the rest of the science class period talking about rules, who makes them and why.

In a similar school, Sleeter and Grant (1991, p. 54) interviewed teachers who

described their purposes as teaching basic skills and academic knowledge, largely at a remedial level, and preparing students for useful lives outside of school . . . they saw their purpose as transmitting to students a body of knowledge and skills that would be practical . . . they explained the students' low achievement primarily by citing deficiencies in the students' home backgrounds.

In this conflict over the school's language and values, these middle-class teachers, who live in the suburbs and generally teach with the best of intentions, rarely acknowledge that children in the inner city bring different historical and cultural experiences and knowledge to school, which is evidenced in diverse motivational patterns, language, meanings, and skills (Boateng, 1990). Although sometimes they acknowledge that cultural, or at least ethnic, differences do exist: "they believe that the first step is to convert all children to replicas of white, middle-class suburban children. A Euro-American-centered consciousness has therefore remained the basis of curriculum development and instruction in the public schools" (Boateng, 1990, p. 75).

One of the dichotomies of my school is the teachers' use of both cultural languages. Teachers would admonish, structure, and control their classrooms, as well as transmit certain knowledge, behavior, and values, within the frame of the dominant official, administrative rhetoric (white, middle-class). Concomitantly in private discussions, aside comments in class, and within the safe confines of the lounge, language and voice would change dramatically. The former was often the voice of authority, power, and control; while the latter was that of the community, alienated and oppressed (expressed both as black and teacher). The second voice constructed most teacher private talk (away from administrators and students) and was as direct, obscene, and angry as that of the students.

In staff meetings, teachers mixed both voices—that of the dominant culture when addressing the principal or the group, and that of the minority culture when speaking privately. Noticeably, the administration was never observed to shift voice.

In a postmodern sense, these teachers moved within multiphonic positions, articulating their language and shifting cultural constructs depending on the respective site. Given the proximity of teachers' and students' cultural voices, it suggests that the voice connected to each space resulted from perceptions, individually and collectively, of their relative power in a particular set of relations.

The meaning of many of these experiences is bound by concerns over issues of difference, culture, language, and dialogue. Much like other critical educators, I found that my "students' cultural knowledge was rooted in their own concrete experience and reflected what was real to them. . . . School knowledge usually concerned matters removed from the students' own existence, and came to the students by way of adults in verbal form without analogues the students had experienced" (Sleeter and Grant, 1991, p. 64).

Similarly, as I dialogued with students, I discovered that for them, school literally had little meaning or relevance to their lives. Increasingly, much of our class time was devoted to stories of their lives and mine (of which they were fascinated; some had never seen a white person, except on TV). Science was learned outside in the grass or exploding on the desk or smelling up the ventilation system. Insofar as what they were tasked with in other classes,

the students dismissed most school knowledge, seeing it as useless. Far from providing students with a way of understanding the world, school knowledge was lodged within students' framework . . . as a relatively unimportant niche . . . the knowledge dispensed was not so much a doorway to the broader society and its culture as it was a series of meaningless tasks to perform. (Sleeter and Grant, 1991, p. 65)

This seems indicated in the school's average of only 10 percent of home assignments being completed, texts were not issued because many were lost or left lying around, and retention of knowledge and skills (per standardized tests) was uniformly below normative grade level.

Although convinced by students' tears and hugs on every graduation day that we had indeed dialogued across our mutual differences and connected intersubjectively, continuing communication with students (many struggling with the dissonance between an urban high school and our shared understandings in class) suggests that it is both possible and problematic to talk across boundaries. In the next section, I want to connect these experiences with the postmodern concerns for difference and dialogue across it, and to suggest (insofar as to similar schools) how teachers might "work with" the Other themselves to create similarities within differences through bridges of empathy.

THE PRACTICE OF "HERE I AM!"

Without being facetious, some postmodernists have tended to polarize the question of difference and dialogue into black and white: difference is commensurable or it is not, dialogue can exist synchratically or is impossible. Contemporaneously it is argued that difference is immutable, while others suggest that its boundaries can be intersubjectively negotiated through empathetic experience of self. In this section, I want to suggest that dialogue across differences is eminently possible, but occurs in a spectrum of lived experiences across a broad range of shifting positions that constitute ephemeral connectivities. Further, that in order to effect "border crossings" and experience similarities within difference, we need to extend from self-experience to experience as an Other and with the Other.

One of the problematics within the postmodern discourse is the lack of attention to urban schools; all too often theorizing of difference and "border crossings" is of generalized Others—students and schools. These urban schools are matrixed by difference, marginality and value, and cultural conflicts. Many teachers fail here (professionally and educationally) because of an inability to project or perceive across the inherent differences (we used to call it "culture shock"); yet others do well. Both my experience and that of these others suggest that it is possible to bridge the gaps of difference and connect with these students and staff regardless of starting points of culture and ethnicity.

Interpretatively, the milieu of the urban school site exemplifies both postmodern camps; the majority of the teachers presuming incommensurability, struggling to move students across the spaces or retreating into survival, and a few, recognizing that it is the curricular and pedagogical that is incommensurable, moving to reach across the gaps and enter into dialogue.

The issue seems initially to crystallize around whether dialogue is even possible. Educationally, we have little choice; if dialogue is impossible for one reason or another, then education is left to the purveyors of the traditional transmission of universalized knowledge and Western values and ethnocentricity. In the inner city, at least, this can be seen as rank failure. To assume, as some do, that dialogue is either impossible or involves the assimilatory imposition of dominance and oppression is itself privileged discourse effectively silencing the Other.

The antidialogue sect would have us presume a permanence of difference and categories, which is negated by the postmodern construct that all categories (hence, differences) are fluid, shifting, and intermixed. As positions, representations, and/or identities shift, it would seem that experiences at some point can connect to initiate dialogic relations. At this point, Burbules and Rice (1991, p. 407) ask: "What positive conditions make dialogue across differences possible? What can educators do to promote those conditions? What is realistic to expect . . . ?"

One stance that educators, particularly in urban schools, can take is to accept the partial: "Dialogue can also serve the purpose of creating partial understandings, if not agreement, across differences. . . . No communication process is perfect; no intersubjective understanding, . . . is ever complete" (Burbules and Rice, 1991, p. 409).

In conditions typical of these classrooms, where communication and connectivity are distorted and/or negated by relations of power and control, teachers must accept that dialogue is omnidirectional, not linear; that this derives of the understanding that voices must be heard to be spoken. Teachers must listen and interrogate both that which is said as well as their reactions to what is heard.

This is not to assert that the cultures and/or experiences underlying the "voice" will be nonproblematic, nor that one's own experience can equate with those of the students or the staff in an inner-city school. In fact, one should assume a stance of humility as to one's own experience and knowledge, since students are equally assertive about their own experiences, knowledge, and values.

In order to bridge the spaces of their individual and collective differences and locate similarities, a teacher in this environment needs to interrogate that which structures his or her own experience, the pedagogy and curriculum, and avoid taking for granted assumptions of student identity: "identity does not follow unproblematically from experience. We are seen to live in webs of multiple representations of class, race, gender, language and social relations; meanings vary within the individual. Self-identity is constituted and reconstituted relationally, its boundaries repeatedly remapped and renegotiated" (Lather, 1989, p. 7).

In order to participate with students in the processing of a dialogic pedagogy across differences, a teacher should not presume a similarity of any difference, but allow articulation without rephrasing into instrumental discussion, nor presume a limitation on the varieties of difference and representations.

As part of the process of developing a pedagogy of difference, teachers need to deal with the plethora of voices, and the specificity and organization of differences that constitute any course, class or curriculum so as to make problematic not only the stories that give meaning to the lives of their students, but also the ethical and political lineaments that inform their students' subjectivities and identities. Border pedagogy provides opportunities for teachers to deepen their own understanding of the discourse of others in order to effect a more dialectical understanding of their own politics, values, and pedagogy. (Giroux, 1988, p. 176)

Ultimately, if an educator desires to be effective in the critical sense within the confines of an urban classroom, to locate the spaces of differences and similarities therein, and encourage dialectic pedagogy to bridge intersubjectivity both teacher and student differences, then I would suggest there are two levels at which this can be attained.

First, the teacher must become familiar with students' voices, conceptually and experientially. "This means giving students the opportunity to speak, to locate themselves in history, and to become subjects in the construction of their identities and the wider society" (Giroux, 1992, p. 135).

Second, in order to be able to initiate any form of bridging of differences, building similarities within and constructing dialogue (partial or otherwise), it is a matter of ethics, not episteme. McLaren (1992, p. 18) describes, in part, a postmodern ethical paradigm that without which I would not have survived my own inner city experience:

> Another in need makes the ethical demand on me—"where are you?" before I ask of the other the epistemological question—"who are you?" We are responsible for the suffering of the other before we know his or her credentials. . . . When a naked face cries "where are you?", we do not ask for identity papers. We reply, first and foremost, "*here I am.*" Solidarity is prior to questions of epistemology. Students need to know we are there for them before we ask them to identify themselves.

I would add that all too often we structure a student's identity (we've heard from other teachers; the student's dress, looks, or language; past grades or test results; etc.) before they can represent themselves. When a student approaches, their identity should be theirs, not what we as teachers impose. In my experience in an inner-city school, it was the teachers who replied "here I am!", who crossed borders, found the similarities, and connected to students—not by structuring a dialogue, but by stepping away from the comfort of authority, power, and control and allowing students to approach within a relationship where dialogue is simply possible, not mandatory.

CONCLUSION

I have attempted in these pages to sketch postmodern concepts within the conditions of urban education, specifically in that place where teacher meets student, where I meet the Other, where I become the Other. Too many teachers fear or fail the inner-city school because, it seems to me, they do not comprehend the potentialities for connections between themselves and the students. Within the boundaries of the postmodern debate over difference and dialogue is to be located the possibilities for bridges or crossings past those differences. In part it requires an understanding of the nature and conditions of education as it is played out in the inner city. It requires an understanding of what it means to be marginalized beyond one's own experience and that one's experiences do not automatically equate with another's. A sensitivity to experience and how cultures and communities frame those differences and the process of dialogue itself provides a basis for this understanding.

The basing of that dialogue, of effecting "border crossings," can not and will not occur without moving away from one's own experience as a totalizing benchmark. It takes the humility of denigrating one's experience for the sake of that of the Other, of attempting without prior assumptions the learning of the conditions of language, culture, and voice. It takes the realization that the knowledge that one brings to the classroom is undoubtedly meaningless to these kids, whose lives are constructed of and by joblessness, violence, and the streets.

It is the sharing of experience through the medium of "voice" that can begin to construct the foundation for a "bridging" dialogue; to locate the similarities within differences. To teach in the inner city is on the one hand to understand the dialectics of language, voice, cultural knowledge, and values, and, on the other hand, to comprehend that the curriculum and pedagogy espoused by those in authority are incommensurate with the realities of students' lives, and that the school and one's experience will be constructed and delineated by the conflict of rhetoric for control of the schools' "voice."

Finally, to teach, particularly within the inner city, is to avoid the official paradigm of constructing students' identities, of forcing the mold, and to place oneself "at risk" by repetitively representing and demonstrating without antecedents or conditions—"HERE I AM!"

NOTES

1. For more description, Jonathan Kozol, *Savage Inequalities* (1991), and Peter McLaren, *Life in Schools* (1989), have written accurate and searing depictions of the conditions of education in inner city schools.

2. The names of schools and personnel are fictitious.

3. I was told later by my teacher friends that there was a $50 pool on how many days I would last—none went beyond two weeks!

4. AAL—African American Language.

5. Racelessness as a construct for a portion of minority school children is conceptualized by Signithia Fordham (1988), and frames the conflicted attempts of certain achievers to assume the dominant values (educationally and culturally) espoused by the school staff versus the often-pejorative efforts of their peers to undercut their achievement in favor of the community (or street) culture. Fordham explains well the often-irregular grades continuity of achievement-oriented minority students (whose academic motivation and grades would fluctuate markedly as they oscillated between the various cultural demands at the school), which was often seen, and rarely understood, at the author's school.

REFERENCES

Boateng, F. (1990). "Combatting Deculturalization of the African American Child in the Public School: A Multicultural Approach." In K. Lomotey (ed.), *Going to School: the African American Experience.* Albany: State University of New York Press.

Burbules, Nicholas and Rice, Suzanne. (1991). "Dialogue across Differences: Continuing the Conversation." *Harvard Educational Review*, 61(4) (November).

Carlson, D. (1989). "Managing the Urban School Crisis: Recent Trends in Curricular Reform." *Journal of Education*, 171: 3.

Comer, J. and Haynes, N. (1990). "Helping Black Children Succeed: The Significance of Some Social Factors." In K. Lomotey, (ed.), *Going to School: the African American Experience.* Albany: State University of New York Press.

Fine, Michelle. (1991). *Framing Drop-Outs.* Albany: State University of New York Press.

Fordham, S. (1988). "Racelessness as a Factor in Black Students' School Success." *Harvard Educational Review*, 58(1).

Giroux, H. (1988). "Border Pedagogy in the Age of Postmodernism." *Journal of Education*, 170(3).

———. (1992). *Border Crossings: Cultural Workers and the Politics of Education.* New York: Routledge, Chapman & Hall.

Glasgow, Douglas. (1980). *The Black Underclass.* San Francisco: Jossey-Bass.

hooks, bell. (1990). *Yearning: Race, Gender and Cultural Politics.* Boston: South End Press.

Kanpol, B. (1992a). *Towards a Theory and Practice of Teacher Cultural Politics: Continuing the Postmodern Debate.* Norwood, NJ: Ablex.

Kanpol, B. (1992b). "Postmodernism in Education Revisited: Similarities within Differences and the Democratic Imaginary."

Kozol, J. (1991). *Savage Inequalities: Children in America's Schools.* New York: Crown.

Lather, Patti. (1989). "Postmodernism and the Politics of Enlightenment." *Educational Foundations*, 3(3).

Marable, M. (1992). *The Crisis of Color and Democracy.* Monroe, ME: Common Courage Press.

McLaren, P. (1988). "Schooling the Postmodern Body: Critical Pedagogy and the Politics of Enfleshment." *Journal of Education*, 170(3).

———. (1989). *Life in Schools.* New York: Longman.

———. (1991). "Critical Pedagogy, Multiculturalism and the Human Spirit: A Response to Kelly and Portelli." *Journal of Education*, 173(3) (1991): 109–139.

Mouffe, Chantal. (1988). "Radical Democracy: Modern or Postmodern." In Andrew Ross (ed.), *Universal Abandon.* Minneapolis: University of Minnesota Press.

Nieto, Sonia. (1992). *Affirming Diversity: The Sociopolitical Context of Multicultural Education.* New York: Longman.

Ogbu, J. (1988). "Class Stratification, Racial Stratification and Schooling." In L. Weis (ed.), *Race, Class and Schooling.* Albany: State University of New York Press.

———. (1990). "Literacy and Schooling in Subordinate Cultures: The Case of Black

Americans." In K. Lomotey, (ed.), *Going to School: the African American Experience*. Albany: State University of New York Press.

Rose, W. (1992). "The Great Pretenders: Further Reflections on Whiteshamanism." In M. A. Jaimes (ed.), *The State of Native America*. Boston: South End Press.

Ruiz, R. (1991). "The Empowerment of Language-Minority Students." In C. Sleeter (ed.), *Empowerment through Multicultural Education*. Albany: State University of New York Press.

Shapiro, S. (1993). "Educational Change and the Crisis of the Left: Towards a Postmodern Educational Discourse." In D. E. Purpel and S. Shapiro (eds.), *Beyond Liberation and Excellence: Towards a New Public Discourse for Education*. New York: Routledge.

Sleeter, C. and Grant, C. (1991). "Mapping Terrains of Power: Student Cultural Knowledge versus Classroom Knowledge." In C. Sleeter (ed.), *Empowerment through Multicultural Education*. Albany: State University of New York Press.

Solomon, R. (1989). "Black Cultural Forms in Schools: A Cross National Comparison." In L. Weis (ed.), *Race, Class and Schooling*. New York: State University of New York Press.

Tabb, William. (1970). *The Political Economy of the Black Ghetto*. New York: W. W. Norton.

Welch, Sharon. (1990). *A Feminist Ethic of Risk*. Minneapolis: Fortress Press.

Williams, S. (1991). "Classroom Use of African American Language: Educational Tool or Social Weapon?" In C. Sleeter (ed.), *Empowerment through Multicultural Education*. New York: State University of New York Press.

11

Emerging Student and Teacher Voices: A Syncopated Rhythm in Public Education

Suzanne SooHoo

Scene 1, An Orchestra: The conductor rapidly taps his baton, signaling musicians to assume their positions. The musicians mentally prepare themselves to read the conductor's commands and to execute the orchestra leader's rendition of the musical piece. They play skillfully as predicated by their many hours of practice and proficiency of following the conductor's lead.

Scene 2, A Jazz Band: A saxophone player, guitarist, pianist, and drummer have just run through a collective arrangement when suddenly the saxophone player solos for four measures. The guitarist appears fascinated and he begins to construct his response, a solo for four more measures. The saxophone and guitar continue to engage in "trading four," the term used for solo improvisations depicting this musical conversation.

Emerging from the traditional public school classroom characterized by the orchestra is a new form: the jazz band (Kerchner, 1990), where students and teachers produce a syncopated rhythm. In the up and down beats of classroom interactions, students and teachers contribute their individual resources to collectively construct unique configurations of sounds and voices. This process unleashes multiple patterns of alternating notes, which has both practical instructional ramifications and theoretical implications. It suggests there are multiple theories that lead toward the understanding of learning in these transformed classrooms.

The prevailing ideology—behaviorism that cast the mold for orchestra-like classrooms—has begun to crack, giving way to constructivism, feminism, and critical theory. These three theories are like a jazz band, warming up in the wings ready to produce an alternative form of music in public education. They represent themes of capability, care, and fairness that have been repressed, according to students, in traditional classrooms.

It is important to understand here, just like the evolving forms of jazz renditions, that the multiple theory framework in understanding student learning is also always moving, always in flux. No one theory dominates the classroom; rather, learning can be best understood as a series of dialectical exchanges between and among various forms of constructivism, feminism, and critical theory (Giroux, 1992). This chapter does not engage in theoretical construction. It does, however, describe a study that gave voice to students in which the possibility that multiple theories of understanding about student learning can coexist. This qualitative study explores the processes and conditions that students learn best. Additionally, this study is action research oriented—where students' strong insistence to develop strategies to influence the power structures at their school were predominant. This methodology became a powerful tool that liberated learning themes and students' collective voices.

PREVAILING PRACTICES

Historically, educators have viewed the process of learning as a transmission process (Iran-Nejad, 1990; Wells, 1986) in which teachers transmit their knowledge into the empty minds of learners. Teachers make decisions about curriculum, pedagogy, assessment, and governance. Students are passive recipients of knowledge who dutifully memorize facts and fill in the blanks (Goodlad, 1984). Standardized expectations and accountability are manifestations of the prevailing ideology. Compliance and obedience are valued over independence and critical thinking, because learners are shaped and molded by adult caretakers (Corsaro, 1983).

The value for humanity takes second place to efficiency and uniformity. Students consequently behave mechanically like robots, moving through a prescribed sequence to achieve predictable results. A growing objectification and mechanization are the results of this blanket of conformity (Aronowitz and Giroux, 1985).

Within this view, educators systematically deny and devalue student voices (McLaren, 1989; Fine, 1989). Teachers make unilateral decisions on what constitutes worthwhile knowledge because they lack faith and trust in students' capabilities (Wells, 1986). They also view students as empty vessels, not contributing resources, and believe they are incapable of contributing toward their own education. At best, they believe that by implementing consistent prescribed standards, they are serving the best interests of students, for they do not possess a sanctioned pedagogy to help them unleash alternative student resources.

METHODOLOGY: STUDENTS AS CORESEARCHERS

The purpose of the project described in this chapter was to understand learning and classrooms as viewed through the subjectivities of the learners. Students were not only key informants but also active collaborators (coresearchers) throughout the investigation. They joined the researcher in the collection of data and organization of research findings at Washington Middle School in Santa Monica, California. (All of the names used in this chapter are pseudonyms.)

One data-gathering technique entrusted students with cameras to take photographs of "meaningful learning experiences" in and out of classrooms. Working on the assumption that what students chose to photograph was influenced by what they believed to be significant (Eisner and Peshkin, 1990; English, 1989), students took several rolls of pictures and prioritized them from most to least meaningful. It was through the oral narratives of explaining their pictures that themes of learning began to emerge.

Students also maintained learning journals, documenting classroom activities period by period, describing meaningful learning. The journals helped students frame their experiences so that they could better describe classroom episodes during the biweekly coresearchers' meetings.

Some students drew pictures of their tacit understandings about learning, thus making their thoughts more explicit. Thinking about schooling and learning was initially difficult. It was like thinking about breathing. How does one begin to deconstruct something that has gone unquestioned in one's lifetime?

Additionally, the researcher "shadowed" students throughout the day in order to gain firsthand experience of a typical day in the life of a middle school student. This meant literally "hanging out" in locker rooms, lunch quads, and hallways for a school year. All of these data-gathering activities served as valuable catalysts for discussion at coresearchers' meetings.

Students had great difficulty with the original research question: "What are meaningful learning experiences?" Instead, their stories delineated more clearly perceived obstacles to learning. Thus the researcher found herself revamping the original line of inquiry to accepting students' narratives about the barriers they experienced in schooling. However, what was not initially anticipated was the dialogues of problematic conditions that prompted student action.

A POWERFUL EXPERIENCE: ENGAGING IN ACTION RESEARCH

By empowering students with research responsibilities, voice was given to a group who historically have not been part of the research community. Coresearchers, equipped with privileges to investigate learning and learning conditions, were asked to define "meaningful learning experiences." At first, they were mute. What followed was a profound discovery. They found they could better understand learning through their perceived obstacles than by understanding the learning process directly.

At coresearchers' meetings, students identified the barriers to learning. They critiqued teachers' attitudes, pedagogy, curriculum, and governance. Originally, this was where the research was scheduled to end. However, once students identified obstacles, their immediate instinct was to resolve the problems. It became clear to the researcher that there was a moral imperative to extend the research parameters to follow through with the coresearchers. Problem identification led to problem solving.

Group solidarity had formed. Collective strength and conviction grew as students shared common episodes of powerlessness and frustration. Consequently, the coresearchers were not content in merely studying their classroom experiences, but pressed instead to actively reshape their learning conditions.

Like action researchers (Sagor, 1992; Reed et al., 1992) they resisted being mere voyeurs (Wexler, 1987) in research, but pressed to engage in constructing a reform agenda. Discussions about alternatives and reform thoroughly permeated weekly meetings. Coresearchers developed group momentum and propelled the study into an action plan.[1]

The desire for action meant negotiating with those who held power. This propelled coresearchers to seek ways to be heard by adults. A political agenda was created and a strategy was developed to "butter up the teachers" with subsequent plans for meetings with the principal.

Students organized the data, prepared papers, and selected, among themselves, speakers for issues. This process resembled Simon's (1988) "project of possibility," where marginalized people develop social alternatives to the dominating power structure. Coresearchers presented their data to the faculty and requested dialogues to address issues in governance, instruction, and curriculum.

IF YOU CAN'T FIND SOMETHING NICE TO SAY, SAY SO

Although students could not articulate meaningful learning processes or conditions, they could vividly describe their perceived obstacles and barriers to learning. Their narratives identified three learning rhythms that were regularly violated in classrooms: the rhythms of learning, care and connection, and respect.

The Rhythm of Learning

What is the rhythm of learning? Is it the undulating movement of ocean waves, the steady purring of a cat, or the irregular staccato patterns of hiccups? Student researchers identified internal learning rhythms and told how their personal rhythms differed from others:

We just read *Call of the Wild* and I thought it was a really good book but we read it so slowly. We read one chapter a month and there were only seven chapters. By the time you're on the last chapter, you have no idea what happened cuz you don't remember it.

We read out loud in class and I don't think that is good. You practice reading but it doesn't help you learn because everybody reads at a different speed. And so you can try to read ahead if you're faster or like go behind. Because of their voice, you can't concentrate because everybody else is with them. And then I don't know, you can't read the way you normally read and how you normally enjoy it.

It just makes you hate reading because you read it so slowly. And it seems like everything you read is gonna be like that. It would be better if we read in class, but to ourselves. (Lori as cited in SooHoo, 1991a)

Fred agreed with Lori and added, "I'm always three pages ahead [of everyone else]" (Fred as cited in SooHoo, 1991a). Emily commented, "I get a better picture when I read myself than when someone else reads to me. I visualize it and I can stop it" (Emily as cited in SooHoo, 1991a).

Students described their internal rhythms as different from the teacher's. Subsequently, much of their energy in the classroom was consumed with attempts to synchronize their learning rhythms to their teacher's instructional rhythm or to catch up at home.

I understand the material, but sometimes she [the teacher] goes way too fast and a lot of other kids agree with me. So I'm just sitting there while she is scribbling stuff on the board that makes no sense to me. I'm just sitting there saying, "Oh my gosh." She goes so fast. She writes and writes and writes. And you know I get so frustrated. So I write everything down, copy things off the board. And so I have to go home and figure out what she said. I have no idea what it means, so I have to figure it out at home. (Angela as cited in SooHoo, 1991a)

The Rhythm of Care and Connection

Rhythm is a kinesthetic body experience like breathing in and out, or rocking back and forth as one cradles a baby. Students identify caring as an important rhythm of feelings that is critical in classroom experiences, particularly in connecting students with teachers, and students with one another.

Students described teachers who don't take time to care as having "an attitude." Students claimed they could not learn from teachers who did not care. When they have an attitude, Juan explained, "they get rude . . . .If they have an attitude, I don't know how they expect us to learn" (Juan as cited in SooHoo, 1991a). Teachers responded that they didn't have time to get to know 120 students each day. Time constraints forced teachers to develop superficial student-teacher relationships.

Furthermore, students reported that teachers devalued students' caring about each other. Two Hispanic males in the coresearchers' group placed loyalty to friends over everything else. This guiding ethos influenced their daily behavior. For example, it was not uncommon to see students risk the wrath of the teacher in order to console or comfort their friends. Angel frequently left the classroom without permission to console a fellow classmate who was kicked out of class. He thought nothing about skipping lunch or cutting class in order to sit with a suspended friend in the counselor's office.

The researcher found that many Latinos scheduled their classes to accommodate their social needs. Interestingly, they represented the greatest number of students who signed up for office work as a course elective. Juan was a third-period office worker who prized this time to telegraph social messages to his peers. This was also a time in which he could be autonomous of regimented classroom routines.

Students also expressed their need to socially connect with others by "roaming the halls." Organized daily by students of color, primarily Latinos, this amoeba-shaped collection of boys and girls moved through the corridors, uncaptained, like a river, flowing around corners and through passages. Homework, hugs, high fives, social gossip, reports of which teacher had "an attitude" today, and who was kicked out of class were typical exchanges. This human glue provided an important social connection that found little to no expression in the classrooms.

Occasional classroom cooperative learning activities allowed students to build temporary communities. But these instances were not predictable. They were dictated by teacher judgment rather than by student choice or needs. Consequently students rushed out of classrooms as the bells rang, not only to relieve their bodies of unyielding furniture but, more importantly, to make precious social connections. For these students, meaningful experiences occurred outside of classrooms. Teachers who were interviewed rationalized that students' social needs should be satisfied outside of the classroom.

The Rhythm of Respect

Early adolescence—a time of significant change in physical growth, cognitive ability, moral awareness, and psychosocial development (Glatthorn and Spencer, 1986)—makes middle schools particularly challenging. Responding to both the developmental instincts to struggle toward adult autonomy and the systematic analysis of their learning conditions, coresearchers questioned their status in their learning environment and rigorously critiqued school governance. Students became aware of their powerlessness as they described oppressive school practices. These practices included a perceived status distance between students and teachers, the unquestioned authority of adults, obsolete disciplinary policies, treating students as children, and treating Hispanic students as less worthy than other students.

The status difference between teachers and students could be observed, students cited, at the teacher-designated rows in the assembly hall, the absence of teachers in the lunch quads and at noontime events, and the retreat of teachers to the comfort of an air conditioned staff lounge. Students concluded that teachers distanced themselves from students to demonstrate that adults were privileged and students were not.

Unequal status was further demonstrated by unequal privileges. For example, students pointed out, teachers could be late for class but students could not. Students needed permission to enter empty classrooms. Teachers could chew gum but the school rules prohibited student gum chewing. Teachers could spit on the overhead to erase the writing while students were expected to treat school facilities with respect.

Physical distancing and status differentiation indicated to students that they were "low life," not worthy to be entrusted with respect, rights, responsibilities, or privileges. The bottom line: teachers did not trust or respect students. Coresearchers hungered for opportunities to demonstrate responsibility but felt locked into a system that could not hear their developmental motors approaching adulthood.

"They treat us like kids" complained coresearchers. "He expects us to be like adults," complained Emily, "but he'll still treat us like kids." Pointing to a beveling machine in woodshop that only the teacher was allowed to handle, "I don't like it when they [teachers] don't let us do things because it's for grown ups," she protested (Emily as cited in SooHoo, 1991a). When I asked her if she thought she could operate the machine safely by herself, she responded affirmatively. She longed for a chance to prove it.

"They think just because we're kids, we don't know anything," added Mike (Mike as cited in SooHoo, 1991a). "Some people say, oh you're 12 [years old]," Angel reported, "you're just a little kid." At a coresearchers' meeting, Kristina stormed into the room, obviously angry, slamming her books on the desk: "The teacher talks to me like a four year old!" (Kristina as cited in SooHoo, 1991a). Mandatory locker and monthly binder clean outs reinforced the message that students could not be trusted. Aba wrote in her journal: "We are treated as if we are not capable human beings" (Aba as cited in SooHoo, 1991a).

Over the public address system, a voice announces, "I smell a lock out today!" This meant students needed to scurry for class or risk getting locked out, only to face the six-foot, 200-pound security guard, the voice from the squawk box. Fred pointed out that if he ran to class to avoid lock outs, he could get a referral for running in the halls. If he followed the rules and walked to class, he inevitably faced a lock out. Either way, coresearchers disclosed, the administration did not notice or care about the apparent contradictions.

Oppressive School Rules

Governance was seriously scrutinized by coresearchers. Not only were there too many rules to follow, they claimed, there was an additive feature about them. Each new problem propagated a new rule.

Every year there is one main problem that happens in school. People start bringing stuff, like Pixy Sticks and then that rule just sticks. That could have happened in 1930. It just stays the rest of the time. No one even notices it or remembers. Like Walkmans were big last year. (Fred as cited in SooHoo, 1991a)

The school's document labeled the Merit System read: "Water weanies warrants three demerits and one detention." When asked, "When was the last time you have a problem with water weanies at this school?" students revealed that the rule was made years ago, designed for a graduated student population.

"They Discriminate Against Hispanics"

The narratives, "They Discriminate Against Hispanics," told by Angel and Juan, describe unequal treatment of Latino students with respect to dress code violations. Due to gang activity in past years, Washington Middle School implemented a dress code restricting students from wearing the colors black and white, and Raiders' paraphernalia. Angel and Juan described a particular incident in which a group of Latino students was singled out to see a movie about gangs by a teacher, the assistant principal, and a police officer. The movie incident was not an isolated case. The boys felt Latino students were routinely treated with suspicion and disrespect by faculty.

I saw this Chinese kid wearing a Raiders jersey, a Raiders jacket, a Raiders hat, and Mr. Brown didn't say anything. And that's not fair. And yesterday, I was wearing some sweats with some shorts underneath and I was like sagging just a little. And Mr. B. said, "Pull 'em up before I pull 'em up myself and write you up!" (Angel as cited in SooHoo, 1991a)

THE REFORM PLAN

Meetings with the Teachers

Biweekly coresearchers' meetings became the forum from which students dialogued with each other about the conditions that oppressed their learning rhythms. These group meetings also equipped students with budding confidence and provided the groundwork for group solidarity. As was stated earlier, problem identification led to an instinct to problem solve and students pushed hard for reform.

This strong desire for action took the following course. Coresearchers invited their four interdisciplinary core teachers and principal to meetings where students shared their perceptions and recommendations about learning and schooling. They plotted a strategy to butter up the teachers; they brought refreshments and started each meeting by telling teachers what they did well and ended with a short list of recommendations. With sensitivity, students unveiled their issues and concerns, conscious of not "turning the teachers off."

Tentative and suspicious, teachers initially debated about attending the meetings. Math teacher, Ms. S. complained, "They're gonna rag on us!" Teachers wondered what was in it for them to respond to the students' invitations. Would the students make suggestions to improve classrooms? "Why change?" asked the history teacher.

Nonetheless, stung by curiosity, the teachers accepted the invitation to a fireside chat, with one proviso: students must meet with the principal separately. Teachers were uncomfortable with the potential vulnerability of the situation in the company of their supervisor.

The following are teachers' reflections about their first meeting with student coresearchers:

After teaching for twenty plus years, skepticism seemed to be a part of my thinking. The way things were seemed to be okay. Why change? The patterns we set up over the years were comfortable as we stood in front of our domain. What could students offer to me or the others to improve what we felt we did well? What did students perceive as faults in our teaching styles? (Mr. O. as cited in SooHoo, 1991b)

The day has arrived! Yes, with much curiosity and more than enough trepidation, the results of students' educational analysis are going to be heard. Of course, I'll need to bear in mind the main characteristic of a good listener—keep quiet. Holding back is definitely going to be difficult for me, who needs to give input or justification for most things. They're going to "rag" on me! (Ms. S. as cited in SooHoo, 1991b)

Sitting with the student coresearchers' tribunal, I listened to students' perceptions of their learning and, most articulately expressed, what blocked their learning. "Teacher attitudes" was a recurring message in that meeting with its stinging reference to uncaring teachers, and with each student comment I grew more disheartened to think that this was me to whom they were referring. Removing my pride from that meeting, it occurred to me that students were becoming active in their learning, the very outcome I wished for the year. And so I listened for their perceptions, their voices, "joined in a journey for metamorphosis," as Megan would say, and made mental notes to file under curriculum and pedagogy and in my heart. (Ms. V. as cited in SooHoo, 1991b)

They, "the students," weakened us with the goodies they provided, and we, "the teachers," were human in the eye of the students for the first time. Time had passed so quickly; we all agreed another meeting would be necessary and fruitful to begin the process of hearing these student voices and try to apply their suggestions to our classes. The ball was rolling. We want to establish a closer student-teacher relationship and jointly formulate strategies for student participation in creating positive learning experiences. (Mr. O. as cited in SooHoo, 1991b)

Student Empowerment

Teachers asked why students had not brought these concerns up before, so students offered two reasons. First, no teacher had ever thought to ask them before about learning experiences. "I've been waiting to get this off my chest," reported Angela, "but there was no one to ever tell this to" (Angela as cited in SooHoo, 1991b). Second, coresearchers attributed their increased understanding and their participation in the project as giving them collective strength to assert their voices.

As a result of the initial meeting, teachers and students planned to work three full days together in the mutual construction of the semester's thematic units of instruction. Improving learning experiences was jointly agreed upon as a good place to start their work together. Instructional pedagogy was overhauled to be more sensitive and receptive to students' experiences, backgrounds, interests, and concerns. Meanwhile, teachers made a concerted effort to get to know the students better. Opportunities were structured to allow students to offer opinions regularly. In addition, teachers frequently made informal inquiries, seeking student feedback.

The principal, in response to coresearchers, developed two student/ teacher task forces to address students' major concerns outside of the classrooms. One task force, called the discipline committee, investigated policing practices by administrators and security guards. The second task force targeted rule-governed Physical Education expectations. "The students presented me with a real dilemma," reported the principal. "Challenging the traditional militaristic P. E. department is not necessarily where an administrator would start restructuring efforts. However, I drew my strength on the students' convictions" (Straus, 1992 as cited in SooHoo, 1991a). End results included student-researchers joining administrators in rewriting the school's discipline plan and students accompanying P. E. teachers to visit alternative programs at other schools.

Coresearchers learned they were capable not only of understanding their learning and schooling experiences but also in reshaping structural conditions. They had joined hands to dismantle those practices that devalued their voice. In turn, they received newfound respect by their teachers, administrators, and fellow students.

Teachers, students, and the principal have coauthored a paper and made

presentations (SooHoo, 1991a) about their experiences. During this process, they became more clear about the values, beliefs, and norms held by
students and teachers. Teachers and students have continued to work hard
through many rough spots. Faculty has had to be thoughtful about re-
minding themselves to include students in decisions.

The original coresearchers' group has moved on to high school. Some
students continue to seek ways to negotiate their learning process and learning conditions with their teachers. A couple have met with the superintendent. Others expressed frustration at revisiting a lack of status and
powerlessness on their new high school campuses.

FROM THE TEACHERS' PERSPECTIVE

Although students were the hub of this research, the role of the teacher
should not be underestimated. The English teacher engaged in a study of
her own and made noteworthy strides in this project. At the beginning of
the project, with law school application in hand, on the brink of burn out,
Brenda V. was ready to throw in the towel. She was dissatisfied with her
lack of success in reaching her students. Questioning if she should remain
in teaching, she wrote in her journal:

If learning is like a heartbeat, then my classes are flatliners. It was only October
[1990] and I was fighting student passivity with all my three years of teaching experiences. Should I waste my talents on students who don't want to learn, who don't
love learning? Should I continue teaching as a career? (Ms. V. as cited in SooHoo,
1991b)

Brenda maintained that she participated in the project because she was
trying to determine her worth as a teacher. Allowing herself to be vulnerable
and humble, she questioned, probed, and critiqued students' accounts of
experiences in her room. Why did she do this? She explained that this project
has been a form of professional growth for her, the most meaningful staff
development she had ever experienced. Her learning was not the result of
mandates from outside her classroom, rather she and her students learned
from each other—organically, rhythmically responding to each other in syncopation.

Starting with student questions, she responded by developing her own
line of inquiry. Three elements were critical to Brenda's growth in this project, elements essential to teachers who are reflective about their classroom
experiences: opportunities to reflect, opportunities to collaborate, and opportunities to challenge conventional wisdom. By examining her own practice and engaging in collaborative dialogue, Brenda, a new teacher
researcher, became a more thoughtful professional and change agent who

would make substantive changes in her classroom practices (SooHoo, 1989).

Opportunity to Reflect

Brenda maintained a journal throughout the project. It helped her become more mindful of instructional decisions and systematically reflective about the days' activities. She filled it with her questions, celebrations, frustrations, and fears. These notes plus students' articulated concerns acted as the catalysts for Brenda to restructure her teaching strategies. Over the course of the project, it appeared that she had matured into a reflective practitioner who identified puzzling, troubling, or interesting phenomena and who tried to make sense of it all by using this information to guide future action (Schon, 1987).

Opportunity to Collaborate

The researcher assumed the role of "critical friend" (Sagor, 1991) with Brenda. Always an available resource, the researcher offered an independent perspective when Brenda sought opportunities to intellectually engage in issues about her classroom. In the mutual construction of meaning and the joint examination of practice, the critical friend from the university and the classroom teacher had the opportunity to connect theory with practice (Goodlad and Sirotnik, 1988). Together they narrowed the gap between "doing research" and "implementing research findings" (Lieberman, 1986).

Opportunity to Challenge Conventional Wisdom

Like a half turn of a kaleidoscope, both Brenda and the principal now viewed their roles from a slightly different angle. They admitted it never occurred to them to include students in their decisions due to firmly held beliefs about adults controlling classrooms. The project had unearthed their unexamined pragmatism and helped to formulate the question: Who should be involved in making decisions about learning and schooling?

FROM THE STUDENTS' PERSPECTIVES

The coresearcher group is a group of students that thought they could not make a difference, but proved themselves wrong. In our school we have changed the way we learn and also our teachers. To me the coresearcher group was a way out of the wrong way of teaching and learning. It was a way that we, the students, could express ourselves and not get in trouble. The teachers could learn from us and we could understand each other. (Angel as cited in SooHoo, 1991b)

Individual students were changed in the process as they engaged in a plan of reform. The transformation of Juan was particularly significant. Juan was Mr. Soc in the halls: sociable, popular, talkative; and Mr. Placid in the class-rooms: quiet, shy, passive. He further reinforced this dual identity by refer-ring to himself as "John" in the classrooms, and "Juan" outside of the classrooms. Juan was socially confident among his peers; John was with-drawn and apathetic.

Although shy initially, Juan was expressive and self-assured at the meeting with teachers as he boldly pointed out instances of Hispanic discrimination that teachers had been unaware of. When Juan spoke up, teachers com-mented: "We saw John take a position, be a leader, dominate the discus-sion." By the end of the year, Juan, previously a C student, graduated with all As and Bs and was voted the most-improved student of the year by his teachers. Juan attributed his transition from invisible student to student of prominence with greater respect and caring from the teachers and his ability to encourage this rapport.

The success of the coresearchers' reform plan can be partly attributed to conditions similar to English teacher Brenda's. Opportunities to reflect as a group, interviews, and journals facilitated a systematic analysis of learning processes and conditions. Student collaboration fueled group unification. Student meetings, structured democratically, gave each person the power to shape agendas and challenge conventional wisdom. These conditions ena-bled coresearchers to become capable ethnographers and agents of change.

FROM THE PRINCIPAL'S PERSPECTIVE

Students: An Unexpected Constituent

This project forced the principal to review her narrow conception of site-based management and shared governance that targeted primarily teacher involvement in school decisions. A new constituency—students—had an-nounced its presence. Previously unacknowledged in decisions of gover-nance and curriculum development, students now promised to be an influential force. Her previous commitment to shared decisions now com-pelled her to include students, unexpected constituents, at the decision-making table.

Before this study began, the leadership at the site was shared among ad-ministrators and teachers. Curricular improvement strategies depended upon teacher leadership and administrative support. Now, students are involved in site leadership in new and more significant ways. Students are often over-heard in the counseling office saying that things are different this year, and that adults really listen to what they have to say. While this does not per-meate the entire institution, no staff member would deny the importance of the student and of the students' perspectives. Student voices are valued and are part of the entire decision-making processes in use at the school (Straus, 1992).

Rethinking Professional Development

The principal also began to reconceptualize professional development on her campus. A new model emerged as she critiqued the existing practices. She started to rethink students' rights in constructing meaningful learning activities.

The traditional staff development model imposes the right method upon the teacher, determining that the leader or the chosen leaders know the best way to do things. This model had guided the intensive staff development efforts under way at the school site during the last six years.

This project provided collaborative time for the teachers and students to work to-gether on issues of curriculum, choice for students, and active learning strategies. Just as teachers have the right to discover what is important to them through peer work, students must also be allowed that right as well.

As the leader, I am gaining comfort in accepting more than one approach to staff development. (Straus, 1992)

Researcher as Critical Friend

The principal attributed some of her professional growth to the researcher as "critical friend" (Sagor, 1991). She told how an outsider helped her gain fresh perspectives about school. Admittedly, neither she nor the researcher were prepared for the total implications of the study.

It is important to understand that the researcher worked painstakingly to develop a rapport and trust with the principal. Without this foundation, allowing a researcher into classrooms, wandering through hallways, and gen-erally collecting information and opinions about the workings of the school through the eyes and voices of students would have been intimidating and confrontive. Even with the trust, I as the researcher collected information that forced me to confront issues I had not chosen to deal with, to see myself and my leadership style through a different lens, and to show vul-nerability often hidden from adults on the campus.

Little did I realize when this project began, how far it would go, how many issues and schoolwide policies would be exposed and addressed, and how strongly the foundation would be laid for the honoring of student voices in schoolwide decision making (Straus, 1992).

Students' organized, political voice had stirred the heart of the leader of the institution. They compelled her to rethink her fundamental beliefs. "Throughout the study, my values and beliefs were challenged," Straus commented.

THE SYNCOPATION OF MULTIPLE THEORIES

Students identified the music they needed in order to optimize their learning capacity. The internal learning rhythm cited by students during reading was the necessary self-regulation of meaning-making ascribed by constructivists. Feminism was manifested in the expressed need to be socially connected to peers and to establish caring relationships with teachers. Coresearchers, like critical theorists, critiqued their governance structure and built an agenda for social change to eliminate student marginality. Consequently, initial attempts were made to deconstruct the curriculum, instruction, and governance of a middle school. Simultaneously, by inviting them as members of the research community, coresearchers became critically conscious and learned about freedom and democracy by experiencing it. These learning rhythms, which students argue are legitimate facets of student learning, have been denied in behaviorist, traditional classrooms. We must move from a single notion of learning to the syncopation of multiple theories of learning.

A practical argument for the syncopation of learning rhythms can be made in the assignment of personal histories, often required in history or language arts classrooms. A teacher, equipped with the knowledge of multiple learning rhythms, can sensitively create a context for which this assignment is made. By establishing a caring classroom community that values diverse contributions, the teacher facilitates the emergence of authentic, oftentimes muted, student voices. Personal histories, depicting lives colored with themes of ethnicity, culture, language, family, gender, or ability, can be the starting point for an emancipatory curriculum. Class meetings that create a knowledge pool can discover common themes such as humanity or dehumanization, belonging or not belonging, hope or hopelessness. All of this depends on the meaning students make as they connect their lives and experiences. These constructive, feminist, and critical exchanges differ radically from the "write an autobiography," which is singularly read by the teacher and furthermore graded.

The looming threat of a national curriculum for each subject matter discipline is yet another denial of multiple learning rhythms. Advocates for uniformed national standards fall again into the "single notion" trap in education. In the interest of excellence, efficiency, and consensual understanding, policymakers choose to standardize and control curricula as if any single curriculum could fully develop human potential. Along these same lines comes standardized assessment, suggesting a single indicator can depict human achievement.

In an institution that is responsive to learning rhythms of capability, caring, and respect, one would expect to find curriculum, instruction, and assessment open to student negotiation. What and how students learn in classrooms must be informed by students. Assessment, or asking "How do we know what we know?" is a collaborative inquiry by students and teacher. They mutually discover what are the best ways of demonstrated knowledge.

During a 1992–93 project of the Partnership Network located at the University of California at Irvine (SooHoo, 1993), a group of high school language arts teachers, representing fourteen school districts, asked their students to engage in a joint research project. Their question was, "What assessments represent an accurate and comprehensive picture of student learning?" Among assessment techniques they identified as authentic in capturing student achievement were portfolios, videotaped performances, peer and self-analysis, and student/teacher interviews.

Constructivist, feminist, and critical influences can be seen in these alternative assessment practices through the sanctioning of individual meaning-making, within a context of caring relationships, to overcome external certification of student achievement and to gain control of learning and teaching lives. Clearly, students and teachers rejected the tradition of achievement being reduced to a single numerical score and a single ideology. They created instead multiple indicators of success, using many theories to inform them. The process that facilitated these results was a syncopated rhythm between students and teachers in responding to a mutual research question.

From a theoretical perspective, the syncopation of multiple theories is also a worthy path to explore. To believe any one ideology could depict human learning is naive. To not search for alternative understandings is irresponsible. To understand both singular and collective contributions of multiple theories is difficult. With the notion (very broadly put) that multiple theories exist within a "text" or class, students in this study can be viewed through this theoretical lens: Constructivism entrusts the locus of control of learning in the hands of the learner as, in this study, the students themselves. Feminism embraces caring, connection, and community as fundamental tenets of classroom environments. Critical theory advocates an emancipatory and liberatory consciousness as the reason for reconceptualizing classrooms. Together, these theories intersect to empower students and teachers to design learning conditions and learning experiences, and to celebrate human resources toward a new reconceptualized moral social order that allows the conditions to help alleviate forms of oppression, alienation, and subordination.

POLICY IMPLICATIONS

Student researchers identified different problems in public schools compared to policymakers. Students did not cite class size, drugs, drop-out rates, or lack of parent involvement as targets for reform. Rather, student core-searchers recommended that educators view students as capable and caring individuals, who are valuable participants and contributors in learning and schooling.

The reform reports of the past decade have sought opinions from teachers, administrators, college presidents, and businesspeople. No opinion from students has been sought to inform the reform movement. The research described in this chapter unleashed student voices and brought forth thoughtful student recommendations because it was informed by multiple perspectives. When we ask ourselves why, historically, students were not considered worthy of consultation, we find that traditionally viewing the student as an empty vessel or a passive recipient has blinded us from seeing students as valuable resources.

No longer a disenfranchised group, the coresearchers have boldly expressed their voices about school reform. The adults in the school have learned valuable lessons from the students and together they have developed alternatives, noteworthy of consideration by practitioners, policymakers, and scholars. Collectively, they, like jazz musicians, respect each other's talent and perspectives as they participate in the syncopated rhythm of negotiating public education.

NOTE

1. Action research is a form of self-reflective inquiry undertaken by participants in social (including educational) situations in order to improve the rationality and justice of their own social or educational practices, their understanding of these practices, and the situations in which the practices are carried out (Carr and Kemmis, 1983, p. 152).

REFERENCES

Aronowitz, S. and Giroux, H. (1985). *Education under Siege*. London: Routledge & Kegan Paul.

Carr, W. and Kemmis, S. (1983). *Becoming Critical: Knowing Through Action Research*. Philadelphia: Farmer Press.

Corsaro, W. (1983). *Friendship and Peer Culture in the Early Years*. Norwood, NJ: Ablex.

Eisner, E. and Peshkin, A. (1990). *Qualitative Inquiry in Education*. New York: Teachers College Press.

English, F. (1989). "Socio-cultural Determinants of the Knowledge Base in Educational Administration: Applications of Visual Data in Illustrating a Theory." Paper/presentation for University Council for Educational Administration, Scottsdale, AZ.

Fine, M. (1989). "Silencing and Nurturing Voice in an Improbable Context: Urban Adolescents in Public School." In H. Giroux and P. McLaren (eds.), *Critical*

Pedagogy, the State and Cultural Struggle. (pp. 152–173). Albany: State University of New York Press.

Giroux, Henry. (1992). *Border Crossings: Cultural Workers and the Politics of Education.* New York: Routledge, Chapman & Hall.

Glatthorn, A. and Spencer, N. (1986). *Middle School/Junior High Principal's Handbook.* Englewood Cliffs, NJ: Prentice-Hall.

Goodlad, J. (1984). *A Place Called School.* New York: McGraw-Hill.

Goodlad, J. and Sirotnik, K. (1988). *School-University Partnerships in Action.* New York: Teachers College Press.

Iran-Nejad, A. (1990). "Active and Dynamic Self-regulation of Learning Processes." *Review of Educational Research,* 60 (4): 573–602.

Kanpol, B. (1992). *Towards a Theory and Practice of Teacher Cultural Politics: Continuing the Postmodern Debate.* Norwood, NJ: Ablex.

Kerchner, C. (1990). Personal correspondence.

Lieberman, A. (1986). "Collaborative Research: Working with, Not Working on." *Educational Leadership,* 43: 28–32.

McLaren, P. (1989). *Life in Schools.* New York: Longman.

Reed, C., Mergendoller, J. and Horan, C. (1992). "Collaborative Research: A Strategy for School Improvement." *Crossroads,* pp. 5–12.

Sagor, D. (1992). *How to Conduct Collaborative Action Research.* Alexandria, VA: Association for Supervision and Curriculum Development.

Sagor, D. (1991). "What Project LEARN Reveals about Collaborative Active Research." *Educational Leadership,* 48 (6): 6–10.

Schon, D. (1987). *Reflective Practitioner.* New York: Basic Books.

Simon, R. (1988). "For a Pedagogy of Possibility." *Critical Pedagogy Networker,* 1 (1): 1–6.

SooHoo, S. (1989). *Teacher Researcher: Emerging Change Agent.* San Francisco: American Educational Research Association. (ERIC Document Reproduction Service No. ED 307 255).

———. (1991a). "Lessons from Middle School Students about Learners and Learning." Doctoral dissertation. Claremont Graduate School.

———. (1991b). "Transforming Classrooms/School through Student Voice." *Claremont Reading Conference Fifty Fifth Yearbook.* Claremont, CA: Center for Developmental Studies.

———. (1993). "Students and Teachers as Researchers." Paper presented to the American Educational Research Association, Atlanta.

Wells, G. (1986). *Meaning Makers.* Portsmouth, NH: Heinemann.

Wexler, P. (1987). *Social Analysis of Education: After the New Sociology of Education.* London: Routledge & Kegan Paul.

12

Safeguarding Empowerment

Jeffrey Cinnamond

INTRODUCTION

R. Prawat (1991, p. 738) recently claimed that "teacher empowerment is no longer simply fashionable in educational discourse, it is almost mandatory." Such a statement indicates the pervasiveness of empowerment as a conceptual and practical process of education. By the nature of being utilized across the spectrum of education, there is a tendency to gloss empowerment's meaning. For this reason I suggest that empowerment is in need of critical examination. A rough examination of the literature suggests that each ideology—conservative, liberal, and critical—has adopted and adapted the term for its uses. However, an examination of the term and topic relative to Michel Foucault and his notions of discourse and power is an underrepresented element of the literature. This chapter will juxtapose Foucault with evidence from an empirical study toward the goal of providing educators new knowledge about critical educational "empowerment" practices.

One way of conceptualizing empowerment has focused upon working within the status quo of the institutional and social context. From such a perspective teachers can be empowered by utilizing the existing school organizational structures (Maeroff, 1988; McElrath, 1988). The process and products of teacher empowerment are articulated and designed from above by those in authority (Richardson and Sistrunk, 1989). As a result the literature does not indicate teachers as having an orientation to move away from oppressive acts (Pugh, 1989). Teachers await those in authority to be the agents of empowerment rather than involving the teachers themselves.

A second mode of conceptualizing empowerment has been identified from a liberal viewpoint. These authors attend to the empowerment of individual teachers who, through reflection, focus upon professional issues (Rice, 1987; Troen and Boles, 1988). These issues may include improved decision making (Greer, 1989), responsibility for planning (Glickman, 1988), development of a knowledge base (Yonemura, 1986), but there is a failure to address institutions and societal impacts that limit empowerment. The liberal tradition has been encapsulated in the following manner: "While liberal reformers tend to use education to promote equality, community, and humanistic social interaction, they do not confront those aspects of the schools which pull in the opposite direction" (Cagen, 1978).

Critical education and feminist writers have been among the more rigorous to address issues of empowerment and the schooling processes, particularity with regard to understanding the contradictions of reform and social context (Aronowitz and Giroux, 1985; Ellsworth, 1989; Freire, 1985; Giroux and McLaren, 1986, 1989; Kanpol, 1992; Lather, 1991; McRobbie, 1978; Shrewsbury, 1987; Simon, 1987, 1988; Weiler, 1988). These authors envision empowerment as resistance to oppressive acts and beliefs and as the self-conscious analysis of teaching for transformative and political work. Empowerment as situated within this literature reflects a "project of possibility" (Simon, 1987) that has as its goal the emancipation of oppressed individuals and groups.

This chapter presents a research project that had as its goal an examination of an urban school setting in western Pennsylvania where empowerment was generally acknowledged by teachers and administrators internal and external to the school as an ongoing practice for several years.[1] Taking seriously the postmodern challenge of problematizing the accepted as real, the goal of this study was to analyze the social practices of empowerment as practiced in an actual location. Because it was accepted and acknowledged that empowerment did exist, the research set out to identify its operational practices. By utilizing Foucault's notion of discourse (1979a), the original research plan was to demonstrate that empowerment is socially produced and transmitted and recursively situated, and that discourse is a constitutive element of empowerment.

However, after the project was completed, a more thorough and careful reading of Foucault, especially his interviews, necessitated a reexamination of the evidence and empowerment relative to his notions of power and resistance. The last section of this chapter suggests an alternative reading of empowerment, which elaborates how teachers and administrators may undo oppressive and subordinative relations rather than only be oppressed and deskilled. While Foucault does not use the expression "empowerment," he does speak of power that "must be understood in the first instance as the multiplicity of force relations imminent in the sphere in which they operate and which constitute their own organizations" (1980, p. 92).

DISCOURSE

Before beginning the body of the text it is important to be clear about Foucault's meaning of "discourse." Discourse is not just text or talk, but also includes the practices that determine them (Foucault, 1979a).

Discursive practices are characterized by the delimitation of a field of objects, the definition of a legitimate perspective for the agent of knowledge, and the fixing of norms for the elaboration of concepts and theories. Thus, each discourse practice implies a play of prescriptions that designates its exclusions and choices (Foucault, 1986, p. 199). Discourse is not about objects, rather it is a means of constitution, which systematically forms objects as well as qualifying speakers. Discourse practices are specific and distinct for each community as it develops subtle, calculated mechanisms, including ritualized forms for disciplining itself and its members. Yet discourse rules are not clearly identified with one author or speaker in the sense of claiming an origin; however, they constitute a specific localized system. A new teacher or outside observer must take a period of time to identify the players and roles because they will be specific for each context and elaborated through the daily interactions of its members.

In this manner, discourse practices act as inclusionary and exclusionary boundaries for each community. Discourse practices "are embodied in technical processes, in institutions, in patterns for general behavior, in forms for transmission and diffusion, and in pedagogical forms which, at once impose and maintain them" (1986, p. 200). For example, to be a community member at a school, one must know and be able to appropriately use empowerment's discourse practices. Gaining entry into the community necessitates gaining a working understanding of its norms, values, and practices embedded in the everyday discursive acts of members. What are the important committees? Who are the more prominent speakers? By what history have they developed their authority?

Discourse practices not only constitute membership, they also regulate members both consciously and unconsciously. As such, discourse practices transmit, expose, anchor, and produce power (Foucault, 1980a, p. 101). To summarize, discourse practices refer to the complex interrelations and representations of language, interactions, context, organizations, and history and treat them as objects for study to comprehend and locate codes of knowledge and power. The production of discourse is controlled, selected, organized, and redistributed according to procedures that act as rules of exclusion impacting both form and meaning that are institutionally and culturally sustained (Foucault, 1983, p. 218). It is through the application of these notions that we can understand more fully how to open spaces of phronesis. That is, how can we work creatively to construct modes of thinking and acting on everyday events to create a truly positive atmosphere for all to work on problems to be solved and goals to be achieved?

EMPOWERMENT

Middleburg was an urban western Pennsylvania elementary/middle school. The building was located in a rural site and was designed and constructed in 1978 as an open school. The previous principal, Mr. Woodall,[2] who now worked in the district's central office, had established and fostered a mode of interaction, decision making, and leadership that utilized shared decision making and multiple points of dialogue and involvement as principles of practice. This formula is the contextual definition of empowerment as a practice of discourse for Middleburg, as identified in the early interviews. Encapsulated in this way, empowerment appears to be a procedure or strategy easily adaptable to other sites and situations.

This definition of empowerment is based upon discussions held with teachers, administrators, and board members prior to the intervention for observations in the school setting. It does not entirely fit with the critical literature, which can be generalized as conceptualizing empowerment as an overcoming of oppression or alienation. In Middleburg's case, empowerment was developed out of the images and goals of a principal, Mr. Woodall, who wanted to develop a particular set of principles for a specific school. The new principal, Jim Bryant, utilized a different administrative approach, and this chapter is in part the story of his failure. Jim Bryant was replaced at the end of his first year.

EVIDENCE

The chapter is based upon evidence collected across a year in the life of a school identified as one with empowered teachers. The year of observation coincided with the hiring of a new principal, Jim Bryant, who was brought in from another district. The evidence consists of the following: a series of site documents that trace the demonstration of empowerment; participant-observations of meetings and activities taking place both within and outside the school setting; field notes; videotapes; teacher-generated documents; organizational narratives; and more than twenty narrative-styled interviews with teachers and administrators involved in Middleburg's daily operation (Cinnamond, 1991).

Involvement with this setting occurred at a particularly significant moment. After thirteen years of leadership, Middleburg changed principals and, as a result, leadership and strategies of discourse. The researchers' participation at this juncture provided a window from which to view empowerment's situated practices of discourse.

For illustrative purposes, two typical examples have been selected that demonstrate empowerment's discursive practices. The first example revolves around the issue of appropriate student dress. It is taken from the narrative of Beth Ingram, a seventh/eighth-grade home economics teacher who had been at Middleburg for three years. The second example involves the issue of principal-teacher evaluations/observations and lesson plans. It is taken from the narrative of Bill Pope, a math teacher who had been at Middleburg for thirteen years. The social facts and discourse practices described by teachers and used as their point of routine were constituted prior to the researchers' involvement with the site.

Appropriate Student Dress

Middleburg's previously established practice permitted students to wear shorts to school if the shorts were stylish and near the knees. This was an unwritten, building-specific practice that had evolved over time. One day Mr. Bryant made an announcement over the school's public address system that students were no longer to wear shorts. Neither explanation nor reasoning was provided for the decision—it was just announced. This strategy of leadership and decision making was the normal pattern for Jim.

As reported in several interviews, the previously established discourse practices of empowerment in this school community suggested that a more typical mode of interaction would have been different. Under the school's discourse practices, Jim would have brought the issue informally to the Program Improvement Council (PIC). PIC's membership was comprised of one representative from each curricular and administrative unit. Meetings were open for everyone, and anyone who attended had equal voice and vote, although typically the same small group of teachers attended each meeting. After discussion, every PIC representative would take the issue back to their learning community for further discussion.[3]

At this juncture, students might also become involved as teachers discussed the concern with students in student government, student organizations, or in their individual classrooms. The PIC representative would return to PIC for both further discussion and possibly a decision. Such a mode of operation has been identified elsewhere as social reflection (Cinnamond and Zimpher, 1990).

It must be emphasized that this stock of knowledge (Schutz, 1962) regarding the processes of decision making and practices of empowerment was not documented in writing anywhere, but had evolved over time and thus demonstrated the embedded and highly contextualized element of discourse. The written statements and official discourse (Smith, 1990) about PIC and the learning communities indicated a more curricular and structural orientation that reflected, to use Smith's terminology, a particular construction for the "relations of ruling." However, through Middleburg's progression and the development of its norms of professional and social involvement and decision making under Mr. Woodall's leadership, the social reflection these organizations constructed were developed through a mode of operations, a discourse practice, that was both empowering and participatory.

The depth to which the patterns of discourse had permeated the school was such that when Mr. Bryant announced his decision on shorts, students were confused. It was not the decision itself that confused them, but their confusion centered on Middleburg's decision-making practices. Students understood that issues were discussed with and by the teachers. In this situation the students were unaware of this happening. Beth Ingram reported in an interview: "One of the students said to me 'I thought that you teachers voted . . . on everything' . . . but in this instance we were not consulted; that has not happened before."

Principal-Teacher Evaluations

Bill Pope, another teacher, elaborated a personal incident attending to an issue that several teachers discussed in their interviews regarding lesson plans and evaluations. He stated: "we had a run in shortly after he was here and I was the first one he observed and it was completely different from what we were used to."

Typically, Mr. Woodall would arrive unannounced for the observation. He would sit in the classroom and take notes. As Bill explained, "you would then have a meeting with him (usually in the teacher's room), and he would go over mostly positive things and then tell you some of the things you might need some help in." However, after Mr. Bryant observed Bill, "he called me up [to the principal's office] and said to bring my lesson plan . . . he said those aren't any good." Bill reported that he pointed out the teacher's manual that outlined objectives for each day and noted that his plans followed the text. Mr. Bryant was not satisfied, and he directed Bill to revise his lesson plans according to Bryant's more structural formula.

Bill continues: "I didn't get one positive feedback, really everything of what he did was negative, then he showed me a check sheet he was using. It was approved by the board and supposedly the association." This was the first time in nineteen years in the system and thirteen at Middleburg that Bill had seen this evaluation form. The form's use by Bryant notes a distinctive discourse practice and orientation toward the teachers.

After meeting with the principal, Bill, in consultation with other teachers, began to talk the matter over with the seventh- and eighth-grade learning community members. It is relevant to note that a special meeting was not called, but the teachers gathered, as was their norm, in the lounge between classes. In interviews the teachers identified this pattern as an element of their empowerment. The teachers tried to meet informally with Mr. Bryant; however, he would meet with them only after they scheduled a time and informed him of the agenda. Later, some teachers from this learning community met with Mr. Bryant, in his office, and asked for an explanation of the evaluation's method. None was given. Following the meeting and after further discussion in the lounge, again at an unofficial meeting, the teachers decided to speak with the superintendent. To meet with the superintendent was an atypical practice for Middleburg's community members. Yet several teachers claimed during interviews that they felt comfortable and enabled to speak directly with the superintendent. Mr. Bryant's evaluation procedures subsequently changed.

DISCUSSION

This analysis focuses on an actual space and site, Middleburg School, and attends to the contextual, plural, and limited nature of empowerment. However, the methods and practices of empowerment, and the label given by the participants for the intricate set of discourse practices at Middleburg, can be identified and are visible for analysis.

Beth Ingram's story points toward significant features of empowerment at Middleburg. The official discourse found in the documents that describe PIC and learning committee activities indicate a curricular function and a structural orientation. Through time this organization's activities and territory had evolved to include *almost* everything related to the school and its operation.

By attending primarily to the literal meaning of the official discourse, Mr. Bryant did not fathom the embedded contextual meaning and related discourse necessary to become a community member. He attended to and claimed a form of professional authority. He saw the textual artifacts of official discourse as objective facts, and as facts he categorized teacher and principal relations into a series of authoritarian principles. By not utilizing the discourse practices of Middleburg, Mr. Bryant indicated an orientation toward a structural regulation of teacher activities.[4] Such an orientation suggests a relation and understanding of teachers and students as objects rather than subjects. Mr. Bryant abstracted meaning of the official discourse and used it to mandate the school's discourse practices and teacher experience and his social relations. He did not focus or attend to the particular and localized practices that had been established over a period of time. The rules of discourse evident everywhere and yet recorded nowhere, were created and sustained by anonymous persons in the sense that everyone knew the procedures, in specific interactional situations. This knowledge was ignored and as a result Mr. Bryant isolated himself. In his isolation the empowerment discourse was discontinuous, abstract, and unintelligible to him. As such, he could not become a participating member utilizing empowerment's discourse practices.

Mr. Bryant attended only to the official renderings. He selected not to dialogue with teachers by disregarding the social stock of knowledge of discourse practices. If the relations and practices were clear to students, who traditionally are outside school leadership and decision-making activities, can one not assume that they were available for the principal's understanding?

This is not a rhetorical question. While teachers were holders and demonstrators of social knowledge and the producers of empowerment's discourse practices, students also knew empowerment's discursive practices. The students saw the discourse practices in evidence through the daily activities of the school. This suggests that if Mr. Bryant had been sensitive to the school's socially organized culture he might have been more successful.

Through the practices of communication and interaction the teachers are able to give voice to their knowledge and experience. Feminist authors, in particular D. Smith (1990), have identified the use of one's own experience and stock of knowledge as a means for claiming authority. Through the teachers' experiences of being students, student teachers, and teachers at other schools, but especially their experiences at Middleburg, they claimed an authority based in this stock of knowledge. Bill Pope's situation with the evaluation and the check sheet is an excellent example of such an orientation.

The official discourse indicated that teachers be evaluated according to criteria and format negotiated by the union and board. However, Middleburg's evaluation practices had evolved in other directions. This is exemplified in the discussion between teachers and the principal that would often occur in the teacher's room. Mr. Bryant attempted to impose a more regulatory orientation, including having the evaluation discussion occur in the principal's office. This indicates a discourse practice running against Middleburg's previously established empowering practices and a distinctively different principle underlying school relations. A feature of empowerment illustrated in Bill's story is how the physical setting for the evaluation discussion has importance in developing and understanding Middleburg's empowerment.

Bill's story lends evidence of another feature. This is the discourse practice regarding the evaluation's content and the way in which it was organized. Bill stated that Mr. Bryant's evaluation began with critical and negative comments and included no positive feedback. Previous evaluation practices began with positive feedback and then moved into suggested areas for improvement.

The tenor and thrust of Bryant's type of evaluation was different. His practice indicates a relation steeped in power and authority coming from one source, the principal. Middleburg's principles of empowerment are oriented toward the goal of improved teaching and social relations through shared discussion of elements that could be worked at together. As well, in previous evaluation processes, there was room for an acknowledgment that on the day of the observation the teacher could be "off" or something could be amiss. There was not a separation between the teacher and the experience of teaching.

By extending the analysis to the events that occurred after the evaluation meeting between Bill and the principal, we can further elaborate features in opposition. This is an illustration of the manner in which Mr. Bryant wanted to structure his interactions at Middleburg. First, rather than calling an official meeting in a meeting room, Bill Pope gathered with other teachers and discussed in an informal setting his understanding of the evaluation. This conversation could not be characterized as just a sour grapes session, because the teachers worked toward action and resolution.

A second group meeting that teachers held with Mr. Bryant occurred in the principal's office. It was a scheduled meeting, by his request. It did not have the mood of an open dialogue among colleagues, but of a confrontation between adversaries. "Official" talk did not occur in the lounge, where others might overhear or participate. For Bryant, official conversations always took place in the principal's office, where he sat comfortably, behind his desk, creating an authoritative distance.

The teachers' alternative result of seeking the superintendent's assistance should be read as an embedded extension of empowerment's discourse practices. Mr. Bryant saw this as a direct threat to the principal's power. The teachers' intent was to gain information through dialogue of the evaluation formula changes. The teachers were not necessarily unhappy about the outcomes in the evaluation procedure; however, they were explicitly dissatisfied about the change relative to the discourse practices.

Discourse practices establish and maintain relations, develop a history and context, and produce a connection that may not be primary or readily evident. The principal, by attending to the official discourse maintained in school and district files, disattended to the school's previous particular social history. This practice silenced teachers' and students' experiences. Mr. Bryant chose to ignore the abyss between the community's social knowledge, the unofficial knowledge maintained by stakeholders, and the official discourse created for the "relations of ruling" (Smith, 1990).

It did not matter that there was a change in school leadership vis-a-vis the principal. The embedded discourse of Middleburg's empowerment lay in the history of interrelations and ongoing interactions of the community's members. The discourse practices provided a framework for the inclusion of plurality, diversity, and difference.

Mr. Bryant could have learned Middleburg's discourse of empowerment. Discourse was not intentionally hidden nor controlled in this school. The stock of knowledge was available for his access in the everyday activities of Middleburg's school members. Whether he chose to ignore it, could not operate within its framework, or was asked by the board to operate Middleburg in a particular way are questions that could not be addressed.

The rubric of Middleburg's empowerment was perpetually unbalanced as the community moved forward and carried empowerment with it. There was a logic of supplementation, regarding the discourse practices, indicating that what was new was added and at the same time endlessly supplanted, left behind, and predominated what was there in the first place. A reciprocal relation exists between empowerment and discourse practices, as each informs, demonstrates, and develops the other.

Bryant's eventual dismissal was a demonstration of Middleburg's teacher empowerment. It is not that they intentionally set out to have his contract terminated; the teachers had a different goal. They wanted to maintain current power and social relations and protect the discourse practices already present and operating in a productive manner for them and the school, and thus became the articulation of a reflective community (Cinnamond and Zimpher, 1990).

FOUCAULT/POWER

To this point the chapter has proceeded as an examination of empowerment supportive of the critical tradition of education (Aronowitz and Giroux, 1985; Giroux and McLaren, 1986, 1989; Freire, 1985; Kanpol, 1992; Simon, 1987). Within this orientation empowerment appears as a partial fulfillment of the Enlightenment project. Among the associated ideals of this project are freedom of the individual, self-rule, individual rights, social justice, and public debate. By using these humanistic principles, teachers feel in control of themselves and involved in school policy and decisions. As the achievement of the Enlightenment's goals, such a perspective can be encapsulated within the expression "critical democracy." Critical democracy has been an explicit goal of liberal/radical educators such as Giroux, McLaren, Kanpol, Freire, and Simon.

Yet a poststructuralist focus to the above evidence challenges the apparently real implications, issues, and questions of empowerment. A reexamination of the evidence with careful attention to the history of Middleburg notes different effects and contradictions within the current use of empowerment. At this juncture the framework of power as outlined by Foucault can be brought to bear on Empowerment for a more critical reading of the events at Middleburg. (From this point on, Empowerment will be capitalized to note its mystic and mythic status.) Foucault's projects are in part an examination of the ideology (my expression) that is presented under the guise of humanism.[5] This makes the selection of Foucault for further analysis of the social practices of Empowerment appropriate. Following Kant, Foucault developed "a self-critical examination of the Enlightenment project of seeking autonomy through reason," while at the same time, Foucault "sees the ways in which reason itself can tyrannize rather than liberate" (Gutting, 1991, p. 262). Foucault (1986, p. 221) identifies humanism as "everything in Western civilization that restricts the desire for power." Humanism accomplishes such a restriction by suggesting that even though one does not have power as an individual, one can at least control or rule the self.

Discipline and Punish (Foucault, 1979b) is in part a demonstration of how liberal democracy's role is to provide conditions for freedom by limiting access to it (Weedon, 1987, p. 121). By questioning the Enlightenment's focus upon individual reason, Foucault questions the possibility of universal or absolute truths (i.e., Empowerment).[6] Utilizing his conception of power and contrasting it with Empowerment permits a more critical engagement of Empowerment as a democratic pedagogical or schooling practice.

Foucault conceptualizes power as a totalizing system that is all inclusive relative to a specific space or location. "Power produced reality; it produces domains of objects and rituals of truth" (1979b, p. 194). However, power is not to be viewed as entirely negative and repressive as it can also have positive features (1980a, p. 137).

Jürgen Habermas (1987, p. 242) notes in his discussion of Foucault that the practices of power are indicative of "asymmetric influences over the freedom of movement of other participants." Certainly Foucault would concur that power and its practices stand in relation to freedom. But the power that Foucault identifies is complex in both its origin and practice, a configuration that is so diffuse that it points toward power and its practices as both authoritative and ignorant. The techniques, measures, rituals of power, and individuals who use them are not always aware of how the practices are those of power, nor are they fully aware of the extent of power's reach. As a researcher or participant, to attend or to see power, one must notice the modifications and transformations of practices, because Foucault (1983, p. 219) states, "power is the way certain actions modify others." Such a notion of power is dissociated from specific individuals (and institutions) so that no one person owns, or is responsible for it (Foucault, 1980b, p. 156). Deleuze (1988, p. 73) states that Foucault's "power does not emanate from a central point." The resultant practices of power move individuals toward the Enlightenment's goal of regulation and governance of self. Self-discipline allows for the imposition of power to be tolerable because power is substantially masked by its own use (Foucault, 1979b, p. 86). Internal control is more tolerable, both individually and socially, to external control.

Empowerment can, in this orientation, appear as an illusion. Self-discipline is a form of obedience. As such, Empowerment, similar to power, "professionalizes and rewards its pursuit" (Foucault, 1980b, p. 93). Teachers and administrators, as they monitor and regulate themselves as individuals and group members, become vehicles of power. Participating in the discourse practices of Middleburg's Empowerment, "the individual is an effect of power and at the same time . . . the element of its articulation" (1980b, p. 98). The web of social networks of power and its effects (Foucault, 1983, p. 224) are amply demonstrated and duplicated in the Empowered teachers as they interact with each other and the administration, all the time moving toward a form of social justice enforced in part by self-regulation.

A conception of Empowerment as the liberatory practice of schools operates at the level of a naive belief that a teacher or group of teachers can free themselves. As Foucault (1983, p. 221) states, "the exercise of power consists in guiding the possibility of conduct and putting in order the possible outcome. Basically, power is less a confrontation than . . . [a] designated way in which the conduct of individuals or groups might be directed." It is a misplaced notion to believe that power or control can be transformed so that everyone is no longer dominated. The power and subtlety of Empowerment is its self-regulation and self-discipline as members regulate and monitor each other for the good and goals of the larger organization. The teachers at Middleburg were encouraged to develop and continue Empowerment because it was a building environment and process that occupied and managed itself with minimal intervention from the district level.

To use Foucault's (1988, p. 105) words, Empowerment becomes a "procedure for training and exercising power over individuals [so that they are] extended, generalized and improved." The discipline of Empowerment occurs within the parameters and limits set by the administrators and agreed to by teachers.[7] Empowerment thus develops into a form and practice of power that is truly anonymous, nowhere and everywhere, while constituted and practiced daily by teachers without the direct input of the administration.

With the above in mind, Empowerment has a limited horizon of practicality in terms of actually liberating teachers. Discourse forms the practices and constitutive features of Empowerment, which the system of power finds useful and develops for its own purposes (Foucault, 1979a, pp. 41–48). The techniques of Empowerment utilized at Middleburg construct a strategy by which teachers and administrators are maintained within a structure that is seldom mutual or reciprocal. As outlined by E. Ellsworth (1989, p. 306), Empowerment "treats the symptoms but leaves the disease unnamed and untouched." Teachers are asymmetrical in their power relations with administrators to be able to make or influence certain decisions relative to the school. One can conjecture that as long as the school operates in an administratively efficient and effective way, Empowerment will continue to be the rationalized and accepted mode of operation.[8]

I do not want to characterize the administration (here to include building and central administrative staff) as acting in the mode of dominant oppressors just because they are of a different organizational class. Foucault's power suggests that the practices of the administration are also the effects of power. Contrary to Marxist-oriented perspectives, such a form of power indicates that power is not necessarily a class conflict nor a measure of exploitation.

Power and its practices maintain a complex and localized web of technology. Deleuze explains that for Foucault "local" probably has two meanings that are relevant for power and the operation of resistance. Deleuze

(1988, p. 26) states: "Power is local because it is never global, but it is not local or localized because it is diffuse." The relations of power are not unified, nor structural in a way to see direct casual relations and mechanisms, because power and its practices are not static. The administration is involved and yet ignorant in the same constitutive practices as teachers.

I suggest that, as generally utilized, Empowerment has become a form of hegemony. It leads the teachers to a false notion of freedom, choice, and control. A bit of history aligns Middleburg more closely with the above discussion of power and Foucault's articulation of the power of the gaze for discipline. Middleburg was designed as an open school. When constructed there were no walls separating classrooms from hallways. Further, the opposite wall from the corridor for each classroom was entirely glass, opening onto the interior courtyards or the surrounding woods. For his analysis of the effects of the Enlightenment, Foucault (1979b, pp. 204–205) draws on the image and design of the panopticon model that functions as "a way of defining power relations in terms of everyday life."

In a manner similar to prisoners in the panopticon, the teachers could be viewed, observed, and objectified at all times and without their direct knowledge. The open school became a practice and technology of domination. The teachers knew they could be observed at all times and comported themselves and their classes accordingly. The power of the gaze operates automatically and impersonally as the teacher disciplines the self, whether or not there is an observer. It is the possibility of surveillance that creates an object and an objectified subject from a fictive relation (Foucault, 1979b, p. 204).

At a later time walls were added to separate the classrooms and hallways. However, most of the walls were constructed of clear glass so the actual changed effect was minimal. As Foucault (1980a, p. 99) notes, the relations of power are not static but are "matrices of transformation." By the time the glass walls were installed, surveillance was accepted. In interviews, teachers spoke of how natural it was for them to be viewed by others while teaching. To continue with parallels to the panoptic schema, after the glass walls were built, their properties or practices of power did not diminish. The teachers were, by this time, docile, normalized, and subdued. Walls made little difference in terms of teacher behaviors as they were now self-regulated. The disciplinary practices that occurred could not be identified by teachers with either a specific institution, apparatus, or individual. Echoing Foucault they spoke of how professional the other teachers were; yet together the mechanism and practices of Empowerment were essentially modalities or apparatuses for the exercise of power. This may lead us to agree with Anderson (1989), who suggested that "Empowerment has entered the main stream" and thus lost "its radical currency."

In the example surrounding the appropriate student dress example, I suggest that Empowerment had become a mode and formula for power relations that silenced teachers and students. This history of Empowerment at

Middleburg was steeped in observation and oppression rather than liberation. The fact that neither teachers nor students responded to the change in policy points to the effectiveness of Empowerment in producing discourse practices that disciplined the teachers and students into a more docile and manageable group.

FOUCAULT/RESISTANCE

Before outlining possibilities for resistance as seen through a Foucault perspective, Empowerment, which has been claimed as a form of resistance, will be discussed as one of power's technologies. Most clearly among authors, Giroux (1988b) has claimed that Empowerment can be a mode of resistance. Educators have developed theories of resistance in hopes of redefining schools and their relation to society (Giroux, 1988b). Yet, given the web of complexity and subtly that characterizes the varied apparatuses of power, one has to be suspicious of such attempts.

Foucault's discussion throughout *Discipline and Punish* (1979b) indicates that in spite of the processes of subjection, subjectivation, and objectivation, there are places for resistance within the carceral community to challenge oppressive conditions. However, such resistance will be at relatively low levels that act in accord with the disciplinary functions of power. Resistance cannot overcome entirely the dissymmetry of power. Middleburg's teachers' Empowerment discourse practices do not operate in the realm of complete resistance to power, because power does not attempt to exclude discourse. I suggest that power's totalizing effects actually encourage Empowerment's practices and act as one of the strategies of power.[9]

Empowerment at Middleburg was an intentional organizational goal. When the building was constructed as an open school, Mr. Woodall set out to create an organizational structure to match the facilities. What seems to have been at the base of this structure was to provide a wide variety of opportunities and encouragements for teachers to talk among themselves and with the principal, as in the case of PIC, learning communities, lounges, and extracurricular activities. I want to indicate that as Empowerment multiplies it also extends power's own utility. The talk and development of Empowerment's discourse practices worked to engage teachers in ways that clouded their conscious awareness of power and its effects. Contrary to Ashcroft (1987), Middleburg's Empowerment became a product of its processes, a completed project rather than an open-ended state of potential.

The effects of the talk and discussions relative to Empowerment by the teachers became a further subjection to power. Empowerment at Middleburg became an extension of power as the teachers moved into different areas of self-discipline and governance (e.g., evaluation). Similar to the confessional, teachers both extended themselves toward a seeming liberatory activity while concurrently submitted themselves to self-regulation. Foucault

(1980a & 1983, pp. 213–216) notes the difficulty of resistance with the development of modern power relations. He grounds these relations in "pastoral power," which he links to the confessional. In the confessional of truth the ritual and discourse are used for salvation. It is the production of truth through confession that takes away an individual's freedom. Foucault links this activity to individuals who become subjects to institutions but also to themselves as they reveal truth and seek knowledge and penance from others. The confessor is in a power relation that transforms acts of power into talk. As talk is formed through discourses, power is diversified and scattered to points of dispersion. The confessee relinquishes power and freedom and in the process constrains and disciplines the self. Middleburg's organized and enacted form of Empowerment worked toward and along this form of subjection as the teachers met and talked in a variety of venues, either with or without the principal present.

Foucault (1980a, pp. 61–62) notes further that those who hear, or require confession, those who console, punish, and scrutinize, have power over those who confess. In a curious twist, teacher Empowerment at Middleburg doubled one's role, as each teacher was both confessor and confesses. A teacher, as a member of PIC, or a learning community, had a duty to both confess and hear the confession of others. The teachers were both subjected and practiced as they sat in collaborative judgment and reconciliation of each other. They volunteered and imposed while the discourse practices of Empowerment developed into procedures of confession that modulated their activities and constructed absolution or penance among and with themselves. The teachers of Middleburg through their variety of procedures were fully enveloped into the polymorphous and polyvocal techniques of power.

Because power is neither centralized nor does it emanate from a single point or person, it is always unstable, moving, evolving. At Middleburg, power can be several operation at once. There is in effect a double subjection and objectification. Teachers bring their own individual or group professional issues as confessions to a group. As in Bill Pope's evaluation, the group listens and either develops a response within the vein of pastoral power, or the issue is taken before another, more knowledgeable, group. The eventual process and response to the issue operates to normalize both the individual teacher and the group. In a second way, the practice of Empowerment also acts to normalize the discourse practices or techniques of power utilized by the individual and the group. As such, I want to downplay the role of Empowerment as a systematically, institutionally, and universally accepted means for liberating teachers. Empowerment cannot be identified as necessarily liberated from domination or power of others. Power is more complex than simple class, organizational, or gendered oppositionals. As Foucault (1980b, pp. 104–108) suggests, power orchestrates time and energies from subjects, and concurrently produces new methods of subjection and regulation.

This discussion may suggest that teachers are entirely powerless. As Anderson (1991, p. 136) asks, should teachers be suspicious of Empowerment when it comes with the full support of administrators? Is there no escape from power such that schools can operate more freely? Foucault (1988, p. 123) states: "as soon as there is a power relation there is a possibility of resistance. We can never be ensnared by power: we can modify its grip in determinate conditions according to precise strategy." Yet he cautions that "one is always 'inside' power, there is no 'escaping' it" (1980a, p. 95). Just as there are multiple points of power, there can be multiple points of resistance. Resistance is "inscribed in the latter as an irreducible opposite" (1980a, p. 96). As soon as power shifts within its web, techniques, and social networks, resistance must change accordingly.

CONCLUSION

Where does this leave students, teachers, pedagogists, and others who are interested in the transformation of schools? Are we to agree with R. Christie (1989), who identifies Empowerment merely as the group's acceptance of a leader's decision based on good communication flow? W. Bain and M. Kiziltan (1991, pp. 98–99) indicate that "Empowerment within the postmodern frame necessitates a form of positive scepticism." While lacking action, such a position suggests an ongoing element of doubt and awareness of the plurality of power and its practices, which tend to homogenize rather than note multivocal and distinct visions. R. Simon (1987) notes that "empowerment should always be linked with critique," while S. Aronowitz and H. Giroux (1985) link empowerment to "a language of possibility."

When speaking of power and resistance, Foucault is clear to indicate that "in human relations, whatever they are . . . power is always present." As long as there is power there is the "possibility of resistance," because power is precisely linked to liberty, freedom, and domination as a strategic game (Bernauer and Rasmussen, 1988, pp. 11–18). Are we to concur with Habermas (1987), who has labeled and critiqued Foucault as a neoconservative because he offers no clear-cut vision or plan of how to operate above, beyond, or within the power game? Or are we to agree with F. Jameson (1981, p. 91), who aligns himself with Baudrillard when he indicates that Foucault's system of power and domination is so pervasive and difficult to step away from that resistance is limited "to anarchist gestures . . . wildcat strikes, terrorism, and death"?

I believe that Foucault would be, to a degree, in sympathy with Jameson and I suggest that this is where we critical educators should locate ourselves. Foucault (1983, p. 212) states that the object of resistance is to attack "a technique, a form of power." Resistance must take on a relationship with power that is "reciprocal incitation and struggle; less of a face-to-face confrontation which paralyzes both sides than a permanent provocation" (1983,

p. 222). To me this warrants that teachers, students, concerned individuals, and groups participate in a particularized site. That in such a space they work to daily recognize and struggle against those forms of power that make individuals into subjects who submit to others. Resistance will look differently at each site as each site constructs its own practices of power. But there can be no universal or global response or resistance to the difficulties in our schools. Empowerment and resistance from this perspective have no center or single point of origin, explanation, or plan of attack.

Further, this suggests that there is no such thing as Empowerment because it must become an element of the discourse of power. Once Empowerment becomes the fabric of school life, it is the instrument of power and not the tool of resistance. When normalized, Empowerment becomes a form that produces specific categories of subjectivities and modes of interaction. Yet, in the case of Middleburg, there are semblances of resistance.

The example regarding teacher evaluations (described earlier in the chapter) does operate as resistance in the manner suggested by Foucault. The issue of Jim Bryant's method of evaluation was the catalyst. Several teachers, led by Bill Pope, developed a specific response to Bryant's activity. As particularized agents who did not act or represent all teachers, they spoke for the self-interests of some. They responded to what they perceived as a shift in the discourse practices of power. Mr. Bryant's demonstration of other preferred discourse practices moved the teachers to action. Contrary to the typical practices of Empowerment and against the new patterns of power relations, the teachers acted against the structures. They did not accept the response of Bryant, nor would they accept the subjectivity Bryant was trying to develop. Their struggle to make visible Bryant's discourse practices and relations of power recognized the partiality of Empowerment as a liberatory practice. The teachers were able to act in accordance with Foucault's resistance because they named the oppression and identified the oppressor for a specific site and space.

There is another dilemma of which Foucault is aware, and which he reminds those of us who wish to transform schools yet do not work in them: What is the role of the intellectual? Foucault (1988, p. 265) problematizes the position of research such as this in the life and activities of Middleburg or other schools:

The role of an intellectual is not to tell others what they have to do. By what right would he do so? And remember all the prophecies, promises, injunctions, and programs that intellectuals have managed to formulate over the last two centuries and whose effects we can now see. The work of the intellectual is not to shape others' political will; it is, through analyses that he carries out in his own field, to question over and over again what is postulated as self-evident, to disturb people's mental habits, the way they do and think things, to dissipate what is familiar and accepted, to reexamine rules and institutions and on the basis of this reproblematization (in which he carries out his specific task as an intellectual) to participate in the formation of a political will (in which he has his role as citizen to play).

As Foucault (1986, p. 207) suggests, we, the intellectuals, the researchers, the writers are ourselves "agents of this system of power." We assist in the construction of the structural features that define agents and the cultural conditions of schools. But theory, the work of intellectuals, can be a form of resistance itself if it is only in the space of the local, and not totalizing; also if it is a specific site or system of struggle where theory reveals and undermines power (Foucault, 1986, p. 208).

To theorize from above and outside schools regarding Empowerment and resistance underemphasizes actual agents and overemphasizes the role of those outside the daily workings of specific sites of struggle. It is an activity of intellectual reduction and domination if it is not coupled with specific action. Theory and research can be a form of passive ideology. As Ellsworth (1989) suggests, without action Empowerment theory is illusionary. While we cannot tell teachers, students, administrators, or parents what to do, we can assist them in the first step of power reversal. Our writings may work to demystify power and its authoritative discourses. In the struggle against existing forms of power, we can "force the institutionalized networks of information to listen, to produce names, to point the finger of accusation" (Foucault, 1986, p. 214).

But we, as outsiders, must leave the development of tactics, strategies, and resistance to those directly involved with the struggles of power and its discourses. Or we can work collaboratively to facilitate their identification of problems and solutions. I can agree with Simon's (1988) identification of projects of possibilities as long as we approach the spaces for Empowerment and resistance as particularized, localized, and the effect of systems of signification—that is, discourse practices that have a specific history.

NOTES

1. This chapter is a more developed understanding of a previous paper presented at the 1991 Ethnography in Education Research Conference and is a part of a project that includes Melenyzer (1991).

2. All participants have been given pseudonyms for the purposes of this chapter.

3. Learning community was Middleburg's term for curricular units. Some were based in subject matter; others were grade-related.

4. Mr. Bryant's activities echo the organizational and structural features identified by McNeil's *Contradictions of Control* (1988).

5. Foucault's work is in part a response to the limits he, as well as other French writers (i.e., J. Derrida), saw with the Marxist-based perspectives.

6. Lather, in *Getting Smart* (1991), suggests the limits of both conservative and radical discourse to move education beyond binary oppositions and proposes a post-structuralist perspective as a potentially more transforming position.

7. As evidence of this, it should be noted that the teachers did not have the opportunity to provide input into the selection of Mr. Bryant as the new principal.

8. As in other schools, high test scores and the volume and intensity of central office interventions were noted by administrators as the marks of success of Empowerment at Middleburg. However, it must be noted that Middleburg was the only school in the district to be using Empowerment as a mode of organization and operation.

9. Anderson's (1990) article notes how meaning management for the purposes of ideological control is an explicit expectation of school administrators and their organizations.

REFERENCES

Anderson, G. (1989). "Critical Ethnography in Education: Origins, Current Status, and New Directions." *Review of Educational Research*, 59(3): 249–270.

———. (1990). "Toward a Critical Constructivist Approach to School Administration: Invisibility, Legitimation, and the Study of Non-events." *Educational Administration Quarterly*, 26(1): 38–59.

———. (1991). "Cognitive Politics of Principals and Teachers: Ideological Control in Elementary Schools." In J. Blase (ed.), *The Politics of Life in Schools*. Newbury Park, CA: Sage Publications.

Aronowitz, S. and Giroux, H. (1985). *Education under Siege: The Conservative, Liberal, and Radical Debate Over Schooling*. South Hadley, MA: Bergin & Garvey.

Ashcroft, L. (1987). "Defusing 'Empowerment': The What and the Why." *Language Arts*, 64(2): 142–156.

Bain, W. and Kiziltan, M. (1991). "Toward a Postmodern Politics: Knowledge and Teachers." *Educational Foundations*, Winter, pp. 89–107.

Bernauer, J. and Rasmussen, D. (1988). *The Final Foucault*. Cambridge, MA: MIT Press.

Cagen, E. (1978). "Individualism, Collectivism, and Radical Educational Reform." *Harvard Educational Review*, 48(2): 227–266.

Cherryholmes, C. (1988). *Power and Criticism: Poststructural Investigations in Education*. New York: Teachers College Press.

Christie, R. (1989). "What Does Empowerment Really Mean?" *NASSP Bulletin*, January, pp. 83–84.

Cinnamond, J. (1991). "Some Principles of Narrative Scholarship." Presented at the Annual Meetings of the American Educational Research Association. Chicago.

Cinnamond, J. and Melenyzer, B. (1991). "Empowerment: An Intersection for Foucault." Paper presented at the Ethnography in Education Conference, Philadelphia.

Cinnamond, J. and Zimpher, N. (1990). "Reflectivity as a Function of Community." In R. Clift, R. Houston, and M. Pugach (eds.), *Encouraging Reflective Practice in Education: An Analysis of Issues and Programs* (pp. 57–72). New York: Teachers College Press.

Deleuze, G. (1988). *Foucault* (trans. S. Hand). Minneapolis: University of Minnesota Press.

Ellsworth, E. (1989). "Why Doesn't This Feel Empowering?: Working through the Repressive Myths of Critical Pedagogy." *Harvard Educational Review*, 59(3): 297–324.

Foucault, M. (1970). *The Order of Things: An Archeology of the Human Sciences.* New York: Vintage Paperbacks.

———. (1979a). *Archaeology of Knowledge* (trans. A. Sheridan Smith). New York: Pantheon Books.

———. (1979b). *Discipline and Punish: The Birth of the Prison* (trans. A. Sheridan). New York: Vintage Books.

———. (1980a). *The History of Sexuality,* Volume One: *An Introduction.* New York: Random House.

———. (1980b). *Power/Knowledge: Selected Interviews and Other Writings* (ed. C. Gordon). New York: Pantheon.

———. (1983). "The Subject and Power." In H. Dreyfus and P. Robinson (eds.), *Michel Foucault: Beyond Structuralism and Hermeneutics.* Chicago: University of Chicago Press.

———. (1986). *Language, Counter-Memory, Practice: Selected Essays and Interviews* (ed. D. Bouchard). Ithaca, NY: Cornell University Press.

———. (1988). *Politics Philosophy Culture: Interviews and Other Writings 1977–1984* (trans. A. Sheridan et al.), ed. L. Kritzman. New York: Routledge.

Freire, P. (1985). *The Politics of Education.* South Hadley, MA: Bergin & Garvey.

Giroux, H. (1988a). *Schooling and the Struggle for Public Life: Critical Pedagogy in the Modern Age.* Minneapolis: University of Minnesota Press.

———. (1988b). "Theories of Reproduction and Resistance in the New Sociology of Education: A Critical Analysis." *Harvard Educational Review*, 53(3): 257–293.

Giroux, H. and McLaren, P. (1986). "Teacher Education and the Politics of Engagement: The Case for Democratic Schooling." *Harvard Educational Review*, 56(3): 213–238.

———. (1989). *Critical Pedagogy, the State, and Cultural Struggle.* Albany, NY: State University of New York Press.

Glickman, C. (1988). "Supervision and the Rhetoric of Empowerment: Silence or Collision?" *Action-in-Teacher-Education* 10(1): 11–15.

Greer, J. (1989). "Another Perspective and Some Moderate Proposals on 'Teacher Empowerment.' " *Exceptional Children*, 55(4): 294–297.

Gutting, G. (1991). *Michel Foucault's Archaeology of Scientific Reason.* Cambridge: Cambridge University Press.

Habermas, J. (1987). *The Philosophical Discourse of Modernity: Twelve Lectures* (trans. F. Lawrence). Cambridge, MA: MIT Press.

Jameson, F. (1981). *The Political Unconscious: Narrative as a Socially Symbolic Act.* Ithaca, NY: Cornell University Press.

Kanpol, B. (1992). *Towards a Theory and Practice of Teacher Cultural Politics: Continuing the Postmodern Debate.* Norwood, NJ: Ablex.

Lather, P. (1991). *Getting Smart: Feminist Research and Pedagogy with/in the Postmodern.* New York: Routledge.

Maeroff, G. (1988). *The Empowerment of Teachers: Overcoming the Crisis of Confidence.* New York: Teachers College Press.

Marshall, C. (1991). "The Chasm Between Administrator and Teacher Cultures: A

Micro-political Puzzle." In J. Blase (ed.), *The Politics of Life in Schools: Power, Conflict, and Cooperation.* Beverly Hills, CA: Sage.

McElrath, R. (1988). "Will Empowerment of Teachers Remove Barriers to Educational Reform?" Paper presented at the annual Council of States on Inservice Education, New Orleans, November (ED 314 364).

McNeil, L. (1988). *Contradictions of Control: School Structure and School Knowledge.* New York: Routledge.

McRobbie, A. (1978). "Working Class Girls and the Culture of Femininity." In Center for Contemporary Cultural Studies Women's Group, *Women Take Issue.* London: Hutchinson.

Melenyzer, B. (1991). "Teacher Empowerment: Narratives of the Silenced Practitioners." Unpublished Doctoral Dissertation, Indiana University of Pennsylvania.

Prawat, R. (1991). "Conversations with Self and Settings: A Framework for Thinking about Teacher Empowerment." *American Educational Research Journal,* 28(4): 737–758.

Pugh, W. (1989). "Moving into the Next Phase of 'School Effectiveness' with Heavy Baggage: An Evaluation of a Districtwide School Improvement Program." Paper presented at the Annual Meeting of the American Educational Research Association, San Francisco, March (ED 307 294).

Rice, K. (1987). "Empowering Teachers: A Search for Professional Autonomy." Information Analyses (ED 282 845).

Richardson, G. and Sistrunk, W. (1989). "The Relationship between Secondary Teachers' Perceived Levels of Burnout and Their Perceptions of Their Principals' Supervisory Behaviors." Paper presented at the Annual Meeting of the Mid-South Educational Research Association, Little Rock, November (ED 312 763).

Schutz, A. (1962). "Common-sense and Scientific Interpretation of Human Action." In M. Natanson (ed.), *The Problem of Social Reality: Collected Papers 1* (pp. 3–47). The Hague: Martinus Nijhoff.

Shrewsbury, C. (1987). "What Is Feminist Pedagogy?" *Women's Studies Quarterly,* 15(3 & 4): 6–14.

Simon, R. (1987). "Empowerment as a Pedagogy of Possibility." *Language Arts,* 64(4): 370–382.

———. (1988). "For a Pedagogy of Possibility." *Critical Pedagogy Network,* 1(1): 1–4.

Smith, D. (1990). *Conceptual Practices of Power: A Feminist Sociology to Knowledge.* Boston: Northeastern University Press.

Troen, V. and Boles, K. (1988). "The Teaching Project: A Model for Teacher Empowerment." *Language Arts,* 65(7): 688–692.

Weedon, C. (1987). *Feminist Practice and Post Structuralist Theory.* New York: Basil Blackwell.

Weiler, M. (1988). *Women Teaching for Change, Gender, Class and Power.* South Hadley, MA: Bergin & Garvey.

Yonemura, M. (1986). "Reflections on Teacher Empowerment and Teacher Education." *Harvard Educational Review,* 56(4): 473–480.

Index

About the Contributors

JEFFREY CINNAMOND is a research faculty member at Eastern Washington University, studying early childhood education in rural areas. His research interests are oriented toward understanding trust within organizations where computer networks are the primary means of interaction and communication.

DANIELE D. FLANNERY is an Assistant Professor of Adult Education and Coordinator of the Adult Education D.Ed. Program at Penn State Harrisburg. She has focused on issues of race, gender, class, and cultural diversity among adults continuing their education. She contributed a chapter to S. Colin III and E. Hayes (eds.), *Confronting Racism and Sexism in Adult and Continuing Education* (1994).

HENRY A. GIROUX holds the Waterbury Chair Professorship in Secondary Education at Penn State University. His most recent books include *Postmodern Education* (with Stanley Aronowitz), *Border Crossings, Living Dangerously, Between Borders* (with Peter McLaren), and *Disturbing Pleasures: Learning Popular Culture*.

BEVERLY M. GORDON is Associate Professor of Education at Ohio State University, where she is also Acting Chair of the Department of Educational Policy and Leadership in the School of Education. Her interests revolve around black studies, curriculum, and feminist issues. She has published widely in such journals as *Journal of Educational Thought, Journal of Education, Journal of Negro Education*, and *Urban Education*.

CARL A. GRANT is a Hoefs-Bascom Professor of Teacher Education in the Department of Curriculum and Instruction and a professor in the Department of Afro-American Studies at the University of Wisconsin-Madison. He has written or edited fifteen books or monographs on multicultural education or teacher education, the most recent being *Research and Multicultural Education* (1993) and *Making Choices for Multicultural Education* (with Christine Sleeter; 1994). He became president of the National Association for Multicultural Education in 1994.

KRIS D. GUTIERREZ is an Assistant Professor in Curriculum in the Graduate School of Education at the University of California, Los Angeles. Her research interests include a study of the sociocultural contexts of literacy development, and understanding the relationship between language, culture, development, and pedagogies of empowerment.

BARRY KANPOL is an Assistant Professor of Educational Foundations at Penn State Harrisburg. His primary concerns are to connect critical pedagogy's many theoretical components to teacher, student, and self-experience. His previous books include *Towards a Theory and Practice of Teacher Cultural Politics* and *Critical Pedagogy: An Introduction* (Bergin & Garvey, 1994).

PETER McLAREN is an Associate Professor in the Graduate School of Education at the University of California, Los Angeles. He is the author of the award-winning *Life in Schools* and the highly acclaimed ethnography, *Schooling as a Ritual Performance*. He is also coeditor of *Critical Pedagogy, the State, and Cultural Struggle* and *Between Borders* (with Henry A. Giroux).

BONNY NORTON PEIRCE is a postdoctoral fellow in the Modern Language Centre, Ontario Institute for Studies in Education, in Toronto, Canada.

MICHAEL PETERS is a Senior Lecturer in the Education Department of the University of Auckland (New Zealand) and Chair of the Policy Studies Group. He was a Lecturer at the University of Canterbury in 1991–92 and a British Council Fellow at the Institute of Education at London University in 1990.

JUDYTH M. SACHS is an Associate Professor and Deputy Dean, Research and Post-Graduate Studies in the Faculty of Education and the Arts at Griffith University (Queensland, Australia). Her current research is concerned with teacher professional development and the work of academics in higher education institutions.

SVI SHAPIRO is Professor and Chair of the Educational Leadership and Cultural Foundations Department at the University of North Carolina,

Greensboro. He is the author of *Between Capitalism and Democracy: Educational Policy and the Crisis of the Welfare State* (Greenwood, 1990), and *Beyond Excellence and Liberation: Toward a New Public Discourse for Education* (with David Purpel; Greenwood, forthcoming).

SUZANNE SOOHOO is an Assistant Professor in the School of Education at Chapman University (Orange, California). She teaches courses on teaching and learning, school leadership, and multicultural education. Her current interest focuses on collaborative action research, with a special emphasis on student researchers and the development of democratic classroom communities.

FRED YEO is an Assistant Professor of Educational Foundations at Siena College (Loudonville, New York). His primary interests are in urban education, critical pedagogy, and multiculturalism.

ISBN 0-89789-307-7

EAN

9 780897 893077

90000>

HARDCOVER BAR CODE